# The Anthropology of Islam

## GABRIELE MARRANCI

Oxford • New York

First published in 2008 by
**Berg**
Editorial offices:
1st Floor, Angel Court, 81 St Clements Street, Oxford, OX4 1AW, UK
175 Fifth Avenue, New York, NY 10010, USA

Berg is the imprint of Oxford International Publishers Ltd.


**Library of Congress Cataloguing-in-Publication Data**

Marranci, Gabriele.
    The anthropology of Islam / Gabriele Marranci.
        p. cm.
    Includes bibliographical references and index.
    ISBN-13: 978-1-84520-284-2 (cloth)
    ISBN-10: 1-84520-284-8 (cloth)
    ISBN-13: 978-1-84520-285-9 (pbk.)
    ISBN-10: 1-84520-285-6 (pbk.)
    1. Islam—Study and teaching. 2. Anthropology of religion—Islamic
countries. 3. Islamic sociology. 4. Anthropology—Methodology. I. Title.

    BP42.M37 2008
    306.6'97—dc22

                                                    2007049376


**British Library Cataloguing-in-Publication Data**

A catalogue record for this book is available from the British Library.

ISBN 978 1 84520 284 2 (Cloth)
ISBN 978 1 84520 285 9 (Paper)

Typeset by JS Typesetting, Porthcawl, Mid Glamorgan
Printed in the United Kingdom by Biddles Ltd, King's Lynn

**www.bergpublishers.com**

# The Anthropology of Islam

Dedicated to the memory of Gregory Bateson

# Contents

# Acknowledgements

This book is the result of my discussions and debates with students and colleagues about what the anthropology of Islam may be. I have benefited from advice, suggestions and criticism during the many years of reflection on the topic and the two years of writing, rewriting, scrapping and rethinking to rewrite again. The words of this book would never have reached your eyes without the time that students and colleagues spent in sharing their thoughts and ideas. Although intended for teaching, this book is a product of learning. I have learnt from my students, both undergraduate and postgraduate, from their questions and from their challenges and curiosity about the anthropology of Islam.

Among my friends and colleagues, I would like to express particular thanks to Professor Daniel Varisco and Professor Bryan Turner for their support and exchange of ideas. I would also like to thanks Ms Hannah Shakespeare, of Berg, for her patience and prompt replies to my questions.

# CHAPTER I

# Introduction

## ELENCHOS[1]

STUDENT: What is Islam?

ANTHROPOLOGIST: Lots of things, of course.

STU: Yeah, but I mean, is Islam its holy books or what Muslims do?

ANT: Neither, I suppose.

STU: Well, it should be one or the other for sure!

ANT: Why should it be so?

STU: I think that the Qur'an and *hadiths*, and the other texts, tell Muslims how to be Muslims and this guides their actions.

ANT: OK, we can try an experiment. Get that copy of the Qur'an on my desk. So, tell me what this is.

STU: A book; a holy book, at least for Muslims.

ANT: What makes it holy?

STU: The fact that Muslims consider it so.

ANT: OK, but if you were a Muslim why would you have insisted that this particular book is the holiest?

STU: That's simple Doc! Because, I would believe the book to be God's words.

ANT: You see, Islam is not just what is written in its books.

STU: Why not? I don't follow you.

ANT: Well, it's very simple. You just said that this book, the Qur'an, is holy because at least one Muslim believes that God revealed it. Now you can agree with me that Muslims, each of them, have to perform cognitive operations to form a cognitive map of what for them is Islam. There is no Islam without mind.

STU: Certainly, you need Muslims to have Islam. Yet I still think that what is written in the sources of Islam shapes how Muslims are. Though there are some cultural differences, I am not sure about your point. I think that something called Islam actually exists.

ANT: OK, we will proceed point by point. Not only do we have different cultures among Muslims but also different interpretations. Which is the most basic element that you need to form interpretations?

STU: First, you need to know at least the language in which the text has been transmitted or trust a translation; but there are also other elements, like personal views and social conditions that surely influence one's interpretation.

ANT: You are discussing a second order of elements. I asked about the basic element without which we cannot have interpretations, or any other mental process, since interpretations are complex mental processes.

STU: Well ... the most basic is that you should be able to think. To have mental processes, like thoughts, we need a mind.

ANT: Yes, because for the 'thing' we call Islam to exist, we need a mind that can conceive of it, making it part of a mental process.

STU: Why refer to Islam as 'the thing' now?

ANT: You have just agreed that Islam exists because of the mental processes allowing some people to make sense of certain texts and practices. Are mental processes 'real' things?

STU: Well, I would say that they are exactly that, processes. We make sense of what is around us through mental processes.

ANT: Exactly, we, as human beings, through mental processes form what we can call maps.

STU: I can see that. So you are saying that Islam is just a map.

ANT: Well, more than one, for sure. It's like one of those maps formed by many other different small maps, which, when put together, represent a vast territory.

STU: And, as you have reminded us many times, the map is not the territory.

ANT: But in this case, we can only know the map, since the territory consists of an endless ensemble of mental processes.

STU: At this point, I do not see the difference between a Muslim and non-Muslim forming mental processes about Islam. What makes them different?

ANT: Nothing, indeed, if we speak of the cognitive processes involved. You know, I have the impression that the most important thing that has been forgotten while studying Muslims is the otherwise obvious fact that they are human beings like me and you.

STU: But, I mean, doesn't the fact that they believe in Islam make their mind different? Sometimes, in some articles, I come across the expression 'Muslim mind'.

ANT: Some scholars, and unfortunately some anthropologists among them, have even suggested that a Muslim mind can exist. But how can a mind, which means cognitive processes allowed through neurological activities, be Muslim? Think if we extend this reasoning to other adjectives: Christian minds, Conservative minds, Jewish minds, Scientology minds, Jedi minds and Flying Spaghetti Monster minds.[2]

STU: So, what makes a person a Muslim? I thought that the fact that a person believes in the Qur'an and the sunna and in the *shahāda*, the profession of faith, makes a person a Muslim.

ANT: You are suggesting that it is the person's act of believing that makes him a Muslim. Let me see ... do you believe that Juan Carlos I is the king of Spain?

STU: Yes, Doc.

ANT: Are you Spanish?

STU: Of course not. You know I'm Scottish!

ANT: Why are you Scottish and not Spanish, though you believe that Juan Carlos I is the king of Spain?

STU: First, I was not born in Spain, I do not have Spanish parents and, by the way, I do not feel Spanish at all. I am not emotionally attached to the idea of being Spanish. Like during the World Cup, if Scotland is not playing, I can support another team, but when Scotland is playing, I am excited and feel something … a particular attachment that tells me that I'm Scottish.

ANT: Indeed, what matters here is that you *feel* to be Scottish.

STU: Are you suggesting that Muslims are Muslims because they consider themselves Muslim?

ANT: Does it sound so strange?

STU: Well, if you are right it means that the most important aspect is neither what the Islamic texts read, nor what Muslims believe, nor how they act, but rather whether or not they believe themselves to be Muslims, and here emotions play a very important role, as in my case of feeling to be Scottish.

ANT: Yes, this is correct. We need to restart our research, as anthropologists, from that 'feeling to be', in this case, Muslim.

## DE-TITLING THE TITLE

*The Anthropology of Islam* is a title that raises questions and certainly expectations. What is the anthropology of Islam? Why anthropology instead of theology or history? Why use the term Islam instead of Islams or Islam(s)? Why focus on Islam instead of Muslims? Is there only *one* anthropology of Islam or can we speak of anthropologies of Islam, or even anthropologies of Islams? How does the anthropology of Islam differ from, say, any other anthropology of religion? How does the anthropology of Islam differ from the sociology of Islam, or Islamic studies, or Islamic anthropology? Of course, I can add many other questions to those I have collected in the two years I worked on *The Anthropology of Islam* – some derived from genuine curiosity, others from healthy academic criticism and yet others from simple sceptical reactions. All these questions have shaped, transformed and re-transformed the book itself. Many of these questions will find answers in the chapters that will follow, in particular Chapter 3. Nonetheless, I want to introduce some relevant points behind the reason for this book. To do so, I need to explain the phylogeny of this project.

When I was a university student in anthropology, with an interest in Muslim cultures, I found myself disoriented by the enormous amount of research and references on the topic of Islam and Muslims produced in the last twenty-five years. Very soon, I discovered that these studies spread among different disciplines with different methodologies, aims, scopes and sometimes, indeed, political affiliations and agendas. My anthropological vocation brought me to focus on the social scientific side of these studies, though I also enthusiastically read and studied historical and traditional Islamic studies works. Although it was not difficult to find ethnographic studies of Muslim communities, in particular devoted to the Middle

Eastern societies, I became aware that an epistemological discussion on what the anthropology of Islam might be never fully developed, despite some reflexive attempts such as those provided by el-Zein (1977) and Asad (1986a). Other scholars have offered critical reviews of the available anthropological approaches to Islam; yet these review articles, such as those written by Fernea and Malarkey (1975), Eickelman (1981b), Abu-Lughod (1989) and Gilsenan (1990), have focused mainly on the Middle East and Northern Africa (MENA). It is not difficult to see how Said, though inexplicably appreciating Geertz's work, suggested that anthropology, despite its 'supposedly disinterested universality' (1985: 95) had not overcome its connections with colonialism and Orientalist views. With Asad (1986a) and Abu-Lughod (1989), I consider Said's observation unfair – without wishing to deny the historical collusions that anthropology as a discipline, and single anthropologists as scholars, had with colonial powers (see Chapter 3 in this book). Indeed, Said superficially ignored the contribution that anthropology has provided to the understanding of North African Muslims and the Middle East through anthropologists such as Eickelman.

Time has since passed, and I find myself on the other side of the desk, teaching students what the university course catalogue calls the anthropology of Islam. If in other anthropological fields, and in religious studies, we can find collections of articles, textbooks and the increasingly successful short introduction (see for instance Bowie 2000; Kunin 2002; Ney 2003; Segal 2006), this is not the case for anthropological approaches to Muslims and their religion. If then we turn to the most widely used anthologies and introductory books on religious studies or anthropology, we can observe a lack – with rare exceptions, such as Morris's *Anthropology and Religion: A Critical Introduction* (2005) – of any reference to Islam or to anthropological research on Muslims. Why? Anthropologists researching topics related to Islam have been, with the notable exception of Geertz, unsuccessful in reaching a wide audience outside their own subdiscipline. Yet there are also other more complex, I would say structural, reasons. Sociological and anthropological research on Islam has developed through specific studies and ethnographies, but without real coherence or discussion among the scholars. During the 1970s, anthropological research on Islam was at its dawn, and el-Zein's challenging article (1977) attempted to reopen a debate, but remained unexplored beyond the scholarly diatribe on one Islam versus many Islams (see Chapter 3, this book). While el-Zein's efforts seemed to fail, the short essays of Geertz's *Islam Observed* seemed to succeed. But it remained an isolated case and certainly did not aim to shape or clarify what the anthropology of Islam might have been. Geertz was just 'observing Islam', and could not forecast the impact that some lectures and a few pages would have produced years later. Finally, in 1986, Asad consciously, rather than by chance as in the case of Geertz's extended essay, offered a challenging reflection on the anthropology of Islam in an attempt to continue the debate that el-Zein started nearly ten years before (Asad 1986b). Asad's effort remained largely ignored, producing response and reflections only after decades had passed (see Lukens-Bull 1999). Hence, nearly thirty years on from el-Zein's intellectual engagement on the definition of the anthropology, we can still say with Asad, 'no coherent anthropology of Islam can be found on the notion of a determinate social blueprint' (1986b: 16). But, do you need a blueprint? I will try to discuss this in the chapters that follow.

The lack of self-reflection on what the anthropology of Islam is or should be, and the lack of a phylogenesis of this anthropological field, can also explain more recent events. Varisco (2005) in his provocative title *Islam Obscured*, has rightly highlighted a certain fossilization of how the anthropology of Islam has been, and still is thought of within university,

> Textual truths engendered and far too often engineered in representing Islam find their way unscrutinized and insufficiently digested into an endless stream of introductory and general texts, even solidly scholarly works. Seminal texts, once canonized as theoretically innovative or simply authoritative by default, have a library shelf life far beyond their usefulness and freshness in the disciplines that generate them. (2005: 3)

Today, after political and social events that have marked the beginning of the new millennium with an increased tension between the stereotyped representation of Islam and the no-less-stereotyped image of a civilizing West, we must reconsider how we have approached Islam from an anthropological perspective.

Anthropologists, as we shall observe in this book (Chapter 4), have preferred focusing their attention on the 'Other' in exotic contexts. Anthropologists researching Muslim societies have for a long time studied Muslim societies within Islamic countries, and often the Muslim was the Sufi or the Bedouin (Eickelman 1981a; Abu-Lughod 1989; Varisco 2005). The west, understood often as a monolithic social and cultural expression, was considered the domain of sociology. The new flux of migrations from Muslim countries changed disinterest, blurring the boundaries between sociology and anthropology, particularly in the case of Europe. As I shall explain later in this book, I strongly believe that we need to observe the methodology employed instead of classical academic divisions. In fact, an increasing number of contemporary sociologists use fieldwork and participant observation as part of their studies. In these cases, I consider their studies as part of the social and anthropological approach to Islam. Nonetheless, even in recent publications, the anthropology of Islam seems still rooted in a nostalgic exoticism. Clearly, as also Varisco has recognized, the anthropology of Islam, today, cannot be other than global. We cannot study, for example, Muslims in Indonesia, Malaysia, Pakistan, Bangladesh, Algeria, Morocco and Libya, without taking into consideration the transnational and global networks they are part of. Similarly, we cannot study Muslim communities in the west without paying attention to their connections with other Muslims in Islamic countries and other communities, both Muslim and non-Muslim. One clear example of the multisided interaction that Muslims living in the west partake in is the campaigns against the Afghan and Iraqi Wars, as well as the recent Israeli–Lebanese conflict. In all these occasions, Muslims have not only shared their activities with other fellow coreligionists, but also with non-Muslim organizations such as the Stop the War Coalition, the No-Global organization and traditional political parties (Yaqoob 2003).

Nonetheless, essentialism affects both academic and popular discourse on Muslims. I tend to call this essentialism the fallacy of the 'Muslim mind theory'. As we shall see in the chapters of this book, surprisingly some sociologists and anthropologists have not been immune to it.[3] This fallacy argues that religion induces Muslims to believe, behave, act, think, argue and develop their identity *as Muslims* despite their disparate heritages, ethnicities, nationalities, experiences, gender, sexual orientations and, last but not least, mind. In other words, their believing in Islam makes them a sort of cloned CPU: different styles, different colours, same process. Sometimes this fallacy is the result of generalizations, some of which are difficult to avoid. At other times, however, it is more ideological and the by-product of an extreme culturalist position. In all cases, the root of it is the, latent or manifest, unrecognized fact that a Muslim person is primarily a human being. In *The Anthropology of Islam,* I shall suggest that emotions and feelings should be at the centre of our studies of Islam. This means reconsidering the relationship between nature and culture – as we shall discuss in Chapter 6.

Participant observation, at least since Malinowski, has been the main methodology within anthropological studies. Fieldwork should have been the main antidote to essentialism. However, fieldwork in itself cannot protect the anthropologist from embracing essentialism. We need to understand that we cannot conduct anthropological fieldwork within Muslim societies and communities as, for example, Geertz (1968) or Rabinow (1977) did about thirty years ago. We have to face, for instance, new challenges, some of which are the product of new technologies. I encountered evidence recently of how the expanding easy accessibility of the Internet in all countries can modify the experience of fieldwork. My PhD supervisor used to tell me about her experience of fieldwork in Africa, and the positive and negative side of leaving the field to start analysis.[4] The anthropologist writing about his or her experience had in the past a certain power in representing the Other. Certainly, the studied community and the anthropologist's informants had less power in publicly presenting their experience of the research. In the case of incidents within the field, there was only one authoritative voice: the anthropologist's voice. Today things are very different. In the era of 'blogging', the informants can tell their story about the research and the anthropologist, as I have recently discovered.[5] Fieldwork, I shall suggest, should incorporate an analysis of the emotional context within which we operate as anthropologists. This means refocusing our attention to how human beings make sense of the 'map' that we call Islam. To do so, we need to observe interpretations of Islam as part of networks of shared meanings; to observe concepts, which we may meet in our interviews (such as jihad, *jāhillyya* and *tawhīd*) as the result of interpretations affected by personal identity, emotions, feelings and the environment, rather than simply a rational textual determinism, or orthodoxy versus orthopraxy.

This also means reconsidering the impact that the anthropology of Islam may have on contemporary issues. Anthropology appears to be the least influential of all the disciplines studying topics related to Islam and Muslims in inspiring policy-making or attracting the attention of the political world and mass media. As I shall discuss in Chapter 4, even an event such as September 11, with its social, political and global consequences, has seen few, scattered influential ethnographic studies, as compared to other disciplines such as Middle East Studies, political studies and even Islamic studies. Why? The anthropologist Hannerz (2003) has rightly answered that the main reason can be found in an inability of anthropologists to reach a wider audience and provide interpretations and future scenarios. This does not mean 'popularizing' the anthropology of Islam but contributing to the debate towards a more accessible engagement with the non-academic world as well as the mass media. Recently, as we shall discuss in Chapter 4, some anthropologists have tried to engage more in the debate surrounding the war on terrorism and the wars in Afghanistan and Iraq. González's edited book *Anthropologists in the Public Sphere* (2004, in particular see parts IV to VI inclusive) presents a good example of the contributions that anthropologists have offered to the current political and social debate concerning the wars in Afghanistan, Iraq and on terrorism. These short articles, mostly written for newspapers and magazines with a wide readership, differ from other political commentaries because they start from the experience of fieldwork and contact with 'the Other'. Other anthropologists have used their methodology to provide new viewpoints on issues such as radicalization, identity, intra-community networks, relations between the state and Muslim communities, and the effects of anti-terrorism policies and legislation on local Muslims, which previously were very much the domain of political sciences (see, for instance. Abbas 2005). The contribution that anthropologists can provide to the current political and general debate on Islam and the Muslim world is extremely important exactly because of the characteristics of anthropology as well as sociology. The anthropologist of Islam can highlight the complexity existing beyond the simplification of the mass media and the populist views of certain politics, and de-orientalize the current debate.

In his research for an anthropology of Islam, Talal Asad, as others after him (see Lukens-Bull 1999), insisted on focusing on Islam as religion. Asad made the fascinating suggestion that anthropologists interested in Islam should rethink their 'object of study' (1986b: 17) as a tradition, which includes, as part of it (and not as part of customs or culture) the Qur'an and the ḥadiths. I certainly can appreciate Asad's viewpoint as a progression from the epistemology – developed, for instance by Geertz (1968) and Gellner (1981) – that affected, and largely still affects, sociological and anthropological studies of Islam. Yet I disagree with his idea of the anthropology of Islam. I think that today we have the possibility of overcoming a pernicious essentialism[6] affecting many social scientific studies of Islam (see chapters 3, 6, 7 and 8 of this book).

We should start from Muslims, rather than Islam. As I have argued above, the main thing that Muslims share among themselves and others is certainly not Islam, but rather the fact that they are human beings. Hence, they communicate, act, interact, change, exchange, with both other humans as well as the environment. These relationships are marked by emotions – which as Damasio has suggested (1999 and 2000) are a reaction to stimuli – that produce feelings. I argue in Chapter 5 that this process has a fundamental impact on how identities are formed. Yet a person defines himself or herself as Muslim because, in one way or another, 'Muslim' has a particular value attached. The value can certainly be explained rationally, but it is not rationally driven. For many people professing their credo in Islam, 'Muslim' has an emotional component attached to it. They *feel* to be Muslims. Then, and only then, the 'feeling to be' is rationalized, rhetoricized, and symbolized, exchanged, discussed, ritualized, orthodoxized or orthopraxized. Of course, people feel to be Muslim in different ways, which are unique to each of them, and they express this feeling in the form of discourse. Some anthropologists, such as el-Zein (1977), have observed that it is impossible to speak of one Islam and we have to move to recognize the existence of Islam(s). Others, such as Asad (1986b), affirm that Islam is something that exists in itself, as, for instance, a tradition. In *The Anthropology of Islam*, I have avoided entering into this diatribe since it inevitably ends in theology. Rather I have suggested that we may understand Islam as a *map* of discourses on how to 'feel Muslim'.

This suggestion has some relevant implications for how we study Muslim societies, also at a methodological level. As I shall explain in Chapter 5, to focus on Muslims as human beings is to acknowledge the role that emotions and feelings have on the informant's discourse of Islam as well as the power that the surrounding environment has in its definitions. In other words, successful fieldwork is based on the capacity of the fieldworker to develop an emotional empathy with his or her studied community. Indeed, if we focus only on the 'object' Islam, we'll miss the relevant processes, existing in identity formation as well as community identification, which can disclose the dynamics of Muslim lives. These dynamics – in other words, the way in which the 'feeling to be Muslim' is expressed, modified by events and environment, established and re-established – are at the centre of what I suggest is a contemporary anthropology of Islam.

I have planned *The Anthropology of Islam* as a multifunctional book. On the one hand, I have tried to offer an unprecedented critical review of studies on Islam and fieldwork among Muslim societies, and on the other, a provocative attempt to reopen a debate that has long been neglected among sociologists and anthropologists studying Muslims. Though my review cannot be exhaustive, and is rather purposely selective, I have embarked on an extended critical analysis of classic and recent social anthropological studies on Muslims. This may provide us with some idea of what forty years of socio-scientific study of Islam have contributed to the understanding of Muslims and their societies. *The Anthropology of Islam* does include, probably for the first time, a dedicated section on studying Muslims in western contexts.[7] In this section I have included some sociologists' studies, since I reject, as sterile and anachronistic, the geo-led division that identifies western-based research as 'sociological' and non-western as 'anthropological' by default. Rather, I have discriminated by methodology, viewing participant observation as a crucial element of an effective approach to the field. Through this extended review, I have tried to highlight two main aspects. The first is the effect that essentialist approaches and analyses have on the overall representation of Islam and Muslims – often bordering on new forms of Orientalism. The second aspect is the lack of socio-scientific, and in particular anthropological, research in some important fields, such as the development and transformation of Islamic and non-Islamic concepts, Muslim aesthetic, the family as a unit, social issues and non-heterosexuality.

The second characteristic of *The Anthropology of Islam*, and perhaps the most challenging for the author, is the attempt to provoke a new discussion within the field. There are many ways of starting a discussion. One of the commonest within academia is criticism, more or less constructive; another is presenting a set of new ideas or views open to debate. In each chapter of this book, I have tried to provide both. I see my suggestions more as an open project, to which improvement and new elements can be added, than a solution. However, I am strongly convinced that we need to move on from conjectural hermeneutics and overcome the idea that symbols can shape human beings, or make them different from the rest of nature. On the contrary, we need to reconsider the relationship between scientific disciplines and anthropology. For this reason, I have based my theory of identity on recent cognitive neuroscientific research on consciousness (Damasio 2000). Although it would be reductive to think that genes, neurons and biology can explain the complex creature that is the human being, it would be obscurantist and rationally blind to reject all scientific studies and research on humans and their minds as not relevant to anthropology.

The culturalist or symbolic approaches to the study of Islam and Muslims cannot be decontextualized from the social and historical context of the 1960s and 1970s. Yet, as we shall see, a perseverance in viewing culture as a special feature, essential to the definition of the human being, may invite us to consider, as Wikan (1999, 2002) has questioned, whether or not culture is irremediably essentialist in itself (see also Grillo 2003). Thus, there is importance in recognizing what we call 'culture' as a natural feature of our being human. In conclusion, I wrote *The Anthropology of Islam* as an appeal to reflect on years of sociological and anthropological studies, which, because they have focused on Muslims as products of Islam, have overlooked the human beings who felt to be Muslims.

## THE PLAN OF THE BOOK

In Chapter 2, I share two encounters, one from my childhood and another from my early anthropological studies, with Islam through the practice and views of two Muslims, Abd al-Kader, a door-to-door salesman, and Abd al Hādī, an imam. I have shown the differences between the two Muslims' interpretations of Islam and compared them with the scholarly presentation of Islam in basic introductions. None of these, however, could be defined as the 'real' Islam. Yet it is helpful, also in this book, to present some of the main aspects of Islam on which most Muslims agree, as far as doctrine and practice is concerned. Similarly, I have presented in this chapter a short history of the beginning of the Muslim community. However, I have stressed that the scholarly representation of Islam should be understood not as Islam itself, but as a map that can help orientate us in a very variegated and confusing territory.

In Chapter 3, I discuss how the study of Islam and Muslim societies did not attract the first anthropologists, who preferred to focus on Native American, African and Polynesian societies. Indeed, they considered Islam and Muslim societies a field pertinent to the so-called Oriental Studies. I present the criticism that Said has advanced in his masterpiece *Orientalism* (1978) and the challenge that, some years later, it presented for anthropologists. In fact, anthropological studies of Islam were not immune from interest-based relationships with colonial powers. The first studies of Muslim societies developed within the French *Ethnologie*, which mainly focused on the French colonies, such as Tunisia, Algeria and Morocco (also called Maghreb). These studies concentrated on the village, since the cities and their orthodox Islam were beyond the aims of the French *Ethnologie*, which focused in particular on kinships, marriages, local tribal Islam and folklore. We shall follow the experience of Gilsenan (1990) and the first reactions to anthropologists who ventured into the studies of the Middle East. Something changed, of course, when for the first time the word *Islam* appeared in the title of Geertz's book. I provide in this chapter a critical analysis of the three main works that have been identified with the anthropology of Islam: Geertz's *Islam Observed* (1968), Gellner's *Muslim Society* (1981) and Gilsenan's *Recognizing Islam* (1982). All these studies focus on the Middle East and North Africa, and together with others, are based on what Abu-Lughod has discussed in her article (1989) as 'zones of theorizing'. I then offer a discussion of the debate regarding the anthropology of Islam as a field of study, which el-Zein (1977) started, Asad answered (1986b) and recently, Lukens-Bull (1999) and, through sharp but necessary criticism, Varisco (2005) re-enhanced. Nonetheless, I suggest that five years since the crumbling of the Twin Towers and in spite of the loss of thousands of lives around the world, Muslims and non-Muslims have still not reflected adequately upon what it means to study Islam from an anthropological perspective in this new era.

In Chapter 5, I move the discussion to study Muslim communities and Islam within Western contexts. At first, anthropologists of Islam privileged exotic villages and cities in which to study local Muslim societies. Today we have to face, even within the local, the challenge of an unprecedented global dimension. From the 1970s until the mid-1980s anthropologists and sociologists focused on the national and ethnic identities of Muslim migrants, suggesting complex processes of integration and assimilation. Yet in the 1980s, thanks to the growing number of the Muslim communities and their new social political activism, Islam, seen as a cultural identity marker, seemed to substitute the previous anthropological interest in nationalism and ethnicity. The concept of identity became central to the understanding of how the Muslim communities would reconcile their religion with Western values. Some influential studies have suggested that Muslim migrants were living 'between two cultures', so that their children could be seen as a product of this 'in-betweenness' possessing fluid, hybrid, multiple identities controlled and shaped by cultural processes. I compare these studies with some of my fieldwork and research experiences suggesting that we should be suspicious of these monolithic culturalist models of identity. I finally discuss the use of the Internet, and the new anthropological studies of the virtual *ummah* that have developed in recent years. In this chapter, I also discuss how the events of September 11 and the war on terror have changed research on Muslims in the west as well as the role of the anthropologists, whose voice is now present within the mass media. I conclude that to study Muslims and Islam within a western context means also to turn the magnifier toward our cultures, our categorizations, and the mechanism in which we make sense of what it means to be a human being in a new dimension that invites the contemplation of the macro within an increasingly shifting micro.

Chapter 6 is devoted to the increasing debate concerning Muslim identity. After summarizing the anthropological approach to identity, I review some anthropological studies focusing on Muslims. In some of these studies, difference and differentiation are presented as the primary reason for the formation of Muslim identities. I also argue that the strong culturalist stand of some research on identity has led some anthropologists to describe western-born Muslims in terms of pathology. Notwithstanding the relevance that difference and differentiation as well as boundary marking processes have in social interaction, I suggest that they may not be prominent in the formation of personal identity. Rather, following recent neuroscientific theories (Damasio 2002), I have argued that, while the self and the autobiographical self are real, identity is a machinery of personal imagination allowing vital coherence between the individual and his or her environment. Hence, emotions and feelings are central to the development of personal identities.

My explanation of personal identity suggests that to the question 'what is a Muslim?' we cannot answer merely by highlighting cultural symbolic elements of reference to Islam as codified religion (a very common practice even in recent anthropological studies). Rather, to the question 'what is a Muslim?' we need to answer 'a human being'. In other words, 'I'm Muslim' means 'I feel to be Muslim'. I conclude that it is by focusing on that 'feel to be' more than on the symbolic 'Muslim' that we can understand how Muslims express, form and develop their identity beyond the imposed stereotypes.

In Chapter 7, I raise some questions about two terms often used within both the mass media and academic studies, Muslim community and ummah (community of believers). I suggest that we need to resolve what I call the ummah paradox. Despite the general use of the terms Muslim community and ummah, the reality is that Muslims are divided into many factions and groups, and what is indicated as one ummah is in reality affected by sectarianism, theological disputes, racism and political divisions. Though Muslims acknowledge the existence of divisions and sectarianism, the majority do not see in this a denial of the ummah. At the same time, social scientists have increasingly employed the keyword 'Muslim community' because of evidence of a sense of belonging among Muslims, in particular during times of crisis, such as the Rushdie Affair or more recently, the global uprising prompted by the Danish Cartoons Affair. I suggest that to avoid essentialism, but at the same time be able to explain the trans-national, trans-ethnic, and often trans-sectarian (Sunni versus Shi'a) sense of belonging among Muslims, we should reconsider the central role that emotions and feelings play, as Maffesoli has argued (1996). Starting from the theory of identity I presented in the previous chapter, I reconsider Hetherington's re-examination of the concept of Bund (1998).

Chapter 8 addresses what Abu-Lughod has called the most investigated of the 'zones of theorizing': the harem. The study of gender in Islam is the field of studies that has suffered the highest level of essentialization. In this chapter I follow the development of the study of gender in Islam, from the silence of the first main studies on Islam to the first feminist viewpoints. I argue that an overemphasis on the debate of women's dress code, and in particular the so-called veil, or *ḥijāb*, has prevented a real study of gender, which in the case of studies concerning Muslims, became synonymous with a study of femininity. Only recently, under the influence of gender studies, have anthropologists started to include masculinity in the study of gender (Lahoucine 2006). As in the case of Muslim women, these studies have focused primarily on the Middle East and other Muslim societies. I suggest that more research should be conducted on masculinity and migration. Nonetheless, I argue that the most overlooked topic within gender studies in Islam has certainly been the study of non-heterosexual Muslims. Only at the end of the 1990s have anthropologists started researching and conducting extensive fieldwork on non-heterosexual communities. Nonetheless, topics such as the relationship between non-heterosexual Muslims and the mainstream non-heterosexual community are still at a pioneering level. I conclude by observing that for a contemporary anthropological approach to Muslims and Islam we need to observe the *dynamics* of gender. This means to focus on femininity and masculinity, more than man and woman, and, in contrast to the more traditional approaches, the role that these dynamics of genders have in Islam, seen as a map of identity discourses.

## NOTES

1. The word 'Elenchos' derives from the ancient Greek ἔλεγχος, which refers to question–answer dialogue that aims to clarify a topic through deconstructing other arguments (May 1997).
2. The Jedi religion, derived from the famous Star Wars series, is now growing and in 2001 was recognized as religion in the UK official Census. The Flying Spaghetti Monster Church started as a humorous initiative, but is now enjoying unexpected success. For more information and possible savoury conversions, you can visit the Church website: http://www.venganza.org/
3. For other examples of criticism concerning essentialist views of Islam and culture see Modood 1998; Donan 2002; Grillo 2003; Matin-Asgari 2004; Geaves 2005.
4. Kay Milton, personal communications.
5. My informant and friend Hasrizal posted his memories of my research and our meetings on his personal blog: http://www.saifulislam.com/
6. Of course, for certain political and ideological positions concerning Islam, essentialism is a positive element in the study of it. Allow me to suggest, however, that even for those who wish to maintain ideological, either apologetic or critical, stands on Islam, essentialism can only lead toward flawed reasoning.
7. I prefer to use the expression 'western context' since even Muslims living outside western countries can have links with the west, understood as a geopolitical dimension, or the West, understood as imagined, often stereotyped, ethnic, moral and political entity.

# CHAPTER 2

# Islam: Beliefs, History and Rituals

## *WHAT IS ISLAM?*

I knew very little about Islam. As a student at the University of Bologna, I discovered my interest in studying cultural phenomena, and among these, religion intrigued me the most. Since my childhood, I had found 'exotic' religions interesting. In my childish mental cinema, Islam projected fantasies of minarets, the *Thousand and One Nights*, Crusaders and Saladins, my colonialist – he fought in Libya – grandfather's stories, and the mysterious garage-mosque in Florence. Beyond fantasies and conspiracies, Abd al-Kader's face, accent and mannerisms made Islam a flesh and bone presence. Abd al-Kader, a Berber door-to-door salesman, used to knock on our door each month or so. As soon as my mother opened the door, he greeted us with his thirty-two-teeth *salām*[1] smile hoping, as usual, that my mother would buy his colourful children's socks. Month after month, Abd al-Kader became a known, and sometimes expected visitor. Soon, the bargains did not take place on the doorstep, but rather in front of coffee, which my mother had prepared for the occasion. Not only was Abd al-Kader a master of bargaining, but also of hypnotic storytelling.

During the winter, when the rain showered outside, he liked spending some time in our kitchen, and entertained us with bright descriptions of his faraway home. Abd al-Kader knew that his stories sold more than his merchandise, and he also knew the effect that his arabesque narration had on my imagination. One day, after he had finished his socks and tablecloths, and probably spent more time with us than he realized, a bip-bip-bip alarm sound abruptly ended the flow of his narratives. At this sound, Abd al-Kader checked his watch and shyly asked my mother, 'May I pray to my God in your home?' She, who has always been curious about religion and tested a good number of them, invited him into the living room. I was very curious and asked if I could stay in the room. Abd al-Kader smiled and showed me how to find the direction for the Muslim prayer; then opened his sports bag, in which he kept his merchandise, and a prayer mat materialized with its colourful design of a black cube in the middle of a mosque building. Abd al-Kader pointed to the cube and told me, 'This is the centre of the universe; this is the Ka'ba, the house of Allah, God'. Then, he stepped, without shoes, onto the prayer mat, raised his hands to his ears and exclaimed 'Allāhu Akbar' and recited the Qur'an. An unknown melody filled our living room. To be honest, the prayer in itself appeared to me, a young curious child, to be like one of those hated physical exercises my school gym teacher required. Abd al-Kader looked pretty expert in this exercise. Later, Abd al-Kader faced the barrage of my questions and I discovered that Muslims must pray five times per day.

This was my first encounter with Islam, as lived religion. Years passed, and the young child became a university student, eager to learn more about the North African community from which Abd al-Kader came. This led me to knock on a door as Abd al-Kader once did with mine. After my shoes joined the others, I entered the prayer hall of a mosque for the first time. My embarrassment and clumsy indecision told the Moroccan *shaykh*[2] Abd al-Hādī that I was not a regular visitor, but one of those entrepreneurs of religious curiosity who sometimes – though rarely – visited his mosque. '*Al-salām 'alaykum.*' He smiled like Abd al-Kader used to do while presenting his goods. I replied with what Abd al-Kader had taught me in the years of my childhood, '*'alaykum al-salām*'. Since those initial salaams, I started to visit shaykh Abd al-Hādī in his mosque for sugary cups of mint tea and a salty chat on Islam. I used to ask him questions, to which he kindly replied, sometimes reciting the mysterious syllable-notes of the Qur'an[3] and interpreting them for me. Among the many questions I asked, one seemed to take him more time and effort to answer: 'What is Islam?' His answer was, '*Dīn* and *īmān*'; a simple answer that became, as the years passed, an intellectual challenge.

Islam is considered a religion. Conventionally the Arabic term '*dīn*' is translated in English as 'religion', while '*īmān*' is usually rendered as 'faith'. The word religion, though commonly used and understood in everyday language, has sparked endless academic disputes over its definition;[4] still today there is no agreement on the subject. The anthropologist Spiro has proposed one of the most widely accepted definitions, '[Religion is] an institution consisting of culturally patterned interaction with culturally postulated superhuman beings'. He went on to explain that superhuman beings, 'refer to any beings believed to possess power greater than man, who can work good and/or evil on man, and whose relationships with man can, to some degree, be influenced by [activities involving values and ritual]' (1966: 96). Although Spiro's definition may show some weakness when applied to 'nontheistic' religions, such as some Buddhist sects (see Herbrechtsmeier 1993), it seems to fit in the case of Islam.

Nonetheless, Abd al-Hādī, who was not aware of Spiro's or others' definitions, taught me that dīn does not mean exactly 'religion'; at least not in the same way we use the term within the Christian western tradition. Abd al-Hādī explained that dīn should be understood through its antinomian: *dunyā*. The term dunyā, of which the main meaning is 'world', also refers to simple matter and, by analogy, the secular. Dīn, in other words, is the opposite of the material world and the secular. It is the domain of spirituality, of the soul. The person's īmān exists within this spiritual domain, of which, according to Muslims, the most powerful and almighty is *Allah*, God, the peace provider. I found Abd al-Hādī's philosophical teaching fascinating. Nonetheless, I came from a Catholic tradition and had attended a Catholic high school. As some Orientalists have argued that Allah is not the same God of the Christians and Jews, so the school priest had taught us that Allah was different from the Christian God. Confident of his understanding and patience, I questioned and challenged Abd al-Hādī on this point. He argued that the priest's argument misled us, the students. Convincingly, Abd al-Hādī demonstrated how a basic knowledge of Arabic can clarify that 'The word *allāhu*, "God", is a combination of the definitive article *al-* with *ilāhun* (meaning "a god"); so Allah means "the God", the only one to whom no associations are allowed, not even Jesus'. In other words, the Arabic term indicating 'God' embeds the main symbol of the strong monotheism that characterizes Islam.

Another of Abd al-Hādī's teachings focused on the term Islam itself. Abd al-Hādī taught me, 'Islam derives from the Arabic three-syllable root *s-l-m*. From this root derives the verb *salima,* to be safe, from which can be derived *sallama,* or to hand over, *istaslama,* to surrender, *salaam,* peace, *salaama,* health or safety and *muslim*'. Abd al-Hādī then told me that beyond this simple group of syllables there was the secret for achieving perfect happiness, 'To be safe by handing over all passions, fears and desires, so that you surrender to Allah following the Prophet; in so doing you achieve peace, and safety from wrongdoing. You become a Muslim.'

During my years of study, books and teachers explained that Islam is a religion based on theological precepts and a particular history. During my research, I learned that the Islam of books, theology and history is nothing other than a ghost hunted for by both the believers as well as the academics. Abd al-Kader's and Abd al-Hādī's interpretations of what Islam is makes Islam a part of reality. And I did not need to spend much time in the anthropological field to appreciate that Abd al-Hādī's Islam differed from Abd al-Kader's. Undoubtedly, they shared similar theological frameworks and history of Islam, but this is not enough to claim that they lived and embodied the same Islam. Their different economic and educational status, their different ethnicities, their different ages, their different worldviews, their different identities – just to mention some divergences – shaped their own practice, idea, ethos and ideology of Islam. Furthermore, like me, they could only have learnt about Islam from others who had learnt about Islam from others, in an endless circle of interpretations. Hence, since interpretations are multiple, multiple are the personal embodiments of Islam.

When I present this argument to my students today, the cleverest – or perhaps the laziest – usually ask, 'Why, if you are right, should I study the basic tenets of Islam and its history?' To which I often answer, 'Because I must mark your essays'. Although this is just a joke, there are some elements of truth in it. What we call the tenets of Islam and Islamic history are nothing else than maps drawn by scholars (Muslims and non-Muslims alike). And although, to use Alfred Korzybski's expression, 'the map is not the territory' (1948: 58), without the map it is very easy to become lost. Similarly, a good knowledge of the theological discourses among Muslims, and historical events related to the foundation and expansion of Islam, can be extremely useful to the anthropological study of Muslims and their religion. The important point – and we shall observe several times in this book that even some anthropologists have missed it – is to be aware that it is not Islam that shapes Muslims, but rather Muslims who, through discourses, practices, beliefs and actions, make Islam.

## ISLAM AND ITS BASIC TENETS

If we could line up, one after another, all the introductory books that have been written about Islam, we would be surprised at the miles we could cover.[5] However, I think that, before discussing sociological and anthropological studies of Muslims and Islam, the reader may benefit from a brief description of 'the map'. I shall divide the summary into two parts. The first part focuses on the official history of Islam (i.e. its origin, community formation and divisions), while the second part observes Muslim rituals as part of a life cycle, which anthropologists have also observed in other cultures (Bowie 2000). I have two possibilities in presenting this section. One solution is to follow the tradition of many introductions to Islam available today. Because the space that this chapter allows me is limited, the reader will certainly be better off with a reading suggestion instead. The second, doubtlessly more attractive for an anthropologist, is to follow my respondents' narrations and explanations about the history and rituals of Islam. Below I follow the second option by providing the reader with a window onto how some Muslims, my respondents and friends in this case, explain, teach and understand Islamic history and Islamic rituals. Are their views and explanations objective? Of course, they are not. Yet on history and the interpretation of rituals, can views and explanations ever be objective? I have only checked that the narrations I am going to present here have been historically 'correct' and have amended only the factual mistakes (such as dates and names). Where have my Muslim respondents and friends learnt this information? From many sources, some common to non-Muslims, such as books, TV and radio programmes, the Internet, and some particular to the 'training' that Muslims, in particular when young, receive within mosques and their home.

Hassan, who is a 53-year-old Jordanian living in London and managing an IT shop, told me, during one of our post-Friday prayer conversations, of the miracle of Islam, 'What I am going to demonstrate to you now is not just a story, but a miracle. The development that Islam brought to Arab people and the short time in which they changed is just that, a miracle of Islam.' Hassan started from pre-Islamic Arabia,

We need to start from *jāhili* times, when Arabia was not Saudi.[6] Well, indeed we can even say that Arabia went full circle, since the Saudi are now jāhili themselves, but this is another story. I was saying ... well yes, Arabs in the peninsula were divided between Bedouin nomads and the more powerful people living in the towns. There were many wars and feuds since the nomads used to attack the caravans and the town merchants. Mecca remained the only real city, nearly a capital. The city was important because of the pilgrimage for all Arab tribes. At the centre of the city, yesterday as today, there was a cube shaped building called the Ka'ba, in which one of the corners housed the *al-ḥajar al-Aswad* [black stone, probably a meteorite]. During the pilgrimage, all the battles were stopped. The Ka'ba, during the time of jāhiliyya was the house of idols, among which there were the representations of both Mary and Jesus. The guardians responsible for the Ka'ba were yesterday and today the powerful *quraysh* family. People respected only two things, the family, the tribe [i.e. kinship] and age, so to be old meant to have more power.

While moving to the café of the mosque in the basement, Hassan had changed his attitude and voice, I could understand that the next part was surely the more important, the centre of his narration,

Now, you see, we are speaking of a feudal society. I mean, they had no respect for anything, not for other lives, and certainly not for women and female children, who they used to kill by burying them alive in the sand when born. You see, the Qur'an for this reason told them [reciting in Arabic Sura 81:8–9] 'When the female (infant), buried alive, is questioned for what crime she was killed.' Muhammad, the Prophet of Islam, *salla Allahu alayhi wa salaam* [*saws*, i.e. peace be upon him] was a very good man but was part of this jāhili society. He was born in 571 CE, and he came from a respected merchant family, at the age of six he was an orphan cared for by his uncle Abū Ṭālib. He had not very many options, but became a manager and took care of the family business and caravans. The honesty of the young Muhammad *saws* attracted the attention of Khadījah, a rich widow. Well, in the end things went further than business, and Khadījah decided to take Muhammad as a husband. Muhammad was fifteen years her junior, but at that time this was not something strange. I can tell you that it was real love and respect, a fantastic relationship. Think that in such a polygamous land, where a man could have as many concubines as he wanted, Khadījah remained Muhammad's only wife until she died.

Hassan, increasingly inspired, went on in his narration. He referred to the sunna and biography of the Prophet, 'All Muslims must know the life of the Prophet *saws*, since he is the perfect example'. Hassan told me that when non-Muslims, who are Christian or of a Christian background, asked him about the Prophet, the first thing that he explains are the differences between how his audience see the figure of Jesus and how Muslims see the figure of Muhammad. He recalled an anecdote, 'One Christian guy who used to work with me told me that Jesus is superior to Muhammad because Jesus was resurrected and is alive while my Prophet is dead. This guy expected some reaction from me. Instead, smiling I answered, "Yes indeed, pretty so. He was so real that I can visit the Prophet's mosque and offer my respect to his grave knowing that his body is there".' Hassan emphasized that the Prophet was only a man, though the best one as guided by God. 'Muhammad *saws* conducted a normal life, between family and work, until the age of forty when he experienced a personal crisis, and questioned himself about the meaning of life, often performing month-long religious retreats in a cave near Mount Hirā', outside Mecca.' Hassan was pointing to an interesting fact. We have no clear idea which religion or religious philosophy Muhammad would have followed before Allah revealed the Qur'an to him. What, however, we do know is that in Mecca an increasing number of thinkers questioned the traditional doctrines and paganism's link to natural events. One of the most influential movements was the *hanīfs*, whose members adhered to local anchorite practices derived from Christian traditions (for more, see Waines 1995: 13–15).

Yet for Hassan and all the other Muslims, it is not a person but a book that is the absolute miracle and God's gift to humanity. Rezeya, a 27-year-old woman of Pakistani origin who studied biology at the Queen's University in Belfast, often highlighted during our interviews how Muhammad could have changed his society using the influence that his family had within the Meccan tribal system and Khadijah's economic power. Instead, Rezeya emphasized how the Prophet followed a very different path, the path of Islam. She observed,

> Now the Prophet did not look for power but for a total change within his society; I mean the end of jāhiliyya, to do so the Qur'an taught him that changes only remain if they change the hearts and minds of people. So when persecuted he preferred to leave instead of fight. So this was the *hijra*, the migration to *yathrib*, today Medina [620 CE] which marks the beginning of the *ummah* [Muslim community]. He went there to sort out the feuds among the tribes and he applied a Qur'anic solution by writing the first known constitution in history.

This was the so-called Constitution of Medina (*dustur al-medinah*). The Constitution of Medina[7] recognized Muslims, Christian and Jewish tribes as separate ummahs (see Chapter 7 in this book), with independent forms of legislation, but united under one God against the idolatrous enemy. The constitution is one of the first examples of divisions between rights and duties among citizens of a multicultural and multifaith society, united, however, in the common belief of the superiority of monotheism against polytheism. Muhammad, now, was not only a Prophet, but also the political leader and main judge of the Muslim community, amalgamating religion and politics into an indivisible entity, which marked the Islamic doctrine of justice and politics in all its future history.

Muhammad, with his new religion based on a radical monotheism, rejected the idols, which were the main reason for the pre-Islamic Arabs to perform pilgrimage to Mecca. It was, after all, exactly because of the Ka'ba that Mecca was an economic and political centre. The Quraysh feared losing their power and control over Mecca while Muhammad, with his increasing number of followers, was introducing a 'revolution' within pre-Islamic Arab society. As we have seen, this society was based on the *sunna* (custom, tradition) of the ancestors, which means that people related to each other following the traditions (or tribal law) of their fathers; Islam challenged society to substitute the tribal sunna with God's law and the sunna of the Prophet of Islam.

The Meccans, and in particular the powerful Quraysh tribe, saw the new city of yathrib as a challenge to both their economic and political power. Muhammad's popularity threatened the centrality of Mecca within the region, and illustrated a new model of governance, which other Arab tribes might have been interested to join. So, the Quraysh, after unsuccessfully executing a plot against Muhammad's life, opted for military expeditions. In 624 CE, the outnumbered Muslims were able to defeat the powerful Meccan forces at *Badr*, near Medina. The miraculous success, which is narrated in the Qur'an, reinforced the faith of the Muslims and increased the number of conversions among Christians, pagans and some Jews to the new religion. The Quraysh, surprised that the Muslims could resist their powerful forces, increased the size of their force and a year later, in 625 CE, attacked the city. This time, however, the Muslims suffered defeat and even Muhammad himself was injured. The Meccans believed they could at last destroy the Muslim community and in 627 CE, they laid siege to Medina. In what would later be referred to as the Battle of the Ditch (the Muslims used a trench to resist the Meccan cavalry), the Muslims won a historical, nearly impossible, battle. The failure of the Quraysh reinforced the image of Muhammad as a divinely guided leader, and many of the Bedouin tribes who supported the Meccans decided to shift their support towards the Muslims. The final act of these short wars took place in 630 CE, when the Meccans did not respect an agreement to permit Muslims to reach the Ka'ba for their pilgrimage (*hajj*). Consequently, Muhammad collected a force of 10,000 Muslims, which nearly without fighting, marched on Mecca, thus ending de facto the Quraysh's rule. Muhammad had not only established a new religion, but also unified most of the Arab tribes under Islam; an unprecedented unity for tribal clans, but a unity that provided one of the most powerful armies, which, side by side with merchants and scholars, would spread Islam to the surrounding regions.

'At the centre of this social and political revolution there was not just a man, but a book, the holy Qur'an', said Rezeya, who continued,

Muhammad *saws* did not want to be a Prophet. At the age of forty the angel Jibril forced the first words of the Qur'an upon him, *iqrā* which means read or recite. He refused and the angel held him stronger and forced him to recite the first verses of Al-Alaq [Sura 96]. The Prophet believed that madness had possessed his mind, but he was supported by Khadijah and his uncle and he started to preach the new religion. The miracle is the Qur'an. The revealed book guided the first Muslim community. There are 114 chapters in the Qur'an and the shortest has only 3 verses, we call the verses in Arabic *āyat*. The Qur'an was memorized and never changed, though the position of the chapters are not in the order they were revealed.

Indeed, the third *khalīfa*, Uthman (644–655 CE) organized a committee to produce an authoritative version twenty years after the death of Muhammad. Uthman's version, which is still the officially recognized version of the Qur'an, arranged the chapters (*surat*) by length with the longest at the beginning. Each chapter has a title derived from a catchword referring to some important event presented in the chapter. Previous systems of classification divided the chapter by the location of the revelation, i.e. Medina or Mecca. The Qur'an is not only the most important text of Islam but also an essential part of Muslim prayers, which should include the first sura *al-fātiha* (The Opening) and part of others. Muslims consider the correct recitation of the Qur'an (*tajwīd*) an art that needs time and practice to master and within which different styles have been developed. The Qur'an is a complex book which addresses not only spiritual matters, such as *tawḥīd* (the Oneness of God), but also narratives and historical content, such as the account of the hijra, and legal injunctions (see for instance Qu. 17:22–39) as well as moral proscriptions, such as the banning of alcohol (Qu. 5:93). The Qur'an recognizes that there have been other prophets, some mentioned in the Bible such as *ibrāhīm* (Abraham), *'īsā* (Jesus), David (*dā'ūd*), Solomon and Moses (*mūsā*), and others whose names have been lost. In other words, each human community had at least a *nabī*, a prophet without a written revelation, or a *rasūl*, a prophet with a written revelation, such as the ones mentioned above. Yet Muslims believe that no other prophet after Muhammad will receive revelations. Finally, Rezeya told me what happened when an imam from London, who was famous for his recitation of the Qur'an, visited their mosque during Ramaḍan,

> The congregation met in one room, with us, the women, sitting in the back. I could see the imam, sitting, legs crossed, with a microphone on the floor, his eyes pointing toward an invisible point behind us. He started reciting the Qur'an and the sound reached our hearts. I cannot describe the emotions that were running through the room; you could have touched it with your hands. People, after a while, started to weep because the imam's recitation was too powerful. The Qur'an can touch your soul not only with its meaning but also with the sounds of its holy letters.

Although the Qur'an is the most sacred source of Islam, Muslims consider the Prophet Muhammad to be the perfect example of what it means to be Muslim. Iqbal, an imam at a local madrasa (a children's school within a mosque) in Scotland, in which I conducted fieldwork, used to repeat to his students 'Muhammad's sayings and actions [i.e. the sunna] gave a physical body to the divine message of the Qur'an.' Islamic scholars have divided the sunna into two main sources: the *sīrahs* and the *hadiths*. The sīrahs are narratives concerning the life and actions of the Prophet Muhammad, which can be compared to Jewish and Christian chronicles. The hadiths are the narratives of what Muhammad said in certain particular circumstances and, after the Qur'an, Muslims consider them the most important source of Islam. Two generations after the death of Muhammad, the hadiths, which in the beginning were transmitted orally, started to proliferate uncontrollably (Burton 1994; Hallaq 1999). It is not difficult to imagine that some Muslims manipulated, or even created, hadiths to justify their own behaviour or to ease the Qur'anic rules. Indeed, it was not long before Muslim scholars recognized this issue and classified the hadiths according to four main different categories based on the reliability of the chain of narrators, or *isnād*. The first category includes the hadiths which are considered *ṣaḥīḥ* (sound or trustworthy), the second the hadiths which, though the chain of narrators shows some weakness, are still considered *hasan* (fair or good), the third those which are considered *da'īf* (weak) and finally the hadiths which have been considered as *saqīm* (sick or infirm, i.e. false). The two collections of hadiths that are considered to be the most authoritative are those of Muhammed ibn Ismā'īl al-Bukhārī (810–870) and Muslim ibn al-Hajjāj (d.875). The science of hadiths, thus, can be particularly complicated and requires years of studies. Yet this is not always the case, and again, today as yesterday, ḥadiths remain very popular among Muslims, in particular in order to support one's opinions. When discussing with Iqbal about the ḥadith, he indeed observed,

> Muslims know that it is important to quote the Qur'an correctly; many can even recite the verses in Arabic. But Muslims do not take care in quoting ḥadith, they do not remember the isnād, even not the book from which they are quoting. The Internet has also complicated the situation. There are hundreds and hundreds of websites reporting ḥadiths and offering ḥadiths, many of which are saqīm or wrongly translated and reported. What can we do? Young people believe more what they read on the screens of their PCs than what I am going to tell them. And believe me, Gabriel, misleading ḥadiths can do lots of damage. In the wrong hands, ḥadiths can justify whatever the Qur'an discourages or condemns. People have not the time to study the ḥadiths and how the ḥadiths should be used. Today we live in a time in which everything should be consumed quickly, and today we have a problem with a ḥadith consumerism. For this reason Muslims are also very confused about what the sharīʻa [Islamic Law] is and how it should be implemented.

Iqbal was pointing out that both the Qur'an and the ḥadiths are central in the formation of what Muslims called sharīʻa. For example, it is from both the Qur'an and the ḥadiths that the five pillars of Islam (arkāna al-islam), fundamental to the sharīʻa, are derived. The arkāna al-islam are the shahāda, or profession of faith (witnessing the oneness of God and the prophethood of Muhammad), salāt, or the five daily prayers, zakāt, almsgiving, sawm, or fasting in the month of Ramaḍan, and ḥajj, the pilgrimage to Mecca to be performed at least once in a lifetime. Yet both the Qur'an and the sunna were still insufficient to resolve all the circumstances in which a legal decision had to be taken. After the death of Muhammad, the ummah had lost its supreme judge and guide for deriving the divine law from the Qur'an. Muslims needed a mechanism to maintain their legal system within God's will. The solution was a process in which ijtihād (individual opinion of a scholar) was based on analogical reasoning starting from the Qur'an and then the ḥadiths. Yet individual opinions could lead to disagreement, khilāf. For this reason, a new law was considered valid only if consensus, ijmāʻ, was reached.[8] Indeed, khilāfa facilitated the formation of many schools of Islamic thought, or madhāhib, of which only four are left within the Sunni tradition (i.e ḥanafīs, ḥanbalīs, mālikis, and shāfiʻīs, all derived from the names of their founders). Yet as Iqbal observed,

> The majority of Muslims born Muslim do not even know that they practise Islam in accordance with the rules of a particular school of thought. They may know that their country, for instance, Pakistan or Turkey, officially follows the ḥanafī school, but this does not mean that they are, say, praying according to it. I came across a brother who was from Pakistan, but he prayed following the mĀliki tradition. The reason was that, of course, he learned to pray from his father who had worked in Morocco for a long time and adapted to the Moroccan style, which is mainly mÅliki.

Surely, the division and differences among the madhāhib are marginal. What instead became the deepest fracture within the Islamic world was – and still remains – the division between Sunni and Shi'i Muslims. In this limited space I cannot provide even a short summary of the complex history and religious tradition of what is known as Shi'a Islam (for more on Shi'a Islam see, for instance, Syed 1981). The division between Sunni and Shi'a is deeply rooted in the history of Islam, and has caused considerable tensions in the Islamic world, since it was often used to increase political struggles and nationalistic or even ethnic clashes.[9] The early divergence between the two parties, which was mainly of a political nature, became increasingly theological. Yet the central debate, if we wish to condense the long dispute, focuses on the political and spiritual role of Muhammad's family. Muhammad died without indicating his successor as leader of the growing Muslim ummah. Hence, Muslims had only two options to resolve the succession issue. The first solution, advocated by the supporters of Alī ibn Abī Ṭālib, the Prophet's cousin, argued that the role of leader of the Muslims, or khalīfa, had to pass from Muhammad to one of his descendants, in this case Alī ibn Abī Ṭālib himself. Alī was a member of the Hāshim family, which, as we have seen, was part of the Quraysh tribe. Alī became Muhammad's son-in-law by marrying Fātima, his daughter. Opposed to the 'party of Alī' (which would later be referred to as the 'Shi'a', whose name means only 'party') remained the majority of Muhammad's companions, or ṣāḥib, who rejected the direct succession as an act against the sunna. They argued that Muhammad had rejected the laws of tribal kinship, and for this reason had not named his successor among his own family. Among the two solutions available to find a leader, the position of the Sunni prevailed, and only four khalīfa later, Alī succeeded in being elected.

Like other khalīfa before him, Alī was assassinated in 661 CE. While the new khalīfa convinced Hasan, Alī's eldest son, to renounce his claim to the khalīfate, Ḥusayn, Alī's second son, refused to recognize Yazid I as the legitimate successor. In 680 CE, Yazid's forces attacked Ḥusayn's small army in Karbalā', in Iraq, exterminated Ḥusayn's supporters, and beheaded Ḥusayn himself. Today we can still visit the marvellous shrine in which the body and decapitated head of Imam Ḥusayn is venerated by Shi'i Muslims. In fact, Alī and his sons are considered martyrs (shahīd) and martyrdom plays a fundamental role in Shi'ism. Revolts against the Sunni khalīfas continued, as did the killing of Shi'i imams. The line of the Shi'i imams eventually numbered eleven, with the twelfth and last imam considered to have concealed himself. However, Shi'i Muslims believe that he will come back on the Day of Judgement, when perfect divine justice will be implemented. Among the many differences, one of the most important is that Shi'i Islam has developed a distinct Islamic school of jurisprudence based on the teaching of Jafar al-Sadiq (d.748 CE), in which human reasoning holds a particularly strong position.

Still, today, tensions mark the relationship between Shi'i and Sunni Muslims. In certain cases, members of the two groups tend to see their opponents as non-Muslims. Yet we can observe some inconsistency, in particular among Sunni, as in the case of the strong support that Hezbollah, the Shi'a militia in Lebanon, received. One of my students, Isham, who was a Qatari Sunni, tried to explain to me this contradiction in these terms,

> I tell the truth, I think that Shi'a are wrong, and I see a lot of *shirk* [idolatry] in what they do. Shi'a perform their prayers by using a stone to remember the grave of Ali, and they believe that their imams have more power when dead than alive. So, they are not real Muslims, I would say. So ... well I do not like them. Yet this is different from the fact that I appreciate what Hezbollah does. They are the last real resistance against the Zionists and they are able to trouble Israel. I mean, if tomorrow the US attacks Iran, all Muslims, even those who hate Shi'ism will support Iran and even go and fight for them. Say that it is politics more than religion! Your enemy's enemy, in this case, is not your friend but your super enemy, since they want to destroy Islam, and not just Shi'ism; Americans and Zionists, as we can see in Iraq, have not even clear the difference between Sunni and Shi'a.

It is clear again, that Muslims' Islam is not monolithic, but a dependent variable which not only is influenced by the identities, memories, experiences, and beliefs of each Muslim and each Muslim group, but also by the surrounding environment and political factors.

## CELEBRATING ALLAH AND LIFE: ISLAMIC RITES OF PASSAGE

Anthropologists have studied religions among different cultures, contexts and places. Certain elements of religion are universal to all; one of these is ritual. We have seen, in the Introduction, that the first anthropologists considered orthodox Islam unattractive from a symbolic and ritualistic viewpoint. By contrast, the village, the Sufi traditions, with their saints, around which devotion and unorthodox practice easily developed, attracted anthropology's curiosity. So, I was not surprised to discover that very few titles of articles (I was unable to find any book) mentioned rites of passage in relation to mainstream Islam. The few existing articles, furthermore, tended to focus on special rituals performed in very remote areas (see Sanadjian 2001), rather than ordinary Islamic practices in urban contexts. Nonetheless, the majority of the Islamic pillars and rituals can be read exactly as rites of passage. Why is it so important to observe these Islamic rituals as rites of passage? Because, otherwise, we are left with only two other analytical solutions: to see them as theological compulsions, or historically fossilized traditions. Before concentrating on the Islamic rites of passage (or life cycle), I wish to summarize some of the main anthropological theories that have tried to explain what the rite of passage may be.

With rites of passage, we refer to a certain form of rituals that human societies have developed to assist and mark the development, and different phases, of their lives. In other words, rites of passage mark a change in status, both biologically (from childhood to adulthood) and socially (from outsider to recognized insider). Van Gennep's book (1909/1960) represents one of the milestones in the study of rites of passage. Van Gennep suggested that a law of 'regeneration', in which rites of passage symbolize forms of the regeneration, controls life. Van Gennep thus explained rites of passage through a threefold model. Firstly, he noticed a phase of separation, followed by segregation and, finally, reintegration. According to Van Gennep, people can change and renew through this process, as their old self dies to make space for the new one. To explain the consequentiality of the phases, Van Gennep employed the metaphor of a house in which people are allowed to move over levels (*limen* in Latin) to reach rooms. He referred to the three different phases of rites of passage as preliminal, liminal and postliminal. The rites of passage, Van Gennep then argued, not only affect the person involved in the ritual but also his own group; in the case of a marriage, he noticed, that the change in status of the groom and bride is accompanied by a change in the status of their families.

Anthropologists soon noticed Van Gennep's theory; among them, Victor Turner. Turner adopted the concept of liminality, but added that people sharing the same rite of passage reinforce their bonds and form what he called *communitas*. Turner believed that Van Gennep's model could find applicability beyond rites of passage (Turner 1967). Bloch followed Turner's invitation and rethought Van Gennep's model. Bloch observed that Van Gennep's model lacks a psychological domain. Therefore, Bloch focused on the difference existing between social status and individual experience. Bloch and Parry (1982), like Turner before them, criticized Van Gennep's beliefs that rites of passage can reduce the 'harmful effects' of the passages between status and groups (1909/1960: 13). They interpreted society not as independently defending itself from change, as Van Gennep seemed to suggest, but rather as an outcome of rituals: 'If we can speak of a reassertion of the social order at the time of death, this social order is a product of rituals of the kind we consider rather than their cause' (1982: 6). Recent and challenging anthropological research on rituals has advanced cognitive explanations for their existence. Whitehouse has provided us with what I consider one of the most convincing. Although I refer to his main book (2004), the theory argues that two divergent 'modes of religiosity' exist, the imagistic and the doctrinal. Religions, according to Whitehouse, show, though with some flexibility, a salient association with one or the other mode. In the 'imagistic mode', rituals, which are often traumatic in their performance, have a lasting impact on people's minds, through their memories, influencing in this way how people conceive of religion. By contrast, in the 'doctrinal mode', religious knowledge is spread through, mainly, intensive and repetitive teaching. For this reason, religious communities in the imagistic mode tend to be small, exclusive and decentred; in the doctrinal mode, religious communities are large, inclusive and centralistic. Following Whitehouse's model, we can say that in Islam, rituals are based mainly on the doctrinal model. Of course, symbols referring to birth, death and resurrection are strong elements of many Islamic rituals. In this section, however, I shall focus only on basic rituals that are common to all Muslims,[10] such as the five pillars, circumcision for men, marriage and death rituals.

All Muslims respect two major festivals ( *'īd*) in Islam and they are *'īd al-fiṭr*, the feast of breaking the Ramaḍan fast, and *'id al-aḍhā*, the feast of the sacrifice (of Isaac), which is celebrated on the tenth day of the month of the ḥajj. Muslims recognize the practice of ṣawm, fasting, as one of the most essential among the arkāna al-islam. Upon reaching the ninth month (Ramaḍan) of the Muslim calendar, Muslims abstain from drinking, eating and sexual relations during the daylight hours.[11] Ramaḍan is a month that emphasizes the unity of the family and the cohesion of society.

Traditionally, every day during the fast, Muslims used to break the fast (*iftār*) with dates and perform the fourth prayer of the day (*al-maghrib*). During Ramaḍan, special local dishes are cooked and family links are reinforced (see Buitelaar 1993). There are three strong emotional moments during the month of Ramaḍan: the beginning of the fast, marked by a visible full moon, the Night of Power *laylat-al-Qadr*, on the twenty-seventh of the month of Ramaḍan, marking the first day of the revelation of the Qur'an, and the 'īd al-fiṭr. I asked Qureshi, an Indian imam living in London, to explain the meaning of Ramaḍan. After some of the standard explanations, he went further saying that, like many other Muslim rituals, Ramaḍan is a metaphor of human life, a teaching in itself. He explained,

> the starting of Ramaḍan represents the hardship that the soul has to undergo to reach happiness. This path is full of temptation, like fresh water and nice food are for the Muslims who fast. Then Allah shows Grace and Mercy and guides humanity with His revelation. So Muslims, during laylat-al-Qadr see that their fast is rewarded with Allah accepting their prayers. Finally, the human soul is freed from hardship and experiences happiness and freedom in the afterlife. Similarly, the Muslims, on the last day of Ramaḍan, stop fasting and celebrate the feast of 'īd al-fiṭr.

The imam, in other words, has described, though with a different terminology from an anthropologist, the phases of a rite of passage: Ramaḍan as a symbol of the transition of the soul through the different phases of spiritual life.

After Ramaḍan, at least once in their lives, Muslims perform another fundamental ritual. The ḥajj is a complex ritual culminating in the celebration 'id al-aḍhā, celebrating the sacrifice of Isaac and reaffirming the Abrahamic origin of Islam. The ḥajj is not just a pilgrimage – it is also a collection of rites, all of which recall the relationship between Abraham, his family and God. Each pilgrim re-enacts Abraham's, and his wife's, actions. To a careful observer, the ḥajj reveals its symbolic emphasis on the different stages of human life. The *ṭawāf*, seven circumambulations of the Ka'ba, the *sa'y*, involving running back and forth seven times between two small hills (al-Safā and al-Marwa) near the Ka'ba, as Hagar did while searching for water for her son Ishmael. The pilgrims then stop at the miraculous well of Zamzam,[12] and drink the water and soak their ḥajj garments (*iḥrām*), which will be used as burial cloth. The most important and emotional part of the ḥajj happens during the ninth day of the pilgrimage, when the pilgrims stand on the Plain of 'Arafa (the so-called ritual of *wuqūf*).[13] If a pilgrim misses this part, the hajj is considered invalid. The wuqūf is a very emotional part of the hajj because the pilgrims ask forgiveness for their sins, and it marks the moment in which the Muslim is 'born again', purified by his or her repentance. After having travelled through the mountain pass of Muzdalifa, sleeping without tents, at sunrise they head towards the valley of Mina, where they imitate Abraham's rejection of Satan's temptations to refuse God's order to sacrifice his son. Symbolically, the pilgrims throw seven pebbles at a tall stone pillar (*jamarah*). Then an animal (normally a sheep) is sacrificed to commemorate God's substitution, at the last minute, of a sheep for Abraham's son. The pilgrims' final two days are spent between Mina and Mecca. Finally, they go back to their normal lives; the change marked by the resumption of everyday dress. The hajj has also another important symbolic value for Muslims. Since about two million or more Muslims take part in the ritual each year, the hajj renders the ummah visible (see Chapter 7), with its different cultural traditions unified under one creed.

The cycle of life is also emphasized in the Muslim prayer (*salāt*), which is traditionally considered to be the second pillar of Islam. Although the Qur'an states the fundamental role that prayers have in the life of Muslims, it does not state exactly when and how Muslims must pray. It is from the sunna, the example of the Prophet of Islam, that Muslims came to know how and when to perform them. Before approaching Allah in their prayers, Muslims have to purify themselves through a ritual ablution (*wūḍu*) in which some parts of the body are washed (i.e. hands, mouth, face and head, arms up to the elbows, and feet). When sexual secretions have been emitted or at the end of menstruation, Muslims have to perform a complete ritual shower, *ghusl*. Muslims should pray five times per day. The position of the sun, i.e. morning (*salāt al-fajr*), midday (*salāt al-dhuhr* and *salāt al-'aṣr*), sunset (*salāt al-maghrib*) and night (*salāt al-'isha'*), dictates the time of the prayer. Since the prayers depend upon the position of the sun, they change in accordance with the latitude of the place in which they are performed. Muslim prayer consists of certain movements repeated in a cycle or *rak'a* (standing–bowing–prostrating–standing), which varies from two to four cycles in accordance with the time of the prayer, while facing in the direction of Mecca (*qibla*). The Muslim worshipper must coordinate the body movements with certain recitations of passages of the Qur'an as well as words glorifying God. It is not difficult to interpret the traditional movements forming a rak'a as representing different stages of life, from being born to resurrection. The prayer breaks the flow of the believer's life into sections marked by the remembrance of God and the afterlife. Muslims can perform prayers anywhere, providing that the place is clean and the time of the prayer has been reached. Yet congregational prayers, *al-jum'a*, are particularly encouraged and attendance at the Friday prayer, *yawm al-jum'a*, in which a designated person delivers a short sermon, is considered *fard*, or obligatory.

I asked many Muslims, and in particular imams, if the prayer had a particular meaning, beyond the theological one. Although I have collected some interesting explanations, including the physical exercise of the movement required to perform the prayer, some pointed out that the prayer represents human life. Mamoun, who has been an imam at an Irish mosque for twenty years, observed,

If you think of how we move during the prayer, you can see that the different parts of the prayer remind you of the journey of life and the different passages. First Muslims stand up, say Allah is great and recite the first sura of the Qur'an (fātiha). This represents the time in which you are fully blessed by youth and strong health, you are young and at the beginning of your journey in life, you need protection, and for this reason we recite fātiha, which is a protection prayer. Then we bend over and, with our hands, reach our knees. This is like when we become older, we are fragile and we feel the weight of our sins and of life. Then we say again Allah is great and we prostate with our forehead to the ground. We are in our grave; we are back to where we started from. And the cycle starts again.

Again, Muslim rituals seem to summarize the passages through which human life journeys. Although Islam rejected pre-Islamic customs and rites as *jāhillya* (pre-Islamic ignorance), circumcision[14] (*khitān*) was retained as part of the Abrahamic tradition. Yet, as in the case of the actual performance of the prayer, the Qur'an does not mention khitān and only the ḥadiths authenticate this tradition. This has facilitated disagreement among the different madhāhib as to whether the practice should be considered obligatory or just part of the sunna. In particular the debate has focused on whether an adult who converts to Islam should suffer the extreme discomfort, with the possibility that this may prevent conversion. There is no prescribed age for khitān, though in general it is performed before puberty. In some countries, such as Turkey, Indonesia, Malaysia as well as parts of Africa, khitān has maintained its ancestral symbolic value of entrance into adulthood. In others, and in particular among the Muslims living in the west, khitān is performed when the child is very young or just a few days after birth, and in hospitals. The ritual of khitān, however it has been performed, becomes a great occasion to celebrate family life so that gatherings and parties are often organized.

However, marriages (*nikāḥ*) are the occasions on which Muslim families organize the most sumptuous and elaborate parties. In Islam, family remains the most important unit of society. Hence, Islam repudiates celibacy and all forms of monasticism and indeed has an extremely positive attitude towards marital sexual relations. Muslims consider marriage one of the most important events in the life of an adult, and the best means to prevent unlawful sexual relationships. Muslim men can marry non-Muslim women, but Muslim women cannot marry non-Muslim men. The fact that Arabs used to be patrilocal can explain this rule so that the education of children within the Muslim community is preserved. Although Muslims can have polygamous marriages (polyandry is forbidden) with a limit of four wives, the Qur'an demands absolute equal treatment among the wives. The majority of contemporary Muslim scholars see polygamy as an exception rather than a right of Muslim men. Indeed, with the exception of some African countries, the majority of Muslims are today monogamous.

In contrast with Christianity, marriage is more a civil than a religious affair, and the blessings of an imam or the mosque are optional. The basic elements for a marriage being valid are the presence of two witnesses and a contract, detailing the bridal gift (*mahr*), which, according to the Qur'an, remains the exclusive property of the bride rather than her father, as in other religions. Islam requires reciprocal respect between the spouses and mutual support, yet the husband has the religious duty to support his family, while his wife can keep her wages if she is working, with anything she spends on the upkeep of the family being considered as charity.

Although the Qur'an and the ḥadīths emphasize that among the allowed things by Allah, divorce (*talāq*) is the most disliked, Muslim men can divorce by repeating three times the statement 'I divorce you' in front of some witnesses, or through a written document. However, the former wife is entitled to compensation (*mutʿa*). Women can also initiate and obtain divorce, and today many Islamic countries have approved legislation that forces the couple to use the courts, such as in Tunisia and Iran. Women can remarry only after a waiting period (*ʿidda*) equivalent to three menstrual cycles. In case of divorce, though the father is responsible for the maintenance of his children until they reach adulthood, they stay with the mother until the age of seven for boys and nine in the case of girls.

If divorce is avoidable, death certainly is not. The Qur'an refers to death as 'the certainty' and it is considered the last rite of passage. In this instance, the rite (prayers and the washing of the body) is the responsibility of the deceased's family. The most important thing is that as soon as possible after the death, a person of the same gender as the deceased washes the body three times and clothes it in a shroud. The body is then brought to the mosque in an open bier, while the shahāda is repeated. A special prayer (*salāt al-janazah*) is performed, usually in the mosque, in which men, children and women take part, though in different rows. Only men, however, can accompany the body to the graveyard, in which the deceased is laid on his or her right, and facing Mecca. The male mourners recite the first sūra from the Qur'an (al-fātiḥah), after which they respect a few minutes of silence, in which each mourner asks forgiveness on behalf of the deceased. The sunna and ḥadīth emphasize that the official period of mourning should be short. Friends and relatives pay visits to the bereaved, often bringing something sweet to eat, and pray for the deceased. The relatives of the deceased visit the grave on the first Friday after the funeral, and on that day they distribute food to the poor. Another important visit is performed on the Friday following the fortieth day after the funeral.

Although I do not have space here to discuss the expansion of Islam, through both peace and warfare, it is important to remember that the first ummah came into contact with other cultural traditions. This explains why, though we can observe a certain unity within Islam, there is a noticeable variety in how the main rituals and practices are performed. Indeed, Islam does not have, unlike most other religions, a unified and recognized church. After the end of the khalīfate, in 1924, no official leader of the Sunni was unanimously recognized. Although Muslims often associate themselves with mosques, local or global Islamic organizations, or a preferred shaykh, there is no obligation for other Muslims to follow them. This, as we shall see, explains the recent proliferation of the *fatwā* (legal opinion or view) on Islamic websites. Islam, in other words, is not monolithic, as the mass media has often presented it, but variegate and heterogeneous, culturally influenced and shaped by the identities of those who interpret its sacred texts and practices. This opens the debate on whether we need to speak of Islam or Islams.

## CONCLUSION

I started this chapter by narrating my encounter with Abd al-Kader and Abd al-Hādī, two Muslims who presented Islam through their everyday practice and views. However, often people learn about Islam not through direct contact with Muslims, but rather through books, articles and the mass media. In this circumstance, Islam becomes texts, history, precepts and tenets. In this chapter, I have briefly highlighted some of these aspects in order to facilitate the understanding of what we'll cover in this book. Yet I have stressed that what we have discussed here is not Islam, but the equivalent of a map, which can help orientate us in a variegated and confusing territory. We have seen that Islam, as any other religion, relies on rituals symbolizing rites of passage. Indeed, while discussing some of the basic rituals shared by all Muslims, I have shown how personal interpretations can go beyond the 'map'. Islam cannot exist without a mind interpreting and making sense of it. So, the Qur'an, the ḥadiths, and the arkāna al-islam would remain mute and without meaning if there were no minds, emotions and feelings informing them and making them unique through the individual professing himself Muslim.

Is studying the textual sources of Islam and knowing its history and theological stances enough to know what Islam is? Being an anthropologist, I think that what Islam *is* depends on how it is interpreted. This means making sense of how Muslims, as a community, organize their social life in different contexts and how individuals interpret their position and identity toward their beliefs. Yet a certain academic understanding of Muslims developed the opposite methodology: starting from Islam in order to understand Muslims.

## NOTES

1. The main religious greetings of Muslims, meaning 'the peace be upon you'.
2. Title of respect for a Muslim spiritual leader.
3. The Islamic Holy Book.
4. For a concise overview of this debate, see Kunin 2002.
5. To mention just a few recent examples: Esposito 1988; Ahmed 2002; Armstrong 2002; Naser 2002; Brown 2003; Riddell and Cotterell 2003; Sonn 2004. Yet, I recommend Waine's excellent book, *An Introduction to Islam* (1995) and the interesting approach of Ernst (2004). From a mainly Christian perspective, see the contribution of Nigosian (2004).
6. The house of Saud took power in 1932.
7. See Watt 1956 for an extensive discussion of the constitution.
8. For a more detailed and historical, yet concise, introduction to the *sharī'a*, I recommend Dien 2004.

9. A clear example of how the division between Sunni and Shi'a has often been reinforced to achieve political goals is the 1980s' war between the Sunni led, but Shi'a majority, Iraq and the Islamic Republic of Iran. Today the division between Shi'a and Sunni is at the base of the bloody civil conflict shaking post-Sadam Iraq.

10. For more information on Shi'a Islam, I suggest Momen 1985 and, specifically on Shi'i rituals, Chelkowski 1989.

11. Children, before puberty, and pregnant or menstruating women are exempt from the fast, while elderly or ill people are allowed to pay the equivalent of a meal instead of respecting the fast.

12. Muslims believe that Hagar, Abraham's wife, ran seven times back and forth between the two hills of al-Safā and al-Marwa, in Mecca, looking for water in order to save her son from dying. Allah sent the angel Gabriel who touched the surface of the ground whereupon the spring appeared, saving both mother and child.

13. Thirteen miles from Mecca, legend has it that this is the place where Adam and Eve met after being exiled from paradise. Indeed, the word 'Arafa derives from an Arabic root meaning 'to recognize each other'.

14. Circumcision in pre-Islamic Arab societies was performed on both sexes. While male circumcision involves the removal of the foreskin, female circumcision (called *khafḍ*) involves the removal of the clitoris or its hood. It is important to emphasize that the practice of female circumcision owes nothing to Islam, and can also be found among Arab Christian communities, particularly in Sudan. Yet some scholars, such as Nigosian (2004: 120), still mislead their readers adducing the barbaric practice of khafḍ to the teaching of Islam.

# CHAPTER 3

# From Studying Islam to Studying Muslims

## BETWEEN REGIONALISM AND ORIENTALISM

Religion has fascinated sociologists and anthropologists since the beginning of their disciplines. However, they focused mainly on the so-called 'primitive cultures'. Indeed, a casual meeting with indigenous people in Mexico, while travelling for the sake of his health, initiated Tylor to anthropology, and led him to advocate a scientific and systematic study of 'primitive people' (Tylor 1881). In *Primitive Culture* (1871), he adopted a unilinear evolutionary theory of societies. Tylor suggested that societies, through the evolutionary process, pass through three progressive stages, animism, polytheism and monotheism. Durkheim, one of the fathers of modern sociology and anthropology, had a stronger impact on how future generations of anthropologists and sociologists would understand religion and its functions within societies. In his seminal work, *The Elementary Forms of Religious Life* (1915), Durkheim introduced his influential distinction between the 'sacred' and the 'profane'. Again, his data focused in particular on Australian Aboriginal people, whom he considered one of the simplest forms of society in existence. Consequently, Durkheim thought that the study of their society could shed light on the origin and formation of the idea of the 'sacred' among more complex societies, such as his own.

Nevertheless, the first anthropologists often developed their analysis from data that they did not collect, and in many cases, were provided by missionaries. Malinowski, who systematically introduced participant observation and fieldwork, can be considered the first modern anthropologist to rely on a planned methodology. Polish, but living in England and teaching at the London School of Economics, Malinowski was in Australia when the First World War began. Forced to decide between internment in Australia and a fieldwork-exile, he left Australia for the Trobriand Islands (Papua New Guinea). The result of his fieldwork was an ethnographic study, *Argonauts of the Western Pacific* (1922), an evergreen that any undergraduate studying anthropology will meet, though the publication of his private diaries in 1967 cast shadows over the real attitude of the author towards his informants. More genuine, perhaps, have been the emphases on participant observation of Franz Boas. Interested in totemic systems, like Durkheim, but paying particular attention to the social psychology of the individual, Boas conducted fieldwork among the Inuit of Canada, and studied their cultural differences. Culture, and how its traits move from one society to another, became a fundamental part of American anthropological studies, while the British tradition would continue to focus on the main structures and functions forming society. Hence, the social anthropologist Radcliffe-Brown not only combined his study of functionalism with structuralism, but he also dedicated a large part of his research to religion. His most famous work is *The Andaman Islanders* (1922), an analysis, based on his fieldwork, of Andaman Islanders' beliefs, religion and rituals.

It is not my intention, here, to discuss the development of anthropology of religion, as other works have freed me of this task.[1] Rather, by showing the first steps of this new field of study, I wish to highlight how monotheistic religions were absent from the interests of these first anthropologists; this notwithstanding the impact that Weber's *The Protestant Ethic* (1920) had on the sociological research of religion. Until the 1970s, ethnographic research on Islam, although potentially 'exotic' and intriguing, was extremely rare. The lack of interest in the ethnographic study of Islam and Muslims was justified by the fact that there was a long and florid tradition of literary and historical studies in the field of Arabic and Oriental studies.

Despite the theological and political conflicts between the Islamic and Christian worlds after the death of Muhammad, and the reciprocal interest in their different theological stands, the first Latin translation of the Qur'an didn't appear until the first half of the twelfth century. Commissioned by Peter the Venerable, the Abbot of Cluny, he used the translation for arguing the weakness and evilness of 'Mohammedanism' (Kritzeck 1964). It is not difficult to think that the Abbot of Cluny started what could be considered the prehistory of Orientalism on the precept that 'to win your enemy you have to know your enemy'. Even after the end of the Crusades, a mainly polemic campaign against the theological stances of the Muslim faith (Daniel 1993) marked the study of Islam under Christian scholarly supervision. Nonetheless, as Robinson has correctly noticed,

> There is a world of difference between those mediaeval polemics and the writings of contemporary Christian Islamicists who are associated, for instance, with Hartford Seminary, Connecticut, or the Pontifical Institute for the Study of Arabic and Islam in Rome. Staff and alumni of these reputable private institutions have done much to correct the distorted images of Islam propagated by previous generations of Christians. (2002: 98)

Robinson, however, has admitted that this is a quite recent development in the Christian–Muslim relationship since 'in the first half of the twentieth century, Christian missionaries in British India were still using an English translation of *The Apology al-Kindi*, an anti-Muslim tract that Peter the Venerable had included in his "Cluniac corpus" 800 years earlier' (Robinson 2002: 99).

If a religious and political leader of those times represented Islam and Muslims as the evil, dangerous 'Other', artists and novelists, in particular during the Renaissance, represented it as the erotic-exotic feminine (Said 1978). Starting from Flaubert's famous personal impressions of Egypt (1972), the distant and exotic

Orient became a cliché in nineteenth-century French (as well as other European) novels. Then painters expressed in colours what the novels had in words.[2] As the novels and the paintings showed no memory of the polemic first Christian studies of Islam,[3] so the new Oriental studies freed themselves of the religious rhetoric. Indeed, these studies developed mainly within the secular environments of European universities, particularly in Germany. Nonetheless, Islam was not a subject of 'scientific' humanistic investigation. Focusing on Arabic, history and philosophy, the Orientalists started to translate and analyse the textual traditions of Islam. Works such Goldziher's *Muhammedische Studien* (1971), first published in 1890, focused on ḥadiths and Islamic history. This nineteenth-century study of the Islamic has offered some interesting, high quality scholarly works, which should not be blindly rejected. The main issue, however, is that, particularly in Germany, these Orientalists studied Islam in the same way as the classic ancient Greek or Latin cultures. If the classic Latin and Greek texts offered to these scholars the otherwise unreachable voices of those societies, Muslim voices would have been easily reachable. Rather, in Orientalist studies, their voices remained mute, not because time had reduced them to ashes and dust, but because Orientalists saw real Muslims, in flesh and bone, as irrelevant. This is hardly surprising if we consider that the majority of Orientalists' works appeared during an expansion of colonialist powers and ideas.

Therefore, Said has argued (1978) that the concept of Orient and Orientalism as a discipline are *European* (i.e. Western) discourses that are far from being neutral; they are ideological and the result of a certain power relationship marked by political interests. Orientalism, to quote Said, '*is* rather than expresses, a certain *will* or *intention* to understand, in some cases to control, manipulate, even incorporate, what is a manifestly different (or alternative and novel) world' (1978: 12, italics in the original). In other words, academics, no less than politicians, are responsible for transforming the Arabs, and Muslims, into the archetype of the 'Other'. This 'Other' embodies the anti-Western per definition. According to an 'Orientalist' perspective, Muslims not only miss some historical events which have enhanced Europe, such as the Enlightenment, but they also lack the capacity for representing (leave aside understanding) themselves. They *need* to be guided by the Western power. Certainly, Said's observations have critical implications for how not only Orientalist scholars, but also contemporary sociologists and anthropologists, have studied and study Muslims.

'Where was The Middle East?' asked Gilsenan, and with cynical humour answered 'interesting enough, nowhere' (Gilsenan 1990: 225). In his chapter 'Very Like a Camel: The appearance of an Anthropologist's Middle East', he has provided a crisp and vivid account, as an 'insider', of the lack of ethnographic studies concerning both the Middle East and Islam. Gilsenan has also suggested that throughout the 1960s, when interest in the Middle East and Muslim societies finally arose among anthropologists, ethnographic accounts of villages and Sufi saints in the Middle East provided the paradigm for the new field, rather than a planned discussion of what the new academic field could have been and aimed at. Inevitably, the anthropological studies of Muslim cities, classic texts and educated scholars remained the domain of the Orientalists. Meanwhile, the wars between the Palestinians and the Israelis, and the consequent geopolitical destabilization of the Middle East, reinforced the competitive, though still new, field of Middle East studies. Middle East studies scholars focused on political, economic and strategic analysis, which provided interesting data for western governments. Increasingly, anthropologists, avoiding the political debate, ghettoized themselves in the villages. If these traditional studies of village kinship and rural leadership had suited the colonialist administration of the previous century, it failed to engage with twentieth-century realpolitik. The anthropologists working on the Middle East and Northern Africa found themselves trapped between the exotic and the ivory tower. If, during the 1960s, the anthropology of the Middle East, as regional anthropology, suffered a difficult identity formation, the anthropology of Islam remained a ghost.

Geertz's *Islam Observed* (1968) delivered the kiss that awakened the sleeping beauty. For the first time, an influential anthropologist wrote a work featuring the word 'Islam' in its title. Geertz's book inspired new generations of anthropologists, who redirected their attention to Islam as religion rather than to kinship, marriages and village rural life (Fernea and Malarkey 1975). During the middle of the 1970s, some scholars started to question the new field and its achievement. One of these first reviews compared studies on the Middle East within the different ethnographic schools, such as French *Ethnologie*, British social anthropology and American cultural anthropology. This review has cast a grim shadow on the overall success of ethnographic studies of Middle East and Northern Africa. Fernea and Malarkey have stated, 'anthropological studies in MENA (Middle East and Northern Africa) have largely failed to attract an audience of scholars beyond those devoted to undertaking such studies themselves... With few exceptions, contributions to anthropological literature based on Middle Eastern research have failed to have an important impact upon theoretical concerns in the field of ethnology' (1975: 183). Even stronger were their conclusions:

> MENA anthropology has, for a large measure, become a set of speakers without listeners. Only a faint murmur of the former, often in an exchange of regrets, is heard in the discourse of general ethnology, of Orientalism, and of the reading public. It is theory which provides academic discourse with depth, just as it is 'history' which gives experience its density, and just as it is connotation which transcends language and liberates speaker and hearer from a state of mutual insensibility. (1975: 201)

The lack of a framework, or better 'a paradigm', has prevented the long list of ethnographic studies, discussed by Fernea and Malarkey (1975), to achieve a convincing discourse. These 1960s MENA ethnographic studies remained at the margin of the anthropological and sociological studies, while by contrast, African ethnographies, such as those of Evans-Pritchard and Turner, became traditional pillars of anthropology. Subsequent critical reviews, though still focusing on MENA and only marginally referring to an anthropology of Islam, have at least forecasted the possibility of a brighter future for the anthropology of Islam[4].

Beyond these few reviews on the ethnographic works of the Middle East and Northern Africa, no scholar has provided a critical study tracing the development of the anthropology of Islam. However, Varisco has rightly observed (2005: 135–6) that perhaps there is no need,

> Imagine the absurdity of writing an anthropology of Christianity by tracing all the ethnography conducted in 'Christian' contexts. What would such a far-fetched and novel text be called? ... I suggest that simple essentializing of the long history of the faith in ideal types, beyond repeating the obvious sectarian splits, offers nothing new. It is easy to create unity out of diversity but seldom does it serve an analytic purpose.

Therefore, in the following paragraphs and sections I do not wish to provide such an 'intellectual trajectory of the anthropology of Islam' (Varisco 2005: 135). Rather, I will discuss the different viewpoints on what the anthropology of Islam might be.

## TOWARDS THE ANTHROPOLOGY OF ISLAM?

As a postgraduate student of anthropology, with a vivid interest in Muslim societies, I was surprised how Islam, as religion, was missing from ethnographies devoted to Muslims. Anthropologists considered studying Islam less attractive than studying 'primitive' religions since many of them perceived Islam as lacking interesting cultural and symbolic features, such as complex symbolic rituals or ceremonies. In other words, Islam, with its iconoclastic traditions, abstract conception of God and focus on orthodoxy, appeared too plain. Thus, anthropologists met Muslims mainly in villages, with saints (Sufis), complex kinships, lineages, and agricultural and pastoral economics. Indeed, as Gilsenan has recalled, Islam remained a difficult element to incorporate within anthropological analysis, 'There was effectively no model in monographic or theory terms to indicate *what* should be done, let alone how, not in what ways such disparate secondary materials might be incorporated into something that would be taken to be recognizably "anthropological"' (1990: 226, italics in the original). Students such as Gilsenan, with an interest in Islam and the Middle East, received the traditional training in anthropology as any other student in the department: spending time reading and studying the 'foundation' of the discipline, such as Durkheim, Malinowski, Evans-Pritchard, Radcliffe-Brown. But, as the student Gilsenan understood in 1963, these authors and their theories hardly would have fitted his research.

The question which Gilsenan, and other pioneers of the new field had to answer, at least to their colleagues, was: 'how do anthropologists studying Islam and Muslims remain anthropologists and not be absorbed into Oriental studies, or the developing Middle East studies?' The solution was found between Chicago and Mexico. Von Grunebaum (1955), an Islamicist working at the University of Chicago, adapted to Muslim societies the findings of an anthropologist colleague, Redfield, whose research focused on peasant communities in Mexico. Redfield had suggested that all the religions bifurcate into 'great traditions' and 'little traditions'. The great traditions are urban and orthodox, they are 'consciously cultivated and handed down' (1956: 70). By contrast, 'the largely unreflective many' (1956: 40) end in practising little traditions, which contaminate mainstream religion through syncretism derived from folklore. He, however, admitted that the two traditions are not isolated from each other but rather interact consensually. Finally, anthropologists studying Muslim society and conducting fieldwork among the 'peasants' of the Middle East and Northern Africa (better known as Bedouins) found the missing link to claim their anthropological pedigree and overcome that 'not always well-concealed irritation' toward anthropologists, labelling Arabists or Islamicists the new 'Lawrences of Arabia' (Gilsenan 1990).

Geertz's *Islam Observed* would provide future generations of anthropologists, conducting research among Muslim societies, with an authoritative precedent, which was not the result of fieldwork in remote areas of South America, but rather a supposed participant-observation of two Islamic countries, Morocco and Indonesia. I shall not summarize Geertz's work here, nor shall I provide a new critique or defence of this seminal study, as many valid summaries, critiques and defences are now available.[5] Rather, I wish to evaluate how *Islam Observed* has contributed to the formation of the anthropology of Islam. What, however, both supporters and detractors of Geertz's *Islam Observed* can agree upon is the lack of real Muslim voices in Geertz's ethnography. The eventual student of the anthropology of Islam hoping to find a Malinowskian inspiration from Geertz's experience of fieldwork in Morocco and Indonesia can only remain frustrated. In *Islam Observed*, fieldwork, we can say, is nothing more than a validating, 'I was there'. But we have to recognize that Geertz has provided two innovative elements, a needed comparative approach to Muslim societies as well the redefinition of the dyad great versus little tradition in terms of scripturalism versus mysticism. Nonetheless, el-Zein (1977) has noted that Geertz, through his famous definition of religion (1966),[6] ended up essentializing Islam. El-Zein has acknowledged that Geertz has considered the particular historical, cultural and social differences between Islam in Morocco and Indonesia, but Geertz, el-Zein has observed, has expressed the contention that all expressions of Islam,

> find unity of meaning through two dimensions of these universal conditions: first as expressions of a particular form of experience, religion, with certain defined characteristics such as the integration of world view and ethos; and second as a historically continuous tradition of meaning in which the original expression and all those following it in time and space do not exist as complete distinct realities but as delicately related developments of an initial symbolic base linked by the social process of shared meaning... This unity of Islam established at the level of his philosophical premises allows Geertz to speak legitimately of an 'Islamic' consciousness at the level of actual experience as well. Each individual experience contains the universal characteristics assigned to the religious form of experience and those particular shared meanings which recall an entire tradition of Islam. (1977: 232)

In other words, despite the useful and challenging contribution that Geertz has offered to the anthropological study of Islam, the ultimate result of his analysis has offered a counterproductive essentialist view of what Islam, rather than a Muslim, is. Furthermore, Geertz did provide, for the first time, that 'paradigm' that the first studies of Muslim societies lacked. From his choice of title to the essence of his interpretation, Geertz has made Islam the protagonist of the anthropological discourse. Albeit, in *Islam Observed*, readers can spot little (if any at all) anthropology.

If Geertz's study had a strong influence on American anthropologists, who started to consider Muslim societies worthy of studying, in Britain *Muslim Society*, a book written by Gellner (1981), would provide British social anthropology with its authoritative work on Islam. Gellner (and then many of his pupils) has forcefully defended his work on Islam, while others[7] have savagely criticized his ethnocentric and monolithic approach to it as much as his total support for an essentialized segmentary lineage theory. As we have seen above, anthropologists who worked on Muslim societies needed to reclaim their challenged anthropological identity. Gellner, like many others, has framed his analysis of North African Muslim societies within the traditional division between little and great traditions.[8] However, he has reclaimed his anthropological identity through the father of segmentary lineage theory, Evans-Pritchard (1940 and 1949), of whom Gellner felt to be a faithful disciple.

Segmentary theory, just to summarize in very few simple words,[9] suggests that families in rural and tribal societies form ties that are segmented in different group sharing interests (such as land or a herd together). So, if in a community there are groups A, B, C, D, E, F, G, H, segmentary theory suggests that through kinship (which, however, goes beyond blood relationships and includes friendships) A and E, C and F, B and G, as well as D and H would form networks aimed at mutual support. This means that if the family C has an argument with family A, E, which has not been challenged by C, will support A against C, while F will support C against A. In certain circumstances, the two main groups, e.g. A and B, to which all the others are tied, could have a feud. In consequence, A would expect that groups E, C and F, would support their cause, while B would trust G, D and H. Of course, power within segmentary societies tends to be diffused. Evans-Pritchard observed, 'Authority is distributed at every point of the tribal structure and political leadership is limited to situations in which a tribe or a segment of it acts corporately. With a tribe this only happens in war or in dealings with outside authority' (quoted in Gellner 1981: 37).

The majority of scholars have interpreted segmentary theory as a way to describe 'not what groups do or not do "on the ground" but how they think or talk about themselves and what they do' (Abu-Lughod 1989: 284). Yet, Gellner has controversially stated, 'to describe a tribal grouping as segmentary is not merely to classify it – it is also in large measure to explain its organization. More than most classificatory terms, perhaps, *segmentation* contains a theory. The theory is simple, elegant, and, in my estimation, to a very large extent correct' (Gellner 1981: 36). Too simple, too elegant and too western, has retorted Hammoudi (1980), who has suggested that Gellner 'brushing aside all history' has just imposed his convenient model on a reality that is instead complex. Because of Gellner's Eurocentric approach to Islam, we should not be surprised to find his segmentary theory rather fixed, unchangeable and totally forgetful of European colonialism. Indeed, Gellner's central argument concerning Islam argues that *Islam cannot change*. Far from being the religion of living Muslims with opinions, ideas, feelings, identities, Gellnerian Islam is an essence that remains constant in its model. So, if segmentary theory shapes Islam in the village, the Qur'an, or, as Gellner has called it 'the Book', shapes the urban Muslim. Because of the lack of references to other anthropologists who have conducted fieldwork in the Middle East and the Arab world (with the rare exception of a few words from Geertz), Gellner's works on Islam are somewhat surprising.[10]

What might students of the anthropology of Islam learn from Gellner's work? Again, as in the case of Geertz, certainly not how to conduct fieldwork, not how to understand their informants and certainly not how to observe the impact that colonialism had on Muslim societies. Gellner is not interested in understanding Muslims; rather, like Geertz, he believed he had provided the ultimate explanation of Islam as a cultural system. But what Gellner in reality provided was a 'simple, elegant' and Eurocentric philosophical-political view of Islam, in which 'the Islam founding Arabs appear only as segmented Bedouins' (Varisco 2005: 75). The influence that Gellner has on British anthropologists studying Islam has been (and remains, e.g. Shankland 2003) relevant. However, Gellner's study of Islam has not provided any contribution to what the anthropology of Islam might be, or even what it means to study Islam. One of the reasons for this lack of reflexivity is that *Muslim Society* is not a monograph based on coherent research, but rather a self-glorifying anthology, which lacks unity. Indeed, we cannot other than agree with Varisco when he notes, 'If there is any one book by anthropologists purporting to explain Islam or Muslim Society that should be avoided because it is so summarily patched together and indignantly indifferent to available scholarship, that text could easily be Ernest Gellner's *Muslim Society*' (2005: 53).

Gilsenan's *Recognizing Islam* (1982) appeared one year after *Muslim Society*. Like Geertz and Gellner, Gilsenan is an anthropologist whose research focused on the Middle East. Yet, in contrast with Geertz's and Gellner's works on Islam, Gilsenan's seminal book succeed in avoiding essentialism. Through an anthropological approach deeply rooted in the practice of fieldwork and reflective tradition, this book provides readers with an inspiring study of the different embodiments of Islam. If I remain stalwartly sceptical towards the suggestion that Geertz's and Gellner's works founded the anthropology of Islam, I have no hesitation in affirming that Gilsenan's study represents a valid start. Notwithstanding that his work remained located within the Middle East and Northern Africa, Gilsenan's *Recognizing Islam* has not privileged the village over the city and has avoided the 'little' versus 'great' tradition dichotomy, as well as the Gellnerian version of segmentary theory. Indeed, Gilsenan, though he never refers to an anthropology of Islam, has highlighted some basic principles in studying the Muslim religion. These principles were hardly a novelty in the anthropological study of religions and cultures, at least since the times of Boas. Yet they were certainly innovative in the case of studying Muslims and Islam. In the Preface of his book, we can read,

> I did not consider Islam to be a monolithic 'it', an entity which could be treated as a theological or civilizational historical bloc, unchanging and essentially 'other' in some primordial way. Nor did I wish to put forward an account of belief, doctrine and history as systematized by Orientalists, theologians or jurists... I was and am concerned with more sociological questions of social and cultural variation in very different societies subjected to the conflict of the colonial and post-colonial periods and of the very turbulent processes we label modernity. (1982: 5)

Gilsenan has, though briefly, outlined the two most important elements of methodology in a sociological analysis of Islam,

> First, to examine the practices and everyday lives of persons describing themselves as Muslims and the discourses of authority that are taken for granted or struggled over; second, to use such an attempt at understanding to reflect back critically on the ways in which Westerners in general tended to approach societies in which such practices, teaching, forms of knowledge and culture are significant. (1982: 5)

In his work as fieldworker and anthropologist, Gilsenan has demonstrated an effort to understand, without patronizing, what both Geertz and Gellner had concealed. Gilsenan has developed clear methodological and analytical paradigms. Part of these paradigms is the attempt to 'dissolve' the essentialist view of a Muslim mind 'explain[ing]' a whole series of events and structures that are otherwise totally baffling and alarming' (1982: 19). Following this anthropological approach means discussing Islam as,

> not a single, rigidly bounded set of structures but rather as a word that identifies varying relations of practices, representation, symbol, concept and worldview within the same society and between different societies. There are patterns in these relations, and they have changed in very important ways over time. My aim is not to persuade the reader to substitute a relativized and fragmented vision for one of global unity. Rather it is to situate some of these religious, cultural, and ideological forms and practices that people regard as Islamic in the life and development of their societies. (1982: 19)

Gilsenan has reversed Gellner's Eurocentric view of Muslim societies, and provided a paradigm for understanding Islam as a discourse within society rather than an essence shaping it. Notwithstanding the weighty contribution that Gilsenan has made towards the formation of the anthropology of Islam, his work has not been widely discussed in reviews within the field.

In the previous paragraphs, we have discussed anthropological works that have been indicated as the 'foundation' of the anthropology of Islam. They are studies, examples, we can say, stemming from the authors' ethnographic experiences, the majority of which are located in the Middle East. None of them, however, offered an answer to the question, 'what is the anthropology of Islam?' In 1977, nine years after Geertz's *Islam Observed*, Abdul Hamid el-Zein provided the first analytical and paradigmatic attempt to define the anthropology of Islam in an article which passed nearly unobserved. Offered in the format of a review, comparing five different anthropological approaches (Geertz 1968; Bujra 1971; Crapanzano 1973; Gilsenan 1973; and Eickelman) against prominent theological viewpoints of Islam, el-Zein's article challenged his reader with a provocative question, 'in the midst of this diversity of meaning, is there a single, real Islam?' (1977: 249) El-Zein answered negatively. The anthropologist wishing to study Islam should recognize that:

> Islam as an expression of this logic can exist only as a facet within a fluid yet coherent system; it cannot be viewed as an available entity for cultural systems to select and put to various uses. 'Islam,' without referring it to the facets of a system of which it is part, does not exist. Put another way, the utility of the concept 'Islam' as a predefined religion with its supreme 'truth' is extremely limited in anthropological analysis. Even the dichotomy of folk Islam/elite Islam is infertile and fruitless. As I have tried to show, the apparent dichotomy can be analytically reduced to the logic governing it. (1977: 252)

El-Zein has suggested that anthropologists should fully reject the essentialist dyad 'true Islam' (i.e. great tradition) versus 'false Islam' (i.e. little tradition), which certain anthropologists have propagated together with Islamic theologians. Rather, he has campaigned for a structuralist approach, which starting from the 'native's' model of 'Islam',

> analyze[s] the relations which produce its meaning. Beginning from this assumption, the system can be entered and explored in depth from any point, for there are no absolute discontinuities anywhere within it – there are no autonomous entities and each point within the system is ultimately accessible from every other point. In this view there can be no fixed and wholly isolable function of meaning attributed to any basic unit of analysis, be it symbol, institution, or process, which does not impose an artificial order on the system from outside. That is, the orders of the system and the nature of its entities are the same – the logic of the system is the content of the system in the sense that each term, each entity within the system, is the result of structural relations between others, and so on, neither beginning nor ending in any fixed, absolute point. (1977: 251–2)

Eickelman (1981b) has highlighted el-Zein's intellectual courage, since, as a practising Muslim, el-Zein advanced theoretical positions that, if misunderstood, as indeed they were, could have been rejected by Muslims. El-Zein has claimed that anthropologists can provide a social scientific analysis of Muslim life through the observation of the diverse interpretations of Islam.

Eight years were needed before el-Zein's critical review found a reply. In *The Idea of an Anthropology of Islam*, Asad finally addressed the questions 'what, exactly, is the anthropology of Islam? What is its object of investigation?' (1986b: 1). Firstly, Asad rejected el-Zein's argument as, 'a brave effort, but finally unhelpful' (1986b: 2), and secondly he criticized Gilsenan's paradigm because,

> like el-Zein, [it] emphasizes ... that no form of Islam may be excluded from the anthropologist's interest on the ground that it is not the true Islam. His suggestion that the different things that Muslims themselves regard as Islamic should be situated within the life and development of their societies is indeed a sensible sociological rule, but it does not help identify Islam as an analytical object of study. (1986b: 2)

Finally, he argued that in an anthropological analysis of Islam, Muslims' theological views could not be ignored, hence, the origin of Asad's harsh comment on both Zein and Gilsenan's views. Abu-Lughod, however, has accused Asad of ideological stances that led him to misunderstand the two authors' positions (1989: 295). Asad has surely provided indications of how scholars should approach the anthropology of Islam,

> If one wants to write an anthropology of Islam one should begin, as Muslims do, from the concepts of a discursive tradition [Islam] that includes and relates itself to the founding texts of the Qur'an and the Hadith. Islam is neither a distinctive social structure nor a heterogeneous collection of beliefs, artefacts, customs, and morals. It is a tradition. (1986b: 14)

For the first time, Asad has proposed the blueprint that this discipline lacked. We cannot understand, however, Asad's paradigm for the anthropology of Islam without grasping his use of the word 'tradition'. Tradition, according to him, 'consists essentially of discourses that seek to instruct practitioners regarding the *correct* form and purpose of a given practice that, precisely because it is established, has a history' (1986b: 14, italics mine). A tradition is conceptually linked to a past (marking the formation of the tradition), a future (marking the strategy of survival of the tradition) and a present (marking the interconnection of the tradition with the social strata). Therefore, Asad has concluded, for analytical purposes 'there is no essential difference ... between "classic" and "modern" Islam' (1986b: 14).

Asad has suggested that a tension exists between historical, political, economic and social dynamics, which through orthopraxy try to change tradition, and the tradition itself, which tries to resist through orthodoxy. For this reason, Asad can claim that anthropologists such as Gilsenan (who has denied the centrality of orthodoxy in Islam) or Gellner (who has transformed certain specific doctrines into the heart of Islam itself) 'are missing something vital; orthodoxy is not a mere body of opinion but a distinctive relationship – a relationship of power'

(Asad 1986b: 15). In conclusion, Asad has argued that the anthropology of Islam 'seek[s] to understand the historical conditions that enable the production and maintenance of specific discursive traditions, or their transformation – and the efforts of practitioners to achieve coherence' (1986b: 17).

Although Asad's view of Islam as a 'tradition' may be an interesting insight, I disagree with his limited and proto-theological paradigm[11] of the anthropology of Islam. First, not all Muslims, though defining themselves as such, have a deep knowledge of the Qur'an or the ḥadiths.[12] Should, according to Asad's definition of the anthropology of Islam, anthropologists consider these Muslims to be bad Muslims? Clearly, this judgmental attitude would contradict one of the main vital aspects of anthropology as a discipline, the avoidance of bias. Furthermore, for the anthropologist of Islam the knowledge of the Qur'an and relevant Islamic literature remains an important good practice; but anthropologists should not necessarily start from where 'Muslims start'. Finally, Asad has limited the anthropology of Islam to an analysis of the power struggle between Muslims trying to maintain orthodoxy and the changing world challenging it. I recognize that Asad has been the first anthropologist consciously attempting to elaborate a discursive paradigm of the anthropology of Islam. Indeed, earlier, anthropologists such as Geertz and Gellner only tried to impose, through their theories, what they saw as the ultimate analysis of *the Islam*. Others, such as Gilsenan, have hidden within the introductory pages of their Middle Eastern ethnographies their partial discussion on the anthropology of Islam. Nonetheless, together with other anthropologists (see Varisco 2005: 151–6), I remain unimpressed, if not sceptically suspicious of Asad's 'brave', but too ideological, efforts to define 'the idea of an anthropology of Islam'.

In recent times, other anthropologists have tried to add their, more or less critical, voices to the development of the anthropology of Islam. Abu-Lughod (1989) has written one of the most detailed reviews of anthropological studies concerning the Arab world.[13] Although she does not directly engage in the Asadian discussion concerning the anthropology of Islam, she has provided insightful observations on the issues affecting Middle East anthropology (but that can be extended to the anthropology of Islam). The first observation points toward the existence of 'three central zones of theorizing within Middle East anthropology: segmentation, the harem and Islam. To switch metaphors, there are the dominant "theoretical metonyms" by means of which this vast and complex area is grasped' (Abu-Lughod 1989: 280). It is surprising to notice how, in particular, the 'zones', 'harem' (understood here as gender studies, see Chapter 8 in this book) and 'Islam' (understood as essentialist approaches) are still part of anthropological studies of Islam. Although, the focus on segmentation has decreased in recent years (yet see Shankland 2003), for more than thirty years, as we have seen, it remained a central topic in the studies of Middle East and Northern Africa. Abu-Lughod has therefore asked,

> Why has there been so much theorizing about segmentation? Even if one grants that some agricultural societies in the Arab Middle East are tribal, and that therefore the analytical issues are relevant to understanding more than the

approximately 1% of the Middle Eastern population who are pastoral nomads or transhumants, the ration of anthropologists, articles, and books to population remains staggering. (1989: 284)

Abu-Lughod has advanced an interesting explanation for this staggering disproportion of segmentary-based studies. We need to take into consideration, she suggests, 'men, politics, and violence'. Indeed, she has advanced the hypothesis that 'a felicitous correspondence between the views of Arab tribesmen and those of European men has led each to reinforce particular interests of the other and to slight other aspects of experience and concern' (1986: 30).

At the beginning of the 1990s, Abu-Lughod felt the need to emphasize that the three 'theoretical metonyms' certainly cannot exhaust all the topics and research available to anthropologists studying the Arab (and Islamic) world. The overemphasis on such limited fields, Abu-Lughod has observed, meant the exclusion of others, such as studies on emotions, economy, psychology, migration in the Islamic world. Yet the main 'missing in action' of these anthropologies remains the lack of historical contextualization:

If Orientalist scholarship looked to the past to define the essence of Arab civilization, anthropology's ahistoricism has tended to produce its own brand of essentialism – the essentialism of Arab culture. Bringing the region into historical time, exploring the ways the complex situations in which people live have been historically produced, and showing how transformations have been and are now being lived by particular individuals, families, and communities are steps the anthropology of the Arab world must take. The result will be to make more fluid the boundaries of the anthropological discourse on the Arab world. (1989: 301)

Abu-Lughod did not aim, like Asad, to develop a programmatic view of the anthropology of Islam. Rather, through an extensive critical survey, she has highlighted some deficiencies in the general understanding of the anthropology of Middle East and Arab World, which, at the beginning of the 1990s, remained (despite the parentheses Geertz, el-Zein and Asad) the only visible 'anthropology of Islam'.

Until the 1990s, the discussion on the anthropology of Islam was proceeding slowly, without clear direction and with few attempts to present a coherent paradigm, marked by tautological ethnographic approaches, which revisited the same villages looking for the same issues. Twenty-two years after el-Zein's seminal article, thirteen after Asad's essay, and ten after Abu-Lughod's review, Lukens-Bull (1999), in his 'Between Text and Practice: Considerations in the anthropological Study of Islam', was still struggling to provide a clear definition and paradigm of the anthropology of Islam. Again, like Asad, Lukens-Bull has to observe 'the anthropological study of Islam is one that has been plagued by problems of definitions. What exactly are we studying? Local practices, universal texts and standard of practices, or something else entirely?' (1999: 1). Lukens-Bull, explicating the obligatory ritual of the critical survey, has measured himself against the exercise of providing a paradigm. To avoid repeating Asad's theological essentialism, Lukens-Bull has rightly acknowledged, 'the theoretical question "What is Islam?" and the theological question "What is Islam?" are not the same' (1999: 10). Anthropology, Lukens-Bull has explained, answers the question at an analytic level, whereas theology, 'addresses the ontological status of things and seek[s] the foundations of faith within the tradition' (1999: 10). Lukens-Bull's argument needs this *distinguo* as his anthropological definition of Islam,

> begin[s] at the same point that a Muslim definition of Islam does. This is not an unusual proposition; many have proposed such a starting point. However, I would like to start with the Islamic definition of 'Islam' as submission to God. All Muslims will agree with this definition. Where they differ is in defining *how* one should go about submitting to God. A comparative study of the different conceptions of how to submit to God (that is, how to be a Muslim) should be the central task of an anthropology of Islam. (1999: 10)

Truly, Lukens-Bull's definition cleverly reconciles both the emic and etic viewpoints on Islam. In my opinion, however, the definition has two effects: it tends to reduce Muslim human beings into Muslim theological beings, and Islam into a powerful all-shaping force. Let me ask, do we need to define 'Islam' in order to define the anthropology of Islam? Certainly, we do not. There is no need of a universal definition of Islam, and there is no need of an agreement between the respondents and the anthropologist in a phenomenological Eliadian style (Kunin 2002, Chapter 8). If anthropology does not need a definition of Islam, Lukens-Bull's paradigm for the anthropology of Islam surely does. Finally, the main weakness in Lukens-Bull's argument is that it reduces the anthropology of Islam to a comparative study of the different styles of Muslim submission.

Lukens-Bull's article and review of previous works, however, highlights an intriguing, though alarming, aspect. All the titles discussed in his review, just like all the titles discussed in Asad's (1986b) and Abu-Lughod's (1989), deals with 'exotic' places. Indeed, we can find titles such as *Gamelan Stories: Tantrism, Islam, and Aesthetics in Central Java* (Becker 1993), *The Political Economy of Islamic Conversion in Modern East Java* (Hefner 1987), *Metaphorical Aspects of Indonesian Islamic Discourse about Development* (Lukens-Bull 1996) and *Islam in Java: Normative Piety and Mysticism in the Sultanate of Yogyakarta* (Woodward 1989) which have mainly located the field within Islamic villages of Muslim countries. Does this mean that the anthropology of Islam suffered from *exoticentrism*? Lukens-Bull could have mentioned some of the available anthropological research on Muslims in the west. Yet, together with many others, he did not. The impression is that still today some anthropologists consider whoever conducts western research on Islam and Muslims to be a 'sociologist'. Have the romanticized descriptions of fieldwork in remote areas and villages something to do with this? Indeed, anthropologists conducting research among western Muslims cannot complain about missing showers and a lack of toilet paper.[14]

Varisco's *Islam Obscured* (2005) has offered the latest attempt to reopen a debate on the anthropology of Islam. The title of this book leaves the reader with no doubts about Varisco's disillusion with forty years of supposed anthropology of Islam. Varisco has presented his argument in the, now classic, format of an extended critical review. Under his critical-cynical-sarcastic axe-sharp style ended the must-be-read Geertz (1968), Mernissi (1975), Gellner (1981) and Ahmed (1986 and 1988). Summarized to the bone, Varisco's book tells us what has gone wrong in the anthropological study of Islam. Acute in his criticism and convincing in his argument, Varisco offers pleasant reading in his sophisticated, yet sarcastic, enjoyable style. So effective has been his criticism that a student of mine has observed, 'whoever reads this book with the intention of approaching the anthropology of Islam would think twice before joining in'. Anthropologists working on Islam after more than forty years are still debating and diatribing something which, at the level of discipline paradigm and theory, remains an errant ghost within the field of social (cultural) anthropology. From Varisco's merciless but convincing reviews, we have the disarming impression that future anthropologists working on Islam are still carrying on without a clear paradigm, without real theoretical discussion, still focusing on marginal aspects, still avoiding the urban areas, and still conducting fieldwork, but discussing Islam without Muslims. In the Epilogue of his book, Varisco has felt that, as an anthropologist working on Islam, he had to face what previous reviewers (with the exception of Asad 1986b) had avoided:

> Iconoclastic deconstruction will never get an author to the right side just because it avoids the wrong side. Now comes the really difficult part: charting a course of safe passage that will stay clear of the same, and perhaps irritatingly resistant, fallacies so prevalent in the texts [discussed]. Having objected to the obscuring of Islam, what is it that anthropologists have, can, and should do to improve their perspectives and methods for a more enlightened but less enrooted understanding of the religion of Muslims? (2005: 140)

Hence, providing a series of Socratic questions and answers, Varisco has outlined what he understands as 'good practice' in the anthropology of Islam.

The first step is fieldwork and participant observation. They lead to ethnography, offering a 'chart [of] how beliefs and ideas are put into practice: not how they are supposed to be or should be, but how they unfold in an observable manner in one small place at one particular time' (2005: 140). Varisco has correctly noticed that ethnography 'is not a panacea for essentializing' (2005: 141) but rather helps to develop debates about realities in continuous change. Varisco has reminded us that the ethnographer has to be something 'between photographer and artist'. The ethnographer not only records the events, but also interprets them, and when s/he writes them down, and ultimately publishes them, they become the domain of the readers who reinterpret the ethnography, and in the case of academics, use them. Varisco, then, moves on to discuss briefly the 'challenges to successful ethnographic fieldwork' (2005: 143). Here, of course, the suggestions could not be other than those any supervisor of doctoral students may provide: be aware of the cultural shock, beware of the health hazards and challenging local traditions, and be ready for emotional issues. Varisco has also strongly affirmed the necessity of knowing the language of the culture, or people, studied. More intriguing is how Varisco avoids the el-Zein vs. Asad disagreement on the existence of one Islam or many Islam*s*. After strongly rejecting any nominalist position, Varisco has endorsed Asad's argument that the problem is not the different attempts that scholars have made to generalize Islam, but how this generalization has been done. In other words, Varisco has told his readers that his problem is 'with "Islam" with a capital "I"' (2005: 146) as presented in the criticism of the work he has discussed in the book. Varisco has rejected the idea that anthropologists can consider local versions of Islam as a 'master blueprint' of this religion,

> Thus, what the anthropologist defines as just another Islam is invariably seen by the practitioner as an attempt to do Islam. The issue is not whether this Islam exists; if there were no concept there would be no meaningful distinction to being Muslim. Theologians have no trouble with an idealized Islam, but should ethnographers among Muslims operate with this conceptualized Islam as a given, as something meaningful in itself, apart from its local appropriation? (2005: 149)

If we wish to radicalize Varisco's viewpoint, we can say that this diatribe on Islam vs. Islams is irrelevant to the anthropology of Islam. But how has Varisco defined the anthropology of Islam?

Varisco considers all these *querelles* on the definition of the anthropology of Islam rather useless, and observes,

> searching for the idea of an anthropology of Islam, I argue, should not lead us beyond ideology and theology but rather probe these very powerful discursive traditions through thick description of ethnographic contexts. Observing Muslims in particular 'Islams' is one of the few things that anthropologists have been able to contribute to the broader academic interest in how Islam is continually defined and redefined and, indeed how religion itself is conceptualized. (2005: 160)

Finally, Varisco argues that what ultimately all forms of anthropology are about is culture. This means that the anthropologists, 'inevitably must go beyond the ethnographic context observed to a broader comparative understanding of how every given human act relates to the potential for specifically human interactions' (2005: 162). For this reason Varisco concludes that the anthropology of Islam could not be other than observing 'Muslims in order to represent their representations' since 'only Muslims can observe Islam' (2005: 162).

Certainly, Varisco's Epilogue leaves open many questions for a coherent paradigm of the anthropology of Islam. Yet, I strongly agree with his views since they move the discussion of the anthropology of Islam away from overused academic clichés and – to use Abu-Lughod's term – 'theoretical metonyms' that have stagnated, rather than advanced, the debate on the anthropology of Islam. Although Varisco has challenged the anthropological approaches obscuring Islam, and, nineteen years after Asad's contribution, renewed the debate on the anthropology of Islam, he has missed a good opportunity to deconstruct one of the most obscurantist elements within the tradition of anthropological studies of Islam: illusory exoticism of fieldwork. Actually, through his examples and the titles mentioned in the Epilogue, he has reinforced (probably unintentionally) the idea that the anthropology of Islam means exotic fieldwork (see in particular Varisco 2005: 138, 144–5). As we shall see in the next chapter, since the end of the 1990s, an increasing number of anthropologists have conducted ethnography 'by living in an Islamic context' (Varisco 2005: 138) but, this time, within the geographical west. Although probably none of these anthropologists had to enjoy the experience of soiling themselves (see the case of Daniel Bradburd reported by Varisco 2005: 144) or fight against exotic intestinal 'flora', as Varisco himself had to face in his Yemenite fieldwork in 1978.[15] Indeed, anthropologists of Islam working in western locations, or trans-regional fieldwork, are providing, in particular after September 11, vital studies to understand Muslim communities and their Islams.

## ANTHROPOLOGY OF ISLAM OR ISLAMIC ANTHROPOLOGY?

We have seen that during the 1980s anthropologists researching Islam and Muslims tried to define the anthropology of Islam. Much of the debate focused on the different role that anthropology should have from theology. Some Muslim anthropologists found unacceptable the suggestion that many Islams, rather than one, could exist. Ahmed is a stalwart defender of the 'one Islam' position. In his controversial *Toward Islamic Anthropology* (1986: 58) he has stated, 'there has been a suggestion by Muslim anthropologists that there is not one Islam but many Islams, a suggestion taken up by Western anthropologists. I disagree with this position. There is only one Islam, and there can be only one Islam'. The anthropology of Islam, as we have seen, has developed from disparate ethnographic studies focusing on Muslims; hence it has lacked a definite paradigm, definition or a theoretical blueprint. In other words, anthropology of Islam is still a debate, an open-ended project and a polyphonic discourse. By contrast, Islamic anthropology has been theorized, provided with a clear paradigm and blueprint: Islam. At the beginning of the 1980s, the project for an Islamic anthropology was not a novelty (Mahroof 1981). In 1984, Ahmed published a short article announcing his book (1986) which would have represented the road map for an Islamic anthropology. Ahmed's *Toward Islamic Anthropology* has received much attention through extended reviews and discusstions.[18] Anthropologists have shown an overall scepticism towards Ahmed's argument, with some vehemently rejecting it (cf. Tapper 1988).

Other Muslim scholars have attempted to Islamicize social scientific disciplines (see Ba-Yunus and Ahmad 1985, Wyn 1988). Nonetheless, Ahmed's polemic attitude toward non-Islamic anthropology and his British anthropological training made his work particularly visible to the western audience. Ahmed defines Islamic anthropology 'loosely' as,

> The study of Muslim groups by scholars committed to the universalistic principles of Islam – humanity, knowledge, tolerance, – relating micro village tribal studies in particular to the larger historical and ideological frames of Islam. Islam is here understood not as theology but sociology, the definition thus does not preclude non-Muslims. (1986: 56)

We can appreciate, as other reviewers have also noticed, Ahmed's emphasis on the inclusiveness of Islamic anthropology. Yet a strong contradiction in terms falsifies all the universalistic framework of Islamic anthropology. Ahmed has stated that Islam, in Islamic anthropology, is not theology but rather sociology. Hence, he has concluded, Islamic anthropology does not exclude non-Muslim anthropologists. Now, I wonder how a non-Muslim, who may not recognize Muhammad as a prophet and be agnostic about God, could apply Islamic anthropological methodology.

Islamic anthropology, however explained or sold, is nothing else than anthropology based on a theological determinism. Any anthropology programmatically based on ideology would face challenging crises of moral and ethical values, which would ultimately prevent the study of certain topics or impose, even before fieldwork, a pre-dictated framework of analysis. To illustrate this point, we can use very simple examples. How can Islamic anthropologists conduct fieldwork, without bias, with Muslim gays and lesbians? How can Islamic anthropologists, such as Ahmed, conduct fieldwork with apostates and study the dynamics of apostasy without compromising the foundation of their own discipline? At this point, it is worth asking if, as Ahmed seemed to imply, Islamic anthropologists must find refuge from contemporary aspects of life studying only the tribal Muslim village.

Ahmed (1986), and Wyn (1988) after him, have not been unsuccessful in their attempt to shape an Islamic anthropology, since, as Eickelman has observed, 'Islamic anthropology ... sounds very much like other anthropologies, except for the efforts to justify it in terms of perceived Qur'anic principles and to encourage Muslim scholars to use anthropological approaches' (1990: 241).

## CONCLUSIONS

In this chapter, we have observed the debate stemming from the question 'what is the anthropology of Islam?' In conclusion, much has been debated, heatedly criticized, sometimes even acrimoniously, but no agreement has been reached. By contrast, Islamic anthropology did not suffer such a lack of identity since its identity was divinely assumed: Muslims could not contradict the Qur'an. Yet this inevitably purges Islamic anthropology from social science and roots it in something akin to theology. Finally, we have observed that the discussion surrounding the idea of an anthropology of Islam is quite recent, since it started during the 1980s. Before that, anthropologists conducted fieldwork in the Middle East and Northern

Africa searching for the 'tribesman' as their colleagues in Africa searched for the 'primitive'. Indeed, we must recognize, as Said has pointed out,

> As primitively, as the age-old antitype of Europe, as a fecund night out of which European rationality developed, the Orient's actuality receded inexorably into a kind of paradigmatic fossilization. The origins of European anthropology and ethnography were constituted out of these radical differences, and, to my knowledge, as discipline, anthropology has not yet dealt with this inherent political limitation upon its supposedly disinterested universality. (1985: 95)

Today, we are more aware of the political influences of colonialism and the impact that it had on the discipline. Yet as Abu-Lughod has discussed in her article (1989), some 'zones of theorizing', affected by Orientalist attitudes, are still present in the anthropology of Islam. What Abu-Lughod has called the 'harem' is probably the most prominent today,[16] together with a new one, 'terrorism'.

The idea of the anthropology of Islam, even recently (see Varisco 2005), is still inevitably linked to 'exotic' fieldwork, often located in the Middle East and Northern Africa, and always in the village. During my bibliographic research for this book, I have tried to find any review or article which, discussing the topic of the anthropology of Islam, mentions fieldwork among Muslims living in the west, or even studying contemporary problems facing Muslims, such as drugs, HIV, secularism, the war on terror and so on. I found none. However, since the 1990s a growing number of anthropologists of Islam have precisely offered glimpses into the lives, and difficulties, of western Muslims; so, why is their work being left aside?

I have found the answer to this question in two main factors. Firstly, anthropologists still seem nostalgic for times of dangerous, challenging, adventurous explorations which, through the rite of passage (often symbolized by general sickness, diarrhoea and lack of toilet paper) of leaving the civilized world for the hardship and pain of the 'primitive' one, could project over themselves a Nietzschean aura of the fascinating superhuman. Secondly, the belief that, despite the methodology used and the training of the researcher, studies conducted within the west are the domain of sociology rather than the anthropology of Islam. If the first reason may be pathetic, the second is certainly illogical. If western anthropologists studying Muslims within western countries are to be considered sociologists (because of the autochthonous location of their fieldwork), why are 'native' anthropologists (e.g. M. N. Srinivas) studying their own 'primitive' societies still recognized as anthropologists? I believe that methodology, rather than location, discriminates between anthropology and sociology. When a study is founded on fieldwork and participant observation, and the respondents' voices are made audible, the distinction between the anthropology of Islam and the sociology of Islam blurs.

In conclusion, though we still cannot define (and probably do not need to do so) what the anthropology of Islam may be (or even should be), we can surely affirm what is not. The anthropology of Islam is not theology. This means going beyond the question of Islam or Islams, and observing the dynamics of Muslim lives expressed through their ideological and rhetorical understanding of their surrounding (social, natural, virtual) environment.[17] Yet many events have changed the relationship between the Muslim and non-Muslim world since Geertz wrote his seminal book *Islam Observed*, and Asad (1986b) reopened the debate on the idea of an anthropology of Islam which el-Zein (1977) had started. September 11 and the resulting 'war on terror' is certainly the most unprecedented and traumatic of these events; an event pregnant with horrible consequences. Six years after the crumbling of the Twin Towers and the loss of thousands of lives around the world, Muslim and non-Muslim anthropologists have still not reflected adequately upon what it means to study Islam from an anthropological perspective in this new era. I shall use the next chapter to begin a debate and (what I strongly believe to be) a much needed discussion.

## NOTES

1. I recommend Morrison 1987, Bowie 2000 and Kunin 2002.
2. See for instance, Delacroix's *Women of Algiers in their Harem* in 1834, and *Fanatics of Tangier*, painted in 1836.
3. Although the Christian polemicists' representation of Islam as a morally depraved and libidinous religion could still be perceived though the eroticizing artworks.
4. For critical reviews of some important works focusing on Islamic regions, some of which, such as those of Bourdieu 1960, Geertz 1968 and Gellner 1981, could be considered as the first attempts to develop an anthropology of Islam, I recommend el-Zein 1977, Eickelman 1981b, Asad 1986a, Abu-Lughod 1989, Gilsenan 1990, Street 1990, Lukens-Bull 1999 and Varisco 2005.
5. To mention just a few, Crapazano 1973, el-Zein 1977, Marranci 2006a, but in particular the superb, (sometimes sarcastically goliardic) Varisco 2005, Chapter 1.
6. 'Religion is (1) a system of symbols which acts to (2) establish powerful, persuasive, and long-lasting moods and motivations in men by (3) formulating conceptions of a general order of existence and (4) clothing these conceptions with such an aura of factuality that (5) the moods and motivations seem uniquely realistic' (Geertz 1993: 90).
7. See, for instance, Anderson 1984; Asad 1986a, 1986b; Munson 1993, 1995; Roberts 2002; Rosen 2002; Marranci 2006a.
8. Yet Gellner has suggested a more complex view in which the two traditions maintain strong links and interrelationships.
9. For a better and more detailed description see Eickelman 1981a, Chapter 6, from which the following examples have been taken.
10. By contrast, he mentioned unrelated European philosophers (*in primis* Hume), writers and historical personages, (see Varisco 2005).
11. For a theological one see Ahmed 1986, which I will discuss below.

12. See Marranci 2006a. Also we may wonder to which kind of ḥadiths Asad is referring: strong, weak or false?
13. But also Islam in general, as the inclusion of works such as those of Geertz 1968 and Asad 1986 and Eickelman 1982 demonstrates.
14. For discussion concerning fieldwork in the anthropology of Islam see Chapter 5 in this book.
15. This does not mean that anthropologists of Islam conducting fieldwork in the west do not encounter cultural shocks, and in particular health hazards, as my experiences of food poisoning may demonstrate.
16. See Chapter 8 in this book.
17. It is important to emphasize that the term ideology here has no negative or political connotation, rather ideology is understood in its primary meaning as a set of beliefs structuring a personal discourse shared through what Mafessoli (1996) has defined as a 'community of emotions'. See Chapter 4 in this book.
18. See for example, Boase 1986, Elkholy 1984, Hart 1988, Tahir 1987, Tapper 1988, Young 1988, Edwards 1991, Varisco 2005, Chapter 4.

# Studying Muslims in the West: Before and After September 11

## *FROM VILLAGES AND SAINTS TO METROPOLISES AND IMMIGRANTS*

In the previous chapter, we have observed that between the end of the 1960s and the end of the 1980s, ethnographic studies of Muslims observed mainly Middle Eastern and North African populations. Even recent article-reviews on the anthropology of Islam have overlooked western Muslims, and Muslims seen as actors within the 'global village' instead of the *duar*.[1] The omission of western-based research on Islam and Muslims does not mean that it does not exist. Indeed, young anthropologists and sociologists have increasingly paid attention to new fields of research, such as Muslim immigrants, second generation Muslims, Muslim transnational networks, virtual ummahs and the integration/assimilation of western Muslim communities. This innovative research, marginalized within mainstream anthropology, found refuge in other more interdisciplinary fields such as migration studies, gender studies, education studies and global studies. Yet as the 'exotic' ethnographies ended entangled in kinship, Sufi saints and segmentary theories, these western-based ethnographies of Muslim lives ended in a cultural hermeneutic suggesting Islam as the ultimate shaper of migrants' lives. The reason behind the essentialist views which some of these western-based ethnographies advocated, and the fascination with the role of Islam in the studied western Muslim community can be traced back to the history of Muslim migration.

During the 1960s, European states actively resourced migrant labour, often from Muslim countries, in order to complete their post Second World War reconstruction. Both the European states and the Muslim workers considered immigration as a temporary rather than permanent arrangement. North Africans, South Asians and Turkish Muslim guest workers left their families behind in their homelands. This first generation of underpaid Muslim immigrant labourers dreamt of their return to the motherland. Year after year, letter after letter, and in many cases, song after song,[2] the desired and planned return metamorphosed into a myth of return.

Isham, who arrived in Paris in the 1970s, told me, after singing a popular *chābi* song, how the 'European dream' turned, for many of them, into the European nightmare:

We left [our country] because since we were recovering from colonialism there were many difficulties. If you were young and Algerian, your country could offer to you nothing more than *trabaco* [expression to indicate contraband]. Colonialism was not dead. It was only different. But if you have family, you have to provide for them. This is the destiny of men and in particular Muslim men,[3] otherwise you play with your honour. Nobody wished to stay here and be a slave of the colonialist. At least during the colonialism we were slaves in our own country. After we were like before, but we had to face migration. All of us left to come back. We counted the days, one by one, like the prisoners do. But to send money back and to live here in France was nearly impossible and our families asked for more and more money. At the end, many of us decided that it was easier to bring our families here. Then children were born here, and the return is just part of the things you say to friends or relatives, repeating again and again 'next year, inshallah'. One 'inshallah' after another and look, I am still here! Yet, now that the children are independent, I'm building my house in Algeria and I am going back next year, inshallah!

At the end of the 1980s, Europe, the USA and Canada saw an increase in the number of second-generation Muslims. The culture of Muslim migrants began marking even the urban spaces of the main western metropolises through new mosques and their minarets, Islamic centres with their Arabic placards and madrasas with their children in *thobe* and *ḥijāb*. Yet in western societies, and in particular France, Great Britain and Germany, political discussion – every time a step behind real life – about Muslim migration failed to address the growing challenges of an unplanned (by both sides!) multiculturalism. On the one hand, marginalization, discrimination, isolationism and ghettoization became an embedded feature of the daily experience of Muslim communities. On the other, autochthonous non-Muslim populations felt threatened and challenged by the unfamiliar, Islamic culture, known only through stereotypes.

It is in this complex social, political and cultural context that ethnographies of western Muslim communities started to be published. We can observe differences between the traditional ethnographic studies of Muslim societies and this new field of research, but also similarities, such as a certain (inevitable?) colonial heritage. Indeed, the western colonial experience explains the presence of the Muslim communities settling in Europe as well as the specific community focus of migration studies. For instance, in the UK the research has concentrated on South Asians, in France on Northern African Muslims and in Germany on the Turkish community. Another similarity with the first 'exotic' anthropological studies of Muslim societies is the political agenda marking some of the studies. For instance, in France the debate is often in the defence of French *laïcité* from Islamic identities, and the consequent strategy of assimilating, in particular, children of Muslim origin. In Germany, the debate focuses more on issues surrounding the level of education within the Turkish community. In the UK women in Islam appeared, until recently, the most popular topic (Haddad and Qurmazi 2000).

As in the case of ethnographies focusing on the Middle East, studies of Muslim immigrants show certain recurrent 'zones of theorizing' (Abu-Lughod 1989). Among these 'zones', which include themes such as integration, westernization, gender (see Chapter 8 in this book), second generations, education and Islamism remain, by far, the most prominent. Although I have neither the space nor the possibility to survey all the sociological and anthropological studies conducted with Muslim communities in the west, I think that it is useful to present below some of the studies addressing these zones.

As we have seen, in post Second World War Europe, Muslim guest workers came, in many cases, from former or current colonies to supplement the drained work force in European countries. In predominantly, and sometimes exclusively, white Christian societies,[4] Muslim workers – with their alien languages and cultures – attracted the curiosity of newspapers and locals. Academia did not understand immediately the dynamics and consequences of these immigrations, and seemed to be unable to forecast the sociocultural consequences of such invited mass of individuals with dreams but no rights. The 'guest worker' had arrived dreaming and hoping for a happy return to the land of his ancestors; in reality, he permanently trapped himself within the increasing suburban proletariat of European cities. From the 1960s, not only did the single male guest worker migrate towards the European dream, but also his family members and in particular, his wife. The presence of women (and then children) with their distinctive dress styles, veils and the fragrance of exotic kitchens intrigued the local neighbours and with them sociologists and anthropologists (Dahya 1965). The presence of the 'other' and the formation of 'ethnic' neighbourhoods challenged the white-Christian homogeneity that had characterized Europe for centuries. This raised social issues, in particular when immigrant children, and then western-born Muslims, reached the doors of European schools and increased in numbers within their classes (Little, Mabey and Whittaker 1968).

The anthropology of the Middle East (or other Muslim countries) originated in serving the colonial administrations by providing an understanding of the 'native' cultures and facilitating their control; the social scientific works on western Muslim communities originated in the increasing need to framework the 'other' among 'us'. During the 1970s, western societies perceived these immigrants as Algerians, Turks, Pakistanis, or in broader categories such as Arabs, North Africans and South Asians, rather than Muslims. Consequently, the immigrants' national and ethnic backgrounds, rather than the religious affiliation, attracted the attention of social scientific research. Studies entitled, for example, 'Pakistanis in England' (Dahya 1972) in the UK, or 'Cultural action amongst Maghrebian migrants in Europe' (Mdaghri 1975) in France, proliferated in the attempt to understand and explain how these migrants could integrate within their host societies (see also Dahya 1973 and 1974). Another important difference between the traditional ethnographic studies of Muslim societies and these new studies existed. The researchers studying the Muslim migrants were part of the mainstream social group, while the Geertzs and Gellners were, so to say, the migrants studying the Muslim autochthons. This simple observation carries, however, important implications for the development of contemporary anthropology of Islam. As I will discuss in the final section, the anthropology of Islam that has focused on western Muslims has lacked reflexivity on the effects that this aspect could have on methodologies and analysis, with a certain disinterest concerning the consequences these anthropological studies may have on the minority population studied.

From the mid 1970s, both the Muslim communities and their host societies became aware that 'the return' would remain what it was: a myth (Anwar 1979). This again shifted how the western host societies saw their Middle Eastern, South Asian and Northern African populations. With the settlement of the guest workers, Islam became visible as part of the identity of these new communities. This changed the way in which sociologists and anthropologists saw their informants. If ethnicity and nationality marked with few exceptions (e.g. Barclay 1969) the first studies, now an overwhelming majority of them started to feature the word 'Muslim' in their titles and abstracts.[5] This does not mean that the focus on ethnicity and nationality completely disappeared. At the beginning of the 1980s, many studies were still referring to the ethnic-national identity of these immigrants and their socio-economic status.[6] Nonetheless, the fact that South Asians in Britain, Northern Africans in France and other parts of Europe, as well as Turkish immigrants in Germany were defining, in the new migration context, their identity as 'Muslim' reinforced the centrality of Islam within social scientific studies. Furthermore, Islam progressively became part of the landscape of main European cities, through the minarets and the oriental-styled mosques, which, for the first time, left the pages of the *One Thousand and one Nights* to materialize in bricks and glass among the curious, or suspicious, looks of non-Muslim neighbours (Metcalf 1996). Unsurprisingly, nationality and ethnicity became less relevant to the understanding of the Muslim communities. New studies focused on 'Muslims in Europe', 'Young Muslims', 'Muslim communities', 'Muslim girls', 'Muslim women' and 'Muslim teachers',[7] thus Islam became the keyword which helped to make sense of the immigrants' *otherness*. The awareness that the, now redefined, Muslim immigration was a permanent feature of western societies, redirected the social scientific research to the difficulties that Muslim immigrants had to face to maintain their Muslim identity and community in the new environment (Saifullah-Khan 1979). The increase in Muslim women, both migrants and of Muslim origin, facilitated a high number of studies, mainly from a feminist perspective, which paid attention to their condition and emancipation (e.g. Saifullah Khan 1975, 1976a; Abadan-Unat 1977). What, however, did remain – and still remains – understudied was the impact that such a massive migration had on the immigrants' countries of origin, extended families, local economies and social structures (for one of these rare studies see Akre 1974). This is hardly surprising, since social policies, often through research funding, suggest, if not dictate, research priorities.

At the beginning of the 1980s, one of these priorities, and certainly a long-lasting one, would become the so-called second-generation Muslims. These young were, at least nationality-wise, considered part of the society in which they were born. The host society of their parents was their own society. This, of course, was the theory (Saifullah Khan 1976b). The reality was, and still is, different.

The question, political more than moral, was asked, and continues to be asked, whether these children would grow up British, French, German, etc. or Muslim. The question of loyalty passed from the concern of the *vox populi* to the *Homo Academicus*, bringing, however, the same faulty essentialism: Islam reduced to the same category of national or ethnic identity.

One of the long-lasting versions of this faulty reasoning reads that young Muslims live in a form of permanent 'in-betweenness' (Anwar 1976, and see also Watson 1997). Anwar (1976) has discussed the relationships between Pakistani Muslims in Britain and their relatives in Pakistan. The author explored the changes which immigration has produced on both the sides of the globe, with a particular attention to identity and traditional values. The study is rooted in comparative anthropology; yet Islam, as tradition, though discussed as a central part of the Pakistani culture, is not topical. The conclusion of this study suggested that South Asian immigrants, and even more their descendants, far from softening or rejecting their commitment to tradition, are mediating and negotiating their cultural and social space between two divergent cultures based on different values. However, Werbner has documented the Pakistani communities' efforts to avoid isolation and ghettoization (Werbner 1979). Indeed, the integration and social inclusiveness of the Muslim communities would become, together with gender and education, one of the prominent 'theorizing zones' of the anthropology of Islam focusing on western Muslim communities.

The tendency to see religion as the main element that could prevent Muslims from integrating within the 'modern', 'civilized' and 'secular' western democracies increased at the end of 1980s. Three events, the less known Honeyford affair (in 1984), the evergreen Rushdie affair (in 1989) and the 1989 *Affaire du Foulard* (the headscarf affair) in France, which would mark the history of the Muslim communities in Europe, seemed to confirm a previously alleged incompatibility between what were indicated as 'western' and 'Islamic' values. With the *Affaire du Foulard* French schools aimed to preserve the ideology of *laïcité* and the affair would culminate fifteen years later in the total ban on 'conspicuous' religious symbols, including the Muslim ḥijāb, in all French schools (see Bowen 2007). For the first time, in all three 'affairs' and in an exponential way, the western mass media played a central role in shaping the debate on Muslims in the west. It is not surprising that two of the three 'affairs' involved the education system. As we have seen, education has been one of the main 'zones' on which sociological and anthropological research on Muslims in the west focused.[8] The presence of Muslim children in the European education system opened the debate on multiculturalism. Of course, politicians, headmasters, teachers and parents had, and still have today, different views on what a 'multicultural' education may mean and whether it may be useful.

Ray Honeyford did succeed in attracting both the mass media as well as the angry attention of the English Muslim community. In 1984, Ray Honeyford, who was the headmaster of Drummond Road Middle School, in Bradford, England, published a controversial newspaper article asking for the rejection of 'the multi-racial myth'. At the centre of his call for the defence of an alleged Britishness stood the rejection of 'barbaric' Islamic customs, symbolized, in this case, by the Islamic slaughtering style. Honeyford mentioned it because of the *halāl* meat his school had to provide to the Muslim pupils. According to him, British people tolerated the 'barbaric' practice, which lacked any British sensitivity, in the name of a dangerous politically correct multiculturalism, which would finally kill what he perceived to be the more civilized British values. Protesting against the cruel destiny of British cows at the hands of Muslim butchers, he called for an assimilation policy, which, through the denial of Muslim children's religious identity, could transform them into perfect 'British subjects'. Despite wide support from the right-wing press and various bourgeois members of the white middle classes, the South Asian protests, and the too visibly racially motivated argument, forced him to take early retirement and to keep his opinions to himself.

The Honeyford affair highlighted the relevance that Islam as a religion and expression of identity had not only for the immigrants but also for their children (Halstead 1998 and Lewis 1994). In conclusion, if we analyse the Honeyford affair from an anthropological perspective, we can observe that four elements were part of it: religious identity, national identity, community affiliation and, in particular, loyalty. The last one would play a fundamental role in the Rushdie affair.

In 1988 *The Satanic Verses* were published, and on 14 February 1989, the Ayatollah Khomeini responded by issuing a fatwa, albeit an ineffective one, calling for the death of Rushdie, who ended up protected by the British government. If the British government could save Rushdie from hell, it could not avoid the global Muslim protests that the publication of the book triggered and culminated in the famous UK book-burning demonstration in Bradford, on 14 January 1989. Journalists, politicians as well as ordinary non-Muslims questioned the 'loyalty' of their host Muslim population. Yet, during my research, ten years later, I was able to appreciate how some of the people who were involved in the riots and book-burning rituals were unable to foresee the socio-political consequences of their acts of protest. One of my respondents, who took part in the protests, holding a placard asking the British government for the severed head of Rushdie, observed, 'We had protested as we used to do in our country'. Indeed, the protests organized in London and Manchester resembled those of Karachi or Tehran.

Culture dictates the act of protesting, in that we learn what is socially acceptable in a protest, so that we can even decide consciously to break the rules to achieve the maximum impact and attention. Yet this was not a conscious decision in the case of the book-burning ritual organized that day in Manchester. To burn an object considered evil is a ritual that is common among certain societies; many Muslims considered it appropriate behaviour to demonstrate in this way their personal commitment to the rejection of evil. Those involved in the famous January protest had no real knowledge that for non-Muslim Europeans the book burning would be nothing else than a horrible historical *déjà vu*. Even the anthropologists who discussed *The Satanic Verses* affair missed this simple fact. Many interpreted the Rushdie Affair as a symptom of the deep frustration of British Muslims and Muslims living in other parts of Europe. Others have emphasized the symbolic value of the event (Asad 1990; Modood 1990; Halliday 1995). Some have provided a cultural symbolic analysis, which, on the one hand, has challenged the Orientalist stereotypes of the 'uncivilized' Muslim, and, on the other attempted to demonstrate that the reactions were not just visceral. Werbner has thus concluded that the British Muslim rebellion against *The Satanic Verses* was the product of the clash between two distinct aesthetics, and between two distinct moralities or worldviews, 'the confrontation was between *equal* aesthetic communities, each defending its own high culture' (2002: 10). The concept of cultural identity would permeate the future studies on second-generation Muslims. Controversy surrounding *The Satanic Verses* reinforced the widespread idea that British Muslims remain a threat for one of the most highly considered values of British society, freedom of speech. Another affair, this time linked to the *foulard* (ḥijāb) would instead reinforce the idea[9] that Islam and secularism were incompatible.

To understand the *Affair du Foulard*, we need to observe the concept of laïcité in France. Not only has the concept of laïcité its origin in the division between church and state, but also in that ideological anticlericalism which had characterized the French Revolution (Bowen 2007). French laïcité is one of the main characteristics of the French educational system. The presence of Muslim schoolgirls adhering to the Islamic practice of covering their heads with ḥijābs (foulard in French) in the French schools was overtly challenging the foundation of the secular state: laïcité (Dayan-Herzbrun 2000). This led to a certain number of schools suspending their Muslim students. The lack of specific legislation proved a problem for the draconian decision of these schools. France started to think that legislation similar to that existing in Turkey, forbidding the wearing of ḥijābs in schools, could preserve the laïcité of French schools for future generations. President Chirac strongly supported the new legislation banning the ḥijāb (together with other 'oversize' religious symbols, such as turbans for Sikhs and yarmulkes for Jewish boys) and in September 2004, with the support of left-wing politicians the ban was imposed. The legislation, as we shall see in the next section, had more to do with September 11 than a definitive solution to an issue that started in the early 1980s. Nonetheless, the affair increased the number of anthropological studies on the ḥijāb, second-generation Muslims and their assimilation (Bowen 2007).

If during the 1970s and the beginning of the 1980s anthropologists working on Muslims in the west had focused on Muslim migrants, at the end of the 1980s their interest was redirected towards the new generations.[10] We have seen that some influential studies concluded that Muslim migrants were living 'between two cultures', so that their children can be seen as a product of this 'in-betweeness'.[11] This reinforced the idea that western-born Muslims had to possess fluid, hybrid, multiple identities controlled and shaped by cultural processes.[12] A good example of these anthropological theories is Jacobson's study on identity among young British Pakistanis living in the London Borough of Waltham Forest (1998). Jacobson's research was based on an extended fieldwork and observed the relationships that these young people formed among themselves as well as with their society. Although very traditional feminist analysis affected Jacobson's conclusions, she selected Tajfel's identity theory (1979), rather than feminist theories, to explain the relationship that her respondents developed with Islam. Tajfel based his social identity theory, as we shall see in the next chapter, on the main idea that people, in order to form their identity, need to be part of an in-group. Yet, because the members of the in-group can make sense of themselves as part of it, they need to identify an out-group. The theory, in other words, tends to emphasize the need of an 'opposition' to form identity. It is not surprising that, directly or indirectly, this theory could be found in many anthropological studies referring to second- or third-generation Muslims.

Therefore, Jacobson argued that her British Pakistani respondents formed their Muslim identity through 'boundary processes [which] promote a certain ambivalence over identity... The process by which a member of the second generation negotiates or determines his or her position within the minority or within wider society is likely to feel like a peculiarly open-ended and *uncertain* project' (Jacobson 1998: 79, italics mine). The Pakistani boys, she suggested, developed 'an assertive Muslim identity', which is 'a *male* phenomenon' and explains the oppression, perpetrated by their brothers, of Muslim girls:

> The 'assertive Muslim identity' is a *male* phenomenon and is probably due to the fact that men are able to take advantage of relative laxity of parents to be largely irreligious in behaviour but Muslim in name. Young women, in contrast, rarely have the opportunity to rebel against the norms of the community and yet continue to be accepted as members of it. In fact, young women may, in a sense, *become the targets of the assertive Muslim identity of their peers*, who find that a convenient way of emphasizing their own 'Muslim' credentials is to insist upon the virtuous conduct of their wives, sisters and daughters. (Jacobson 1998: 121 emphasis mine)

Islam, in Jacobson's understanding, characterizes the in-group and makes it different, and opposite, to the out-group (i.e. the host society). Furthermore, Jacobson argued that young male Muslims use Islam like a tool to enforce on women an Islamic moral code, which exalts the Islamic identity of the male relative, who is said to be often just a 'Muslim in name'. Going through the available social scientific literature concerning young Muslims in the west, we can observe that the above approach has become a model; a misleading and dangerous one, as I shall argue below.

My experience of conducting fieldwork among western Muslims in several European countries has made me suspicious of monolithic models of identity as well as certain culturalist feminist analyses, which, in an attempt to denounce the patriarchal oppression of women, ended in representing women as disempowered passive objects without real will. These authors have interpreted Islam as a cultural force capable of overwhelming nature, environment and time. But do Islam really – seen as a cultural domain – and the 'west' – seen as a geo-cultural space – impose in-between, 'mixed up' and 'confused' identities? Or rather, are they an illusory result of radicalized cultural symbolic interpretations? Some anthropologists have gone so far in their cultural-essentialization as to pathologize young Muslims' identities. Here is a clear example of this pathologization: 'Second and third generation young Asians *suffer* from "mixed up" and "confused" identities because of the *"cultural clash"* that results from occupying a *contradictory* location between *conflicting* "majority" and "minority" *cultures* and *identities*' (Archer 2001: 82, emphasis mine). Other authors have provided examples which could convince the reader that identities can be mixed as colours or the ingredients of a cake, so that Qureshi and Moores (1999) have employed the metaphor of 'remix music' (a genre of music that mixes Indian with western styles) to explain the identity of 'Pakistani Scots'. They have argued,

> [they are] positioned between two sets of cultural values with often contradictory expectations. On the one hand, there is the social world of family, community and religion – while on the other, there is a western world which is experienced through institutions like education and media. However, ... the demands upon women within certain interpretations of the Islamic tradition make any translation between those value systems especially difficult for 'second generation' girls. (1999: 318)

The symbolic cultural analysis can be so radical that the personal identity of young people becomes the dress style they select. Again, we can find this in an exemplary passage from Qureshi and Moores's article: 'We could say, then, that each style of clothing involved "putting on" a different feminine identity and performing the situationally appropriate role' (1999: 319).

Let me point out some of the reasons that a contemporary anthropology of Islam should overcome simplified cultural symbolic analysis; reasons that have confused, more than clarified, the understanding of the new Muslim generations. Just a very simple observation can show how flawed the above essentialist hermeneutics positions are: no culture is monolithic; all cultures contain diversity. I have often had the impression that we, the anthropologists, are trapped in the academic presuppositions we have built up, and this explains why they are difficult to deconstruct. One of these presuppositions is the idea that cultural features are unequivocally related to identity. So if an individual (or a group) expresses specific cultural traits, they are often assumed as anthropological evidence that the person has a particular identity rather than another. In the case of a person expressing cultural aspects that are part of two different cultures, it is often assumed that the person ought to have more than one identity. Consequently the person has to suffer a clash between them when, as in the case of many western-born Muslims, the person was born within heterogenic environments. Although I have been trained as a cultural anthropologist, during my fieldwork I started to question whether the indefinable concept of culture, as understood, for instance, from Geertz on, was the real problem to be addressed. Within such abstract theoretical frameworks and models, something needed to be reinstated: the human being.[13]

## AFTER SEPTEMBER 11: BETWEEN TRADITION
## AND INNOVATION

On 12 September 2001, I decided to visit the mosque in Belfast. I used to visit it every Sunday as part of my observation of the so-called Sunday school for the Muslim children (*madrasa*) organized within the Belfast Islamic Centre (Marranci 2006b, 2006d). Instead of the usual joyful laughs and high-pitched voices of children, lugubrious silence and smashed windows welcomed me. Like many other Islamic symbols in the west, the Centre had been vandalized, its Muslims frightened, and even the prayers suspended. The Muslims preferred to remain protected by the walls of their homes rather than face the impromptu vigilantes who, with illogical and blind hysterical revenge, took the lives of innocents. September 11 brought visible changes to the mosque. Muslims had removed the green insignia, welcoming the visitors in Arabic and English, to the Belfast Islamic Centre. The identity of the detached house was thus concealed. Muslims had lived in Northern Ireland for more than thirty years, witnessing disruptive sectarian 'Christian' terrorism spreading fear within Northern Irish society. Now, the terror that Northern Irish people could see them as the archetype of terrorism forced them, though for just a few days, to seek refuge in a fearful low profile.

'Never, since the time of the persecution of Muhammad and his followers by the Meccans' pagan hands, had Muslims needed to hide their identities as they had to in Europe the day after September 11', said Ahmed, one of the eldest members of the community. The idea that a new *hijra*[14] might be required circulated among the Muslim community. A hijra, however, towards nowhere since many became *muhājirūn*[15] in the west in order to save themselves and their families from pro-western or western-sponsored Muslim dictators, such as Saddam Hussein in Iraq. The aftermath of September 11, however, changed the mood. Rage substituted the fatalistic *inshallah* attitude when the highly technological, expensive and devastating American bombs ripped apart the poor and tormented land of Afghanistan (Marranci 2004). Muslims in the west felt that a double standard language was employed in which the 'others' were often defined as terrorists if they did not agree with the mainstream secular positions. The networks of relatives and friends, which any multinational and multiethnic western Muslim community possesses, became a sort of Babel of news which often reached the community members before even Al-Jazeera could spread it through parabolic dishes.

The double standard was not only visible in the words of politicians in news-papers but also 'watchable' in the self-censorship implemented by the western mass media. But what had been censored found its way to Muslim audiences through other mediums. Pictures of dead children, tortured Muslims, destroyed mosques and boot-stepped Qur'ans reached Muslims in the west through email or mobile phones.[16] Tragedy, blood and death, so traumatically broadcast in the case of the Twin Towers, remained mostly hidden in the case of Muslim death and suffering in Afghanistan and Iraq. When a terrorist attack strikes our cities, the indignation, fear and rage we experience leads politicians, commentators and laymen to ask for the punishment of the evil others, new draconian laws to fight the invisible but ever present enemy of 'our civilization', democracy, secularism and freedom. This Manichaean political populism, invoking violence as a legitimate defence from somebody else's belief in justifiable violence, is not an exception, but rather the rule of the rhetoric of fear and empowerment. The same dynamics, as I have argued in *Jihad Beyond Islam* (Marranci 2006a), explain the existence of the rhetoric of jihad in some Muslims, particularly when young.

September 11 has certainly changed the world and the lives of millions. It has transformed the world into a less secure place than before, raised the tensions between different worldviews, challenged our intellectual and religious beliefs and shaken rights which we had taken for granted in the western part of the world after the end of the Second World War, such as freedom of speech. Like me, many other anthropologists were conducting their research and fieldwork when the tragedy took place. Some of these anthropologists, I trust, were researching topics related to the Muslim world, living among Muslims, sharing the experience of September 11 from the side of otherness. At the same time, other anthropologists were surely living the collapse of the World Trade Centre (WTC) in New York and its aftermath minute by minute.

Six years after the terrible event few publications devoted even marginally to Islam avoid mentioning, in one way or another, September 11. How did the anthropologists of Islam react to this tragedy and its aftermath? Were they among the many commentators of those unfortunate days and their consequences? In what way has September 11 and the war on terror changed their research and fieldwork? Is the anthropology of Islam, in particular when dealing with Muslims living in the west, still the same? Are the theorizing zones, which we have discussed above, still central to the discussion of Muslims in the west?

Let me start from a first important observation. Publication of academic work is inevitably a slow process with an average of seven–eight months for a journal article and one year and five months (sometimes even two years or more) in the case of an academic book. This means that the first articles discussing September 11 and its aftermath were available from the end of 2001/beginning of 2002, with books forthcoming in 2003. Moreover, in the case of anthropological studies, which are normally based on ethnography, time for conducting fieldwork, analysing the data and writing the article stretched even further the time-relationship between the event and its interpretation in comparison, for example, with political science or media studies. This explains why an extended collection of articles focusing on Muslims in the west, such as Haddad (2002), did not even mention the attacks on the Twin Towers and its consequences for Muslims living in the west. Nevertheless, we should recognize that, six years after the collapse of the WTC, though September 11 is virtually always mentioned in any recent articles, books, or applications for research funding concerning Muslims and Islam, real ethnographic studies on September 11, its aftermath and consequences are few, scattered and often affected by a lack of reflexivity. But the lack of reflexivity is not the only problem that the anthropology of Islam faces in the globalized, fast, world of communication. Social scientists have been able to reach a wider audience and present their interpretations and future scenarios. Anthropologists, in the majority of the cases, remain trapped in their ivory tower (Hannerz 2003).

Hannerz has observed that anthropological comments on 'current events and contemporary history' have been marginal; consequently, even after September 11, they have been unsuccessful in reaching a 'wider audience',

> 'One big thing' stories are indeed a genre from the borderlands between journalism and academia: among the authors we can identify a political science professor at one leading university (Huntington, at Harvard) and a history professor at another (Kennedy, at Yale); a think tank intellectual (Fukuyama, then at Rand Corporation); a journalist publishing most regularly in a magazine (Kaplan, in *The Atlantic Monthly*); and then again Friedman, three times a Pulitzer Prize winner, at what is arguably the world's leading newspaper. There is not an anthropologist among them. (2003: 173)

Of course, Hannerz is not suggesting a 'popularization' of anthropology, rather he is rightly interested in seeing 'an expansion of anthropological work into kinds of commentary that may or may not be immediately identified with the discipline..., but which over time may become recognized as part of the public repertoire of anthropologists' (2003: 186).

If it is true that some anthropologists of Islam, working on traditional studies of Muslim villages and rural communities, have published monographs without considering the impact that these events might have had on the studied community,[17] others have, often for the first time, engaged with the mass media and tried to reach a wider audience. González's edited book *Anthropologists in the Public Sphere* (2004; see parts IV to VI inclusive) presents a good example of the contributions that anthropologists have offered to the current political and social debate concerning, among other topics, the war in Afghanistan, Iraq and terrorism. These short articles, mostly written for newspapers and magazines with a wide readership, differ from other political commentaries because they start from the experience of fieldwork and contact with 'the Other'. For instance Beeman (2004) has pointed out that the anti-terrorist messages of the Bush administration would not win the hearts and minds of Muslims. On the contrary, they would sound suspicious and neocolonialist because of the historical memory of a certain political rhetoric during colonialist times. Other anthropologists and sociologists have resorted to the Internet in order to express their concerns and analysis in the aftermath of September 11.[18] I agree with Hannerz that anthropologists working, in this case, on Muslims and Islam may achieve a significant 'mediating role'. Hannerz has indeed emphasized, 'bringing us into scenario-writing may be a way of bringing people into those scenarios, "fellow human beings", ... people whose actions can be seen to make a difference, whether in one direction or another – and who can thereby instruct audiences that their actions can make a difference, too' (2003: 168). For this reason, together with other anthropologists working on Islam, I decided to co-edit a blog with Daniel Varisco (www.tabsir.net) focusing on Islam and Muslims in the aftermath of September 11. The intention is to counterbalance, through the experience of ethnography and fieldwork, other more established blogs kept by so-called Neo-Orientalists, such as Daniel Pipes and Martin Kramer. To bring the fellow human being into the scenario is certainly one of the main aspects of a contemporary anthropology of Islam, as I will discuss in the following chapters.

The war on terrorism and the wars in Afghanistan and Iraq have, for the first time, forced anthropologists and sociologists of Islam (or at least some of them) to leave their ivory tower to make their opinions available to the wider public. Their academic research aim, more often than before, is to provide a reading of and answer to contemporary issues. Even the Internet itself has become a locus of anthropological fieldwork and analysis. I will mention here two different and inspiring studies, Varisco 2002 and Bunt 2003.

Varisco has suggested an intriguing reality involving not only the activities of Muslims within cyberspace, but also the representation and stereotypes affecting Muslims and Islam post-September 11. He has observed how the Islamic world has been reduced to the face of Osama bin Laden in, for example, the interactive page of *The Washington Post*, 'On the main web page there is a portrait of bin Laden astride a map of Asia. By clicking on individual countries on the map, short summaries of each country pop up. Thus, bin Laden himself becomes the iconic portal for obtaining contextual information on the region and Islam' (2002: 934). Varisco has also highlighted the role played in constructing and reinforcing anti-Muslim stereotypes by apparently innocuous cyber-videogames and cartoons, which appeared in the aftermath of September 11, in which bin Laden is reproduced.

In his extensive and interesting monograph *Islam in the Digital Age* (2003), Bunt has instead focused on the online activities of Muslims. He has observed forms of e-jihad, the uncontrolled proliferation of fatwa websites of dubious authority and the dependence of the young Muslim generations upon the Internet for acquiring knowledge on Islam. In the conclusion of his book, Bunt has also observed the positive role that the Internet has on the concept of ummah itself. He has suggested, 'It is through a digital interface that an increasing number of people will view their religion and their place in the Muslim worlds, affiliated to wider communities in which "the West" becomes, at least in cyberspace, increasingly redundant' (2003: 211). Yet there is more research needed in this new field, particularly in the domain of gender. In his detailed and interesting study, we cannot find the word 'woman' even in the index. So, for instance, we may wonder how Muslim women are taking part in 'cyber Islamic environments', using online fatwas as well as conducting e-Jihad shoulder to shoulder with their Muslim brothers.

It is an unsurprising fact that with the 'war on terror' social scientists, and among them anthropologists of Islam, have increasingly focused on issues concerning radicalization, identity, intra-community networks, relations between the state and Muslim communities, and the effects of anti-terrorism policies and legislation on local Muslims. Approaches to these topics have been very different, from the analysis of mass media representations of Muslims and the war on terror, to ethnographic studies focusing on ordinary Muslims. A good example of recent research in this area, which offers diverse social scientific styles, is Abbas's edited book *Muslim Britain: Communities Under Pressure* (2005). Many of the contributions show the complex reactions of the British Muslim community to the tragic events of September 11 and its aftermath in a way that other political scientific studies did not. The voice of the communities is made audible. At the same time, some contributions tend to highlight the emotional critical responses of western-born Muslims (see Marranci 2005), which have often been silenced. The explanation for this can be found in two main points: firstly, the fear that the angered opinions could misrepresent the respondents as radical (i.e. a form of conscious self-censoring); secondly, because analysis of emotions has often been overlooked to privilege social-political analysis.

After September 11, anthropologists working on Islam have felt pressure to advance a counter-hegemonic discourse against certain simplifications that affected not only the political but also the academic discourse, in particular in the USA. The relationship that certain anthropological traditions have with colonialism and post-colonialism is now felt as a burden that has to be resolved once and for all. We can observe a new and fruitful reflexivity, which was previously missing within the field of anthropology of Islam. For instance, Price has suggested, 'we can help to reveal the complexity behind an oversimplified picture and to de-exoticize those who are being marginalized as uncivilized or reactionary ... Anthropologists can enrich public discussions of terrorism by "studying up" and examining state terrorism' (2002: 5). Others have gone even further; for example, Sluka, Chomsky and Price (2002) have argued for a direct involvement of anthropologists in the field of human rights, not only as scholars, but also in roles ranging from activists, to 'witnesses, alarmists' or even 'shock troopers' (2002: 12–13). One attempt to deconstruct a certain hegemonic understanding of the war on terror through stereotyped cultural premises is Mamdani's article, published in the *American Anthropologist* just one year after September 11, where Mamdani has rejected what he has referred to as 'cultural talk', since

> on the one hand, cultural explanations of political outcomes tend to avoid *history* and issues, By equating political tendencies with entire communities denned in no historical cultural terms, such explanations encourage collective discipline and punishment – a practice characteristic of colonial encounters. This line of reasoning equates terrorists with Muslims, justifies a punishing war against an entire country (Afghanistan) and ignores the recent history that shaped both the current Afghan context and the emergence of political Islam. On the other hand, culture talk tends to think of individuals (from 'traditional' cultures) in authentic and original terms, as if their identities are shaped entirely by the supposedly unchanging culture into which they are born. In so doing, it dehistoricizes the construction of political identities. Rather than see contemporary Islamic politics as the outcome of an archaic culture, I suggest we see neither culture nor politics as archaic, but both as very contemporary outcomes of equally contemporary conditions, relations, and conflicts, Instead of dismissing history and politics, as culture talk does, I suggest we place cultural debates in historical and political contexts. (2002: 767)

The relationship between history, politics and culture is a complex one and anthropologists of Islam had, and have, to face a new challenge in the post September 11 era, which means reconsidering this variable in the context of a global war without clear enemies as well as a global strategy which affects the lives of local people and communities.

To study Muslims and their understanding of Islam also means passing the magnifying glass over our own cultures, our categorizations, and the mechanism through which we make sense of what it means to be a human being in a new dimension that asks us to contemplate the macro within an increasingly shifting micro. Thus, the anthropologist Sundar (2004), who in his article has analysed mass violent events, such as the 2002 Gujarat massacre of Muslims and the 2003 US occupation of Iraq, has argued that social scientists need to reconsider how public morality is constructed. This is because the culturalist explanation of mass violence had for a long time set up an unacceptable hierarchy of cultures, the heritage of a colonialist past which has avoided looking:

> at the transnational flows of ideas of security, terror, and 'normal' states of the economy and the global reach of a few media organizations. Yet to see the perpetrators or supporters of violence not merely as warped individuals but as subject to powerful discourses of hate that translate in unhealthy ways into their everyday lives does not lead one to condone their acts. (2004: 157)

Since the war on terrorism, and the terrorist attacks that have shocked not only western but also Muslim countries and the wider world, instability and violence have reached an unprecedented global level. Any incident that may involve Islam, as tradition, in one country, through the mass media, the Internet, and also through personal networks, will receive attention at a global level.

## CONCLUSIONS

The anthropological study of Islam has changed deeply since the beginning of the 1980s. At first, anthropologists of Islam privileged exotic villages and cities to study local Muslim societies. Today we have to face, even within the local environment, the challenge of an unprecedented global dimension. The shift of interest from, in the majority of cases, the Middle Eastern village to the western cities in which Muslim immigrants settled, firstly as guest workers, then as citizens, has characterized the last twenty years of this discipline. Nonetheless, even in these new generations of studies, focusing on integration, identity, emancipation of women, education, multiculturalism and Islamophobia, many of the post-colonial themes, which marked the first anthropological studies of Muslim societies, may still be recognized. Essentialist understandings of Islam affected the first ethnographic studies of Muslim societies. Similarly, essentialization of the concept of culture has favoured dyadic representations of the western-born Muslim generations. During the 1970s and until the mid-1980s anthropologists and sociologists focused on the national and ethnic identities of the Muslim migrants, suggesting complex processes of integration and assimilation. Yet in the 1980s, thanks to the growth of the Muslim communities and their new social political activism, Islam, seen as a cultural identity marker, seemed to substitute the previous anthropological interest in nationalism and ethnicity. The concept of identity became central to the understanding of how the Muslim communities would reconcile their religion with western values; yet before September 11, it was not democracy or terrorism at the epicentre of this discussion, it was education.

September 11 and the war on terrorism has asked anthropologists working on Islam to reflect on their works and role. For the first time since the anthropology of Islam became a self-conscious field, scholars started to reconsider their position in face of global turmoil. Some anthropologists started to show how the life of western Muslims was entangled not only with the rest of the Islamic world, but also with the western one. Local had to become global, from the study of the cyber Islamic environment to the mass media representation of tragic events shocking the world. New ethical and moral issues have opened the door to a difficult dilemma inviting anthropologists of Islam to wonder which role they may have in this political scenario. A recent incident illustrating the connection between the very local and the very global was the Danish Cartoon affair. On 30 September 2006, a Danish conservative newspaper, the *Jyllands-Posten*, decided to publish a series of cartoons depicting the Prophet of Islam ridiculously; one of these badly designed caricatures represented Muhammad with a turban in the shape of a bomb imprinted with a gold *shahāda*. According to the cultural editor of the newspaper, Flemming Rose, the intention was to provoke a discussion about freedom of speech and censorship. The result has been Muslim mass protests, at a global level, some of which resulted in fierce outbreaks of violence at the cost of human lives. Of course, as in the case of *The Satanic Verses*, the majority of western commentators emphasized the incompatibility of Islam with freedom of speech, and consequently democracy, while the Arab and Muslim opinions highlighted the western attack against Islam, reinforcing Muslims' suspicions that the war on terrorism was nothing else that a war on Islam.

Although an anthropological interest in the Danish Muslim community existed before the cartoons, at the time of writing, no anthropological study is available on the new affair, with a surprising delay with respect to the case of, for instance, *The Satanic Verses*. As I have mentioned above, anthropology is an ethnographically based discipline, and published studies are inevitably behind 'real time'. Yet the complexity of connections that these post September 11 events have with others, such as the Abu Ghraib scandal, secret detention of Muslim prisoners, torture, invasions, and the collapse of social relationships between Muslim communities and governments, challenged the capacity of the anthropologist of Islam to understand reality by observing the local, the micro. As we shall see in the following chapters, this requires that we start to reconsider methodologies, ideas and paradigms.

## NOTES

1. They are small villages often formed by related families.
2. There are many repertoires of Muslim migrants' songs whose texts describe the pain of being distant from their family and the imminent return to their homeland. For instance, one of such repertoires among the Algerians in France was the *chaabi* (see Marranci 2000a).
3. Muslim men have the obligation, according to the Qur'an, to be the breadwinner.
4. It is also important to notice that before the Second World War, societies such as the Italian, German and Spanish used to migrate instead of being harbours for migration.
5. Sometimes maintaining in the titles the ethnic or national denomination as in 'Muslim Pakistanis' or 'Muslim Algerians'.
6. See for instance Aldrich 1981; Bhatti 1981; Werbner 1980 and 1981; as well as Wilson 1981.
7. To cite just some examples, see Nielsen 1981; Mildenberger 1982; Qureshi 1983; Anwar 1982 and 1984; Barton 1986; Andezian 1988.
8. See for instance the studies conducted by Little, Mabey and Whittaker 1968; Anwar 1982; Ahsan 1988; Afshar 1989; Hewer 1992 and 1996; Haw 1994; Basit 1997; Archer 2002.
9. At least before the last few years of Blair's government, which has shown an unprecedented intolerance of freedom of speech.
10. See, for example, Anwar 1982, 1984, 1990; Nielsen 1987; Krieger-Krynicki 1988; Mirza 1989; Modood 1990; Gardner and Shukur 1994; Aronowitz 1998; Shaw 1998, 2002; Glebe 1990; Chon 1994; Geaves 1995.
11. Brah 1979; Mirza 1989; Bhachu 1993; Knott and Khokher 1993.
12. See for instance, the anthropologist Jacobson 1998; Shaw 1998 and 2002; Qureshi and Moores 1999; Dwyer 2000; Archer 2001 and 2002.
13. See Chapter 5 in this book for a discussion on Muslim identity.
14. Muhammad's decision to migrate from Mecca to Medina in order to preserve the newly born Muslim community.
15. *Muhājirūn* were the Muslims who performed the hijra.
16. I myself have received some through the people who I met during my research.
17. See for instance Shankland 2003. Although his book is presumably based on his 1998 research in Turkey, we must notice that there is not a reflection of the impact that the war on terrorism might have had for the Alevi Turkish community and their possible reactions.
18. For instance, anthropologists such as Abu-Lughod, Werbner, Asdar Ali, Smith and Henfner have published easily accessible papers on September 11. See the Social Science Research Council's web pages 'After Sept. 11: Perspectives from the Social Sciences', http://www.ssrc.org/sept11/

# CHAPTER 5

# From the Exotic to the Familiar: Anamneses of Fieldwork among Muslims

## *INTRODUCTION*

Fieldwork has been the central feature of anthropology at least since Malinowski's *Argonauts of the Western Pacific* (1922/1978). Since the 1970s we have witnessed a proliferation of epistemological discussions about fieldwork: from what fieldwork means, to the role of the fieldworker in the field and on the field;[1] discussions about the impact that gender,[2] age[3] and ethnicity[4] may have on fieldwork as well the impact the fieldwork may have on the fieldworker's emotions.[5] Other reflections of fieldwork have paid attention to the ethical and political challenges which fieldworkers may face since they do not operate in a social vacuum.[6] More recently a great number of anthropological textbooks have provided practical instructions on how to plan and conduct fieldwork, how to collect fieldnotes[7] and how to transform the experience of fieldwork into meaningful ethnographies.[8] In other words, fieldwork has been discussed from every imaginable viewpoint and through a plethora of examples derived from various theoretical positions and ethnographic experiences. Because of such diverse typologies of experiences of fieldwork, one might expect that those who have researched Muslim societies had contributed profusely to this 'fieldwork epistemology'. A review of the diverse ethnographic examples provided in these 'know-how' guides to fieldwork leaves that expectation largely frustrated. Beyond the anecdotes offered in the now classic studies of Muslim societies (e.g. Crapanzano 1980; Dwyer 1982; Gilsenan 1982; Geertz 1995; Rosen 2002) or short introductions to specific ethnographies, anthropologists of Islam have refrained from discussing and reflecting upon their own experiences of fieldwork, as well as those of others. The reasons are various; for instance, some anthropologists consider fieldwork among Muslims no different from, say, fieldwork among Eskimos. However, I expect that the strongest reason remains the fact that an explicit focus on Muslims as Muslims (instead of as villagers or members of a certain national or ethnic group) is rather recent.

When I was a student and realized that I could not find any epistemological reflections concerning fieldwork among Muslims, pending my own experiences of conducting research, I could only ask senior colleagues and teachers for insights. The answer I received from experienced scholars, with years spent in their fields, incredibly resembled the one Paul Rabinow collected in the 1960s. Rabinow reported that when questioning scholars about the lack of information available on fieldwork and Islam he received the same answer repeatedly, 'I thought about it when I was young. I kept diaries, perhaps someday, but you know there are really other things which are more important' (1977: 4). Young anthropologists today have only to type the keyword 'anthropological fieldwork' into an electronic library catalogue, and they will be spoiled for choice. Yet few would provide something approximating a discussion of fieldwork among Muslims. In the paragraphs below, I shall provide a critical review of these few discussions and reflections, taking the liberty of adding to them my own experiences.

## EXPERIENCING THE EXPERIENCE: FIELDWORK BEYOND MUSLIMS

We can trace introductions to ethnographic works and anecdotes that mention some aspects of conducting fieldwork in a Muslim space back to the end of the 1960s. Nonetheless, we may consider Peneff's article (1985) one of the earliest examples of a reflection on fieldwork in an Islamic country. Based on his freelance fieldwork in 1960s' post-revolutionary Algeria, Peneff has reflected on the effects that political scenes and economical circumstances have on fieldwork. However, the main topic in the article centred on his ethical dilemma between conducting overt or undercover fieldwork. It was the 1960s, so, after some attempts to resist the temptation, and little danger of criticism from contemporaries, he finally gave in to undercover fieldwork. Peneff, the anthropologist, became Peneff, the French businessperson looking for deals with Algerian entrepreneurs. The article offers some interesting insights, from a reflection on the impact of undercover research to the ethical implications of academic funds and sponsorship for ethnographic research. Yet as other reflections on fieldwork among Muslims written during the 1980s and 1990s, Peneff seems more interested in experiencing the experience of fieldwork than in seeing fieldwork as a medium through which to make sense of his informants' realities. Indeed, Peneff was conducting fieldwork in a recently decolonized Muslim society. At that time, post-revolutionary tensions shook Algeria, which, among other things, was trying to redefine the role that Islam had to play within the new post-colonial social order. The voices of these Muslims and the anthropologist's experience of living among them during such social turmoil would have been relevant. However, one cannot find a single example of Peneff's personal experience of Muslims. They are just good or bad businessmen.

As we have seen in Chapter 2, scholars used to see the study of Islam and Muslim societies, in particular within urban contexts as opposed to rural, less intriguing and 'exotic' than adventuring into traditional African or Polynesian societies. I am therefore not surprised that in authoritative works such as Geertz's classic, *Religion of Java* (1960) or his most quoted *Islam Observed* (1968), the informants' voices, as well as the anthropologist's experience of living with them, have been silenced, overpowered by the anthropologist seen mainly as author rather than fieldworker.

Nonetheless, even when the anthropologist as author wished to offer a keyhole through which to view the mysterious alchemy of practising fieldwork among Muslims, this ended in making the anthropologist not only the author but also the Prima Donna. An excellent example of this genre remains the only monograph still available that combines, at least in the title, the words 'reflection', 'fieldwork' and a Muslim country, Morocco (i.e. Rabinow 1977). In this book, Rabinow has narrated his first experience of fieldwork in Sefrou. Chapter after chapter we are introduced to his experience of everyday fieldwork, from a frustrating attempt at learning local Arabic through the locals, to the frustration of dealing with local informants; from the successful access to a hostile village, to the informants' manipulations that successfully transformed the anthropologist into the village chauffeur. Rabinow's book is fascinating and easy to read cover to cover during a warm summer evening, as I did. We surely cannot criticize Rabinow for a lack of honesty. In his fieldwork account, he has revealed what Malinowski tried to hide in the violated secrecy of his diaries: sexual relationships during fieldwork,

> After tea and another set of exchanges in Arabic, it was clearly time for bed. Ali took me into the next room and asked me if I wanted to sleep with one of the girls. Yes, I would go with the third woman who had joined us for dinner. She had her own room next door, so we could have our privacy... Aside from the few pillows and charcoal burner for tea, there was only the bed. The warmth and non-verbal communication of the afternoon were fast disappearing. This woman was not impersonal, but she was not that affectionate or open either. The afternoon had left a much deeper impression on me. (1977: 68–9)

What has surprised me the most about this paragraph is neither the anecdote, with its chauvinist final comment (probably socially excusable at that time), nor the lack of discussion on the ethical implications and the informant–anthropologist power relationship (we would need another decade to find such self-critical views). Rather, it is the detachment from the informant's reality. Rabinow was experiencing the experience of being an anthropologist more than observing through participation the different experiences of his informants' Islam. Indeed, Newton (1993: 7) has observed,

> Most of Rabinow's description is disingenuously offhanded and is made to seem – despite the unexplored admission that this was "the best single day I was to spend in Morocco" – primarily about validating his manhood to male Moroccans while fending off "haunting super-ego images of my anthropologist persona" [Rabinow 1977: 63–9 quoted in Newton 1993].

Rabinow was surely an observer, yet too defensive to become a participant (beyond the sexual indulgences of youth). For instance, as in his narration of the sexual encounter with a 'not impersonal', but 'not that affectionate' Berber prostitute, and also in his account of a healing Sufi ritual, he remained an outsider 'negotiating a delicate balance of power across the gulf of the anthropological project' (Ewing

1994: 573). So much an outsider was Rabinow that he perceived Islam as an obstacle, which finally forced him out of the field and towards his national identity,

> Yet, there was one further question to ask; Are we all equal, ben Mohammed? Or are Muslims superior? He becomes flustered. Here there was not possibility of reformist interpretation or compromise. The answer was no, we are not equal. All Muslims, even the most unworthy and reprehensible ... are superior to all non-Muslims. That was Allah's will. The division of the world into Muslim and non-Muslim was *the* fundamental cultural distinction, the Archimedean point from which all else turned. This was ultimately what separated us ... The lesson of tolerance and self-acceptance which ben Mohammed had been teaching me during the past months held sway. I had a strong sense of being American. I knew it was time to leave Morocco. (1977: 147–8)

He left Morocco for good, at least as an anthropologist, since Rabinow's main research today focuses, among other non-Moroccan things, on molecular biology and genomics. Rabinow's book does not tell us very much about the relationship between the respondents' Islam(s) and the fieldworker's experience of it. Yet, if read carefully, this book shows the difficulties and challenges that fieldworkers working on Muslim societies can face when they have inadequate or absent knowledge of theological rhetoric and the discourses existing within it.

*After the Facts. Two Countries, Four Decades, One Anthropologist* (Geertz 1995) demonstrates greater reflexive spirit and intentions. Published in 1995, the book represents an anamnesis of being an anthropologist back in the 1950s. Notwithstanding Geertz's famous storytelling and writing style, which is surely fascinating, this book is reminiscent of a hero's memoir: half narcissistic satisfaction, including nostalgic disillusionment in a changing world, and half inspirational guide for future generations (of ethnographers). I cannot dismiss the power that this Geertzian inspirational guide had on me: I became an anthropologist. Nonetheless, though writing in the middle of the 1990s, the nostalgia left Geertz in the 1950s. Despite the fact that the two countries are again Morocco and Indonesia, twenty-seven years on from his *Islam Observed*, Muslims, as believers in Islam, remain reflexively unobserved; or better, Islam itself becomes *the Muslim*, so much that even the entry *Muslims* in the index redirects the reader to *Islam*! As we have discussed in the beginning of this book, Muslims cannot be reduced to their religion, since Islam exists only through interpretations. Another, and probably the most questionable aspect of *After the Facts*, is that after two Muslim former colonies, four decades between colonialism and post-colonialism, one anthropologist in 1995 has still missed a good occasion to offer a reflection on the impact that colonialism had and has on Muslims and their interpretation of Islam. Missing is also a recognition of the influence, positive or negative,[9] of Said's *Orientalism* on the study of Islam. One can agree or disagree with Said's idea of Orientalism, but one cannot ignore it, not even *the* anthropologist. Therefore, when the reader turns the final page of *After the Facts*, what remains in his or her mind are neither the two Muslim countries, nor the four decades dedicated to the study of Muslim societies, but rather *the anthropologist*: the undoubtedly unique way of being Geertz; Clifford Geertz.

Although we need to recognize the limitation of these first reflections on fieldwork among Muslims, these authors at least offered a glimpse of their experiences. Others, such as Gellner who worked on Muslim societies during the same years, remained very quiet, if not secretive, about their fieldwork and relationship with their Muslim respondents. This, as we have seen in the previous chapter, brought Said (1985) to include ethnographic studies of Muslim societies within the domain of Orientalism. What Geertz in his counterargument to Said's *Orientalism* (1982) has missed is that 'interpretation' gives the anthropologist the power to 'create' his or her object of study, which in this case are human beings and societies. The lack of informants' voices or the essentialization of a people, in this case Muslims, to their religion or cultural system, can produce the same effect that traditionally oriental studies of Islamic texts, and artistic representation, did. The power of fieldwork, meant as sharing experiences and emotions, is lost in favour of the super-power of the anthropologist as trans-cultural hero, who can explain and make sense of the web of symbols and meanings hidden to his or her 'people'.

At the end of the 1980s, however, authors such as Clifford and Marcus (1986, and Clifford 1988), Fisher (Marcus and Fisher 1986) and Rosaldo (1989) shocked the traditional way of interpreting fieldwork and anthropology. This, of course, also had an impact on the anthropology of Islam, where the voices of the researched started to be represented, and the complex human relationships between the fieldworker and his or her 'people' were not only acknowledged but also made into an integral part of their ethnographies. To this, I would like to add in the next section the role that emotions have in an effective fieldwork and in preventing those Orientalist temptations that still haunt anthropologists studying Muslim societies.

## EMOTION, EMPATHY AND ORIENTALISM

As with any other anthropological fieldwork, those conducted within Muslim societies and with Muslims are based on the capacity of the fieldworker to build relationships and links with the studied communities. The complexity of this process not only affects the strategy through which fieldwork is conducted but also the epistemological question of what the ethnographer could learn from it and how the experience could be translated into ethnography. There is a long debate within anthropology of how anthropologists might achieve the understanding of different cultures and practices. Rosaldo (1993) for instance, has expressed a rather radical viewpoint on this issue. He has argued that the ethnographer's personal experiences determine the level of empathy or understanding s/he could have of the studied community. Rosaldo has reinforced his argument through his personal experience of loss, arguing, for instance, that only those who have suffered a serious personal loss may be able to write ethnographies on death. In other words, according to Betty (1999: 74), Rosaldo has suggested that, 'Understanding comes with empathy and empathy derives from common experiences'.

This position, if accepted, raises serious problems for anthropologists studying religion. For instance, we may wonder whether an atheist or agnostic anthropologist may be able to understand religious people fully. Even anthropologists professing faith in a religion would not be able to understand other believers if they have not experienced the same categories of emotions. Rosaldo's argument can make sense only if we accept a strict cultural hermeneutic understanding of emotions, feelings, empathy and identity. Notwithstanding the widespread and hegemonic relevance, after Geertz, of cultural hermeneutic positions, some anthropologists (see for instance Milton 2002, Milton and Svasek 2005 and Marranci 2006a) have ventured into new approaches, which, without denying the relevance that social interaction has within the human species, do not reduce the essence of being human to an undefined system of symbols. Although we shall discuss the role of emotions in Muslim identities in the next chapter, it is important to mention here Milton's view. She has suggested that emotions 'are an ecological rather than a social phenomenon, that they are a mechanism through which an individual human being is connected to and learns from their environment' (Milton and Svasek 2005: 32).

It is clear that Milton has not rejected the idea that emotions are generated during social interactions, but rather that they have a 'social ontology' (2005: 35). This means that the 'other' producing the emotional behaviour 'does not have to be a social or human other; it can be anything with which the individual organism engages, for emotion is part of that engagement' (2005: 35). This leads to the conclusion that through the engagement with different environments 'people learn to love, hate, fear, or be disgusted by different things, so that their body reacts differently when things are encountered' (Milton and Svasek 2005: 36). Following this interpretation of emotions, we can see how fieldworkers should not need to experience the same category of emotion through cultural symbolic expressions in order to understand, and empathize with, their informants – or even the environment in which the social interaction takes place. We, as human beings, though unable to share the deepest of feelings, can make sense of emotions, even if the category is different, by associating them with those we have experienced during our lifetime. In other words, an ethnographer studying death rituals within a certain society does not need to have suffered the loss of a relative or friend in order to make sense of the emotions of bereavement. Moving this reasoning to the study of religion, and in this case of Islam, although religious affiliation has an impact on how emotions are expressed, the emotions are not ontologically different from others expressed in non-religious contexts, or in other religious contexts. Hence, emotions are accessible to investigation and analysis, even if experience, as we shall see, is not. This explains the relevance that personal human bonding relationships have not only in achieving access to the community studied, but also in making sense of its world and viewpoints.

Magnarella (1986) has disclosed those 'human bonds' that became an integral part of his Turkish fieldwork in 1963. As many other anthropologists conducting research in villages, a local family 'adopted' and integrated him within its economic, social and emotional life. Central to his experience of Turkish culture was his 'adoptive mother', who, thanks to her age, could overstep the gender rules existing in the Sunni Muslim village. Being the 'son' of this old woman gave him, as a male anthropologist, an unprecedented opportunity to observe the role that women had in the village and the networks and dynamics of power existing within it. If Rabinow was, with difficulty, trying to establish himself as an anthropologist through fieldwork, and if Geertz established himself, successfully, as *the* anthropologist, at least in a sort of Jungian archetype, Magnarella has shown the, often blurred, delimitation between friendship, emotional involvement and anthropological awareness, 'My Turkish mother died in 1977. I miss her folk wisdom, the biscuits she baked specially for me whenever I went on a trip, her ritualistic pouring of water to ensure that my journeys and returns went smoothly, and they always did. I miss her' (1986: 37). Magnarella empathically became part of the emotional life of the Turkish family he was working with.

Another anthropologist, Ewing (1994) has provided us with a good example of the influence that the environment may have on the ethnographer. Ewing, during her fieldwork on Sufi practice in Pakistan, experienced a challenging event. Although a self-defined 'agnostic Westerner', she tested, in the best tradition of cultural anthropology, the spiritual power (*baraka*) of the local saint, who visited her during dreams, as he himself had promised. Indeed, Ewing experienced what many of her informants told her, during her research, about the practice of visiting saints. In a certain sense, Ewing was 'going native'. To 'go native' as Ewing has reminded us, is one of the 'taboos' of anthropology. Ewing has challenged this misconception, which, according to her, 'results from a refusal to acknowledge that the subjects of one's research might actually know something about the human condition that is personally valid for the anthropologist: it is a refusal to believe' (1994: 571). Her experience is useful for us for another reason. By reading her accounts of her story, we can observe the impact of what I call the 'emotional environment'. She experienced the saint as many of her informants did because she had become part of the community of emotions her informants shared.

During my fieldwork in Northern Ireland, I witnessed and experienced something similar. I was attending a meeting organized by NIMFA (Northern Irish Muslim Families) whose main guest was a Sufi from West Africa who talked about the relevance of life and family. However, when I asked the others present at the talk, everyone had the impression that the Sufi had answered each of our questions personally speaking differently to each of us, despite the fact that he delivered the talk to the assembly. Moreover, many of the youngest among the group, myself included, received further teaching from the Sufi during our dreams, which continued for weeks. As an anthropologist, I can try to explain this event in different ways. Is the scientific, or esoteric, explanation, however, the more relevant for understanding how my respondents made sense of this experience? Or, was the shared emotional experience that I had with them more relevant? It is my contention that it is the shared emotional experience.

In the case of studies focusing on Muslim societies, it is even more important to remember that a Muslim is a human being. I am aware that this seems simplistic; yet while teaching a course on 'fieldwork and Muslim societies', I came to appreciate how what might seem to be simplistic could be actually unobvious. For example,

I normally start my class by asking two students to join me in front of the others. Then, I ask the class to tell me what makes a person a Muslim. Often the first common answers point to Muslim dress style, such as women wearing the ḥijāb (veil), and men wearing caps and long beards. I ask two non-Muslim students, male and female, to wear respectively a Muslim cap and a ḥijāb. I then ask the class if these items make their fellow students two Muslims. Of course, the class agree that dress style is not enough to make them Muslim. I challenge the class to find the element that makes a person a Muslim. The commonest second answer is that s/he believes in the Qur'an and Allah. I tell the class that a Jesuit I know believes strongly that the Qur'an is a revealed book and Allah, God, is its author. I ask the class if this makes my Jesuit friend a Muslim. The class, after suggesting that he may be a Muslim Jesuit, recognize that even believing in the Qur'an does not transform a person into a Muslim. I test other cultural elements, such as the profession of faith, the pillars, Ramaḍan and so on. Even in these cases, any non-Muslim could follow the practice and not for this reason be himself or herself a Muslim. The final, and most radical, example I provide is the case of a person who says that s/he is Muslim because other people recognize him or her as Muslim. The class agrees that this is not enough to say that the person is a Muslim. So, I insist, if a Muslim is not what s/he wears, what s/he eats or avoids eating, what s/he celebrates or essentially believes, and what other people say s/he is, what, in essence, is a Muslim? Somebody sometimes provides what I consider to be the only possible answer: a human being who *feels to be* a Muslim. As we shall see in the next chapter, feelings and emotions are correlated in a particular way. So, it is that *feel to be* which makes an enormous difference when we try to understand Muslim societies through participant-observation. Indeed, this awareness prevents the essentialization of Muslims to their religion and consequently the trap of Orientalized ethnographies.

The approach I suggest can clarify another important aspect. As everybody can agree, conducting fieldwork among Indonesians is certainly not the same thing as doing so among Pakistanis. Similarly, conducting fieldwork among Sufi Muslims is surely a different experience from doing so among Salafi Muslims. In which way can we speak of the anthropology of Islam? How can we share, as we have done in this chapter, experiences of fieldwork among such heterogenic communities? As we have seen, central to the understanding of Islam, as expressed in different social interactions, is the human being who in this case *feels to be Muslim*. Hence, I can suggest that anthropology of Islam should, in different times, spaces and realities, try to explain how Muslims 'feel to be Muslim' and express it.

## *STAYING HERE, BEING THERE: FIELDWORK ON MUSLIM COMMUNITIES IN THE WEST*

John came back from his fieldwork. Together with four other anthropologists, we decided to celebrate the event with a dinner at the local Chinese restaurant. It was a nice night of a splendid summer. We were sitting in the restaurant waiting for our dishes, while John entertained us with his adventures in Papua New Guinea; dangerous animals, uncomfortable sleeping, exotic yet challenging food, infected water, annoying insects, lack of toilets but certainly not of diarrhoea; in one word: fieldwork. Others joined the conversation adding difficulties to difficulties, unpleasantness to unpleasantness, exotic countries to exotic people, obscure languages to unwritten grammars. Then the time came when they expected my additions to the list: comfortable beds; European capitals; fantastic food in western-based mosques; drinks in cafés; English, French and Italian as main languages; the only dangerous animal was my neighbour's frantic dog; modern and efficient toilets; the worst illness (at that time) flu. Yes, I was at home, in familiar Europe. Notwithstanding I had lots of anecdotes with which to entertain my guests, despite having no exoticism to offer. One of my colleagues openly questioned me, 'Do you not feel that you lack the real sprit of fieldwork?'

D'Alisera (1999) has provided us with one of the best descriptions of unrealized expectations of fieldwork. The civil war in Sierra Leone forced her to exchange an adventurous research on Islam in the Kambia district with a home doorstep fieldwork on Sierra Leonean Muslims in Washington. She has vividly painted her disappointment,

> This was not my dreamed-of entry into 'the field.' The landscape evoked too many personal memories – of family, holiday fun, undergraduate idealism. Inscribed with these multiple remembrances, the landscape seemed void of adventure. 'This isn't Africa,' I mused. 'This isn't even rural. This isn't really fieldwork.' Horns beeping, angry traffic faces, icy river below, English spoken all around me – all left me with the same feeling: familiarity. 'This is the place where I'm going to become an anthropologist?' – I hated every moment of this 'entry into the field.' (1999: 6)

The idea that fieldwork in anthropology means strange places and strange diseases is an old one. In other words, 'cool' fieldwork is to non-Western as 'un-cool' fieldwork is to Western. You may ask why I have used the term Western and non-Western, instead of, for instance, exotic and familiar. During a conversation with some African and South Asian anthropologists, I discovered that they did not consider fieldwork conducted in a Western city as exotic (i.e. interesting). By default of logic, I expected that surely for a Pakistani anthropologist living in Pakistan fieldwork in Paris among the Muslim Algerians should be at least 'exotic'. Yet the Pakistani anthropologist did not think so, and the African colleagues agreed with him. Why? We may ask.

Firstly, although an increasing number of studies have focused on Muslims living in the West, there is hardly any reflection on the experience of conducting fieldwork among them. Secondly, a conceptualization of 'distant' and 'remote' – hence 'exotic' – is still haunting anthropology at the beginning of the new millennium; and heritage, according to Passaro of 'the colonial mentality that once delighted in harrowing ethnographic accounts of the conquest of physical landscapes and of native reticence, when wresting "secrets" from remote "natives" was the *raison d'être* of the endeavour' (1997: 147).

Nonetheless, there are many similarities between conducting fieldwork with Muslims in the West and in the Islamic world. Trust, networking, gatekeepers and even kinships are part of the research here as there. However, in exchange for village life there are urban spaces and their challenges instead. Mobile phones, trains, subways, emails and the Internet become fundamental tools to stay in contact with informants, organize interviews, and participate in rituals and ceremonies. Technology, indeed, is at the centre of this kind of fieldwork because of the lack of a centre that, for instance, a village could provide. As with many other anthropologists conducting urban research, the main issue I had to face was 'disorientation' and what Marcus (1995) has called 'methodological anxieties'. One of these is the difficulty of conducting fieldwork among different nationalities, ethnic groups, religious affiliations (e.g. Shi'a and Sunni), Islamic theologies and opinions at the same time. In fact, even if one particular Muslim community is studied, this one will be never isolated, but rather interconnected with the Islamic environment existing in the field location, as well as with non-Muslims agencies, individuals and social actors.

The fact that Muslims living within the West interact mainly with non-Muslims asks us to pay particular attention to such a dynamic. Unfortunately, this has often been overlooked, even in recent studies. The main reason for this is the familiarity with the surrounding environment in which the fieldworker is conducting research, as D'Alisera had occasion to notice,

> At times the familiarity seemed intrusive, and I often became angry when it invaded my research space. The taxi drivers [one of her informants] with whom I rode would often stop midsentence to point out to me the usual tourist attractions – the White House, the Washington Monument, the Supreme Court – sites that they either assumed I wanted to see or had probably just grown used to announcing to their passengers as a matter of habit. I would smile, then try to ease them back into whatever we happened to be talking about. It never occurred to me to ask what these so very American places meant to them. I was not, after all, in Washington to sightsee. I did soon become aware of my mistake, but I am not convinced that I fully realized its import. (1999: 17)

Another example is the case of a British anthropologist conducting fieldwork on Muslim students' experience of British secondary schools. The anthropologist will have not only direct experience of the education system attended by his or her informants, but also memories of being a student herself or himself. Although this is certainly an advantage, again, this could affect the capacity of fieldworkers to observe and note important factors.

Personally, I became aware of the relevance of participant-observing informants' continuous criss-crossing of Muslim/non-Muslim cultural and social spaces while researching the Islamic activities of a Muslim women's group in Northern Ireland (Marranci 2006b). During this research, I was focusing on how the Muslim women's group, Al-Nisa, positioned itself within the overall local Muslim community as well as the main Islamic Centre at the central mosque. At a certain point, the central mosque felt challenged by the activities of these women and in particular their progressive and Islamically feminist approach. I expected that the Al-Nisa Women's Group would have tried to remain associated to the central mosque. Yet they did not. The reason was clear. I had focused on Al-Nisa as a Muslim support and service provider for the Muslim community. Yet the members of Al-Nisa saw their association as part of the complex network of associations and NGOs existing in post-Friday Agreement Northern Ireland. I had to reconsider my findings as well as methodology. Nevertheless, the experience was extremely useful for understanding that to conduct fieldwork on Muslim communities in the west means becoming part not only of the studied community (or communities or network of communities) but also of the dynamics of relationship with the non-Muslim environment surrounding them.

More than in any other research reality, anthropologists conducting fieldwork among western Muslims have to be very aware of the role and impact that mass media may have on their research. It is undeniable that the western mass media have subjected the Muslims living in the west to the highest level of invasive scrutiny that a community has ever received (Poole 2002). Surely September 11 has been at the centre of an unprecedented rise in the number of newspaper articles, magazine and TV reportage, cartoons, and editorials on Islam and Muslims. Sometimes, new ideas for academic research are the result of this mass media exposure of the western Muslim communities. More often, the ruthless approach of certain mass media jeopardizes anthropological research, or even manipulates them. In certain cases, however, the anthropologist becomes the point of contact between the Muslim community studied and the mass media. This is certainly a recent aspect of the anthropology of Islam, and surely, a challenging one, since, as Pécoud (2004) has noticed, anti-essentialist views tend to be unpopular with the mass media and the policy-makers. This is because – Pécoud has argued – the dominant discourse 'is characterized by a construction of cultural difference in which they represent the "most different" category and share some specifically "Turkish" or "Muslim" characteristics' (2004: 22). Anthropologists of Islam, working within a western context, find themselves within webs of 'intellectual competition' in which 'the most powerful sources of knowledge [i.e. the mass media and policy-makers] will not only impose itself as the central authority in the field: it will also impose what could be called its Weltanschauung [worldviews]' (2004: 22). Hence the relevance of being aware of this process, in particular in the aftermath of September 11 and the war on terrorism.

## CHALLENGES AND OPPORTUNITIES IN THE AFTERMATH OF SEPTEMBER 11

I have not collected other accounts, but I trust that other anthropologists found themselves in my shoes. In 2001, a few days after September 11, I had to change my long planned research in France. During a previous fieldwork, I had developed some contacts with Algerians from the so-called *al-Jabhah al-Islāmiyah lil-Inqādh* (The Islamic Salvation Front). I was invited to conduct research about identity and migration among them. However, some days after September 11, several phone calls, some of which were anonymous, made clear that my research was no longer welcome. The high security alerts had worsened the previously uneasy relationship between the North African community and the gendarmerie.[10] My informants were too scared and worried to devote time to my research; they wished to keep a 'low profile'. Consequently, my flight tickets ended in the bin, and I had to find another field. The war on terror has also affected the possibility of obtaining visas for intense research abroad. Increasingly, particularly in the case of the Middle East, even when anthropologists have been lucky enough to be granted a visa, they may discover that instead of the standard six months, only a couple of weeks have been allowed. From experience Hegland (2004: 575) has observed,

> For those anthropologists fortunate enough to get a visa at all, it may allow them no more than a few weeks of in-country research time. This poses a challenge to our understanding of the time it takes to do useful and serious social scientific fieldwork. As such, limitations have become frequent for social scientists working in Iran, though, we need to rethink the ways we customarily conduct fieldwork research and try to adapt some research methodologies to these restrictive conditions – not as an ideal or a norm, but out of necessity. Such salvage efforts might not live up to our professional standards, but as my own experience has shown, they can yield rich material and make the effort quite worthwhile.

Nonetheless, September 11 has not only disrupted, at the time, ongoing fieldwork, and made access to non-western fields more cumbersome, but also increased the academic and, even more, the non-academic interest in Islam.

So, if at the beginning of this book, we met a young Gilsenan (1990) lamenting the lack of interest in anthropological research on Middle East and Islam, today, I can affirm that the situation is the opposite. So much so, that September 11 has produced a new phenomenon: academic-conversion to Islam. For instance, I came across the tragic-yet-comical case of an anthropologist who had worked and published for a decade on Tibetan Buddhism, proclaiming himself, on his institutional web page, to be an 'expert' on political Islam after merely reading some books on the Middle East and fundamentalism but never having conducted fieldwork in the region nor publishing on the topic. Unfortunately, these improvised 'academic-converts' are often more interested in the postgraduate market, and chatty-trash publishing, which their recently discovered anti-terrorist expertise could provide, rather than real academic interest in understanding Muslims and their lives. To these (fortunately) few (but tragically increasing) academic entrepreneurs of the September 11 business, we have to add an army of journalists, improvised anti-terrorist experts, commentators, novelists and, last but not least, politicians, all ready to theorize and tell us what 'political Islam', 'Islam' or even 'the Muslim' might be. In the majority of cases, none of these self-styled 'experts on Islamic terrorism' have spent time conducting fieldwork among Muslims, leave aside among radicals.[11] For these reasons, fieldwork focusing on Muslims as human beings, rather than cultural agents, is today central to an anthropology which aims to understand Muslims beyond stereotypes and Orientalist, freak-show representations of their lives and beliefs.

Yet this massive, often negative and biased, attention has made Muslims around the globe very suspicious of any research or researcher. Therefore, it is not surprising that anthropologists of Islam may face a hard time achieving the much needed trust. Successful fieldwork can only be conducted once the anthropologist has achieved a certain degree of trust and confidence from part of the studied community or at least some of its key members. People can decide to collaborate on a piece of research for many reasons: from personal to political interest; from real friendship to curiosity; from visibility to necessity. Never has it been so important for anthropologists working with Muslim societies to be clear and open about the research and the reasons for which they are conducting fieldwork. Even more important, without compromising the academic value of the research, is making informants aware of what is intended to be written. Today, any research involving Muslims has a political value, for states, individuals, agencies as well as the Muslim community. So, although living within the studied group is an essential factor in decreasing the suspicion of the fieldworker, even simple incidents, which may be apolitical, could easily be interpreted through the existing political tensions within some Islamic societies and western nations. Of course, this is not just a September 11 novelty; as for instance the incident experienced by Nourse (2002) can demonstrate. During her 1995 fieldwork conducted in an Indonesian town, a local well-known thief stole some of her belongings:

> I impulsively walked over to knock on Farhan's door. His younger brother, sister, and mother, all nice people, answered. I told them about the theft. They commiserated. Then Farhan appeared in the back of the house and I saw him look at me and sneer. He began to laugh. That was the last straw. I looked at him and vehemently exclaimed, 'It was you! I know it was. Don't think I don't.' I will never forget the look of horror on everyone's face when I said that. Farhan's sister, my friend, looked at me in shock and said, 'I know Westerners accuse each other publicly, I've seen it in TV shows, but this is not something we do here.' I walked back to my house. I knew I had crossed a line here, but also felt someone had to confront Farhan so that no more thefts would occur. About thirty minutes later I noticed a crowd had gathered out in front of our houses. I walked outside and saw several of my friends as well as strangers. Everyone looked at me. One young man – I never learned his name – pointed a finger at me and said, 'You foreigner – you American – who do you think you are, accusing Indonesians of theft?' 'Go home, foreigner! Go home, American!' (2002: 34)

The simple mishandling of the accusation, in a way that contradicted local traditions, acquired an unexpected political connotation. After September 11, western anthropologists conducting fieldwork within Muslim societies do not even need similar incidents; they are questioned, examined and evaluated starting from the political actions of their countries.

This has a psychological and emotional effect on the fieldworker, on his or her ability to approach the field, to work within it, as Gardner, for instance, experienced during her fieldwork on the British Bangladeshi community,

> For a phase in my fieldwork, I became actually paranoid about what people thought of me. I was terrified that I would meet direct hostility, or even aggression, and would not be able to continue. More profoundly, the experience of being held in suspicion and not always being welcome is deeply unsettling. Discussing these issues with friends who did fieldwork with people who welcomed their enquiries, and who were vociferous in their desire to be written about, I realise that postmodern critiques of anthropology have fewer emotional resonances for them than for me. (1999: 70)

Indeed, one of the topics that scholars have often discussed regards the power relationship between the ethnographer and the studied community. Some authors (e.g. Clifford 1983; Marcus and Fisher 1986; Geertz 1988) have highlighted the power that the ethnographer has over the studied subjects. Recently, some anthropologists (e.g. Nourse 2002; Kalir 2006) have criticized this position and suggested that, particularly during fieldwork, the informants can be the more powerful within the relationship. For instance, Kalir has observed,

> Persuading them [the informants] to cooperate with my research therefore depended crucially on my ability to gain their full trust. This in turn endowed my informants with considerable power to determine the nature of our mode of engagement. It also reduced my pre-designed research method to secondary significance for the way in which my fieldwork unfolded. Put differently, conducting semi-structured interviews, tape-recording formal and informal conversations, taking photos, and being able to participate in regular as well as special events, were all dependent on my ability to generate trust and establish meaningful relationships with informants. (2006: 235)

I have recently experienced something similar during a sensitive research project on religious identity formation among Muslim prisoners and former prisoners in the UK. I have found that the Muslim people I contacted for interviews or to discuss the topic (including administrators of Muslim organizations and mosques I visited) have spent time 'Googling' my name, reading my blog, articles and even delaying meetings until they had finished my last book. Surely, neither Geertz or Rabinow, nor Gilsenan or Gellner had undergone such pre-fieldwork scrutiny by their studied communities and informants. This has a tremendous impact on how we conduct fieldwork today. In these circumstances, is it still the anthropologist who chooses his or her studied community and informants? Or do the community and informants, after studying the student, choose the anthropologist by deciding whether or not to collaborate with him or her? And moving from fieldwork to ethnography, is there a risk of self-censoring our own studies and findings because of the fear that they may compromise any future research (or in some cases personal or informants' safety)? Of course, the answer is 'yes'. Yet as for instance Kalir recently has acknowledged, 'we should be mindful that an "embodied" bias could in some cases be a *sine qua non* for carrying out fieldwork' (2006: 244).

Trust, as we have said, is central to fieldwork, in particular today in the case of research on Islam and Muslims. Evergeti, who has conducted fieldwork in a Greek Muslim village (1999, 2004, 2006) has emphasized that 'establishing trust was an ongoing process that was an integral part of my ethnography and as such lasted throughout my fieldwork' (2004: 45). As in the case of Geertz (1973) the incident that helped Evergeti to achieve the trust of the Muslim village she was studying was the unwanted attention that the local police paid to her visit in the region. This transformed Evergeti into a sort of antagonist presence against what the villagers saw as an oppressive and suspicious authority.[12]

Although these kinds of incidents can demonstrate to the community that the anthropologist is not a 'spy' or an agent of the government, it is not the incident itself that may allow them to understand the community and become part of it. I strongly believe, as I have experienced many times during my research, that it is the empathy that the anthropologist experiences, through emotions, which allows him or her to feel the other as a fellow human being. It is through this humanization of the anthropological fieldwork that difficulties can be overcome. We cannot understand, for instance, my friend Muhammad, the Muslim, if first we do not understand Muhammad as a human being. As I will explain in the next chapter, it is through emotions and feelings that Muhammad experiences and embodies Islam. Participant observation, in my opinion, does not mean just taking part in activities and sharing actions, which we can observe, note, report and analyse. This, in the best case, would remain a useful exercise. Participant observation means taking part in the emotional processes involving the formation of feelings. So, for this reason, studying Muslim societies and communities requires a good knowledge of the main aspects of Islam and its texts, and being acquainted with a certain rhetoric existing in the Islamic world. This facilitates the possibility of observing, through participation, how informants transform, manipulate and make their own these elements.

## CONCLUSIONS

Books and 'how-to' guides about anthropological fieldwork are increasing in number within publishers' catalogues. Among this large production, it is unusual to find even chapters addressing the experience of conducting fieldwork among Muslim societies and communities. In the few cases in which some examples have been provided, they describe and discuss what I call 'exotic' fieldwork. Even less available is material containing reflections on the impact and issues that an anthropologist may face in conducting fieldwork within Muslim communities, in the west and in Islamic countries, during this endless 'war on terror'. In this chapter, I have tried to start a reflection and discussion on what it means to conduct fieldwork among Muslims today. In doing so, I have provided examples from the experiences of some anthropologists as well as my own. I have suggested that at the centre of a contemporary anthropology of Islam should be the human being even before the Muslim. This is vital if we wish to overcome a certain Orientalism and suppression of self-represented identities, as we can observe in classic works, from Geertz to Rabinow and Gellner.

To focus on Muslims as human beings is to acknowledge the role that emotions and feelings have on the informant's discourse of Islam as well as the power that the surrounding environment has in its definition. In other words, successful fieldwork is based not only on knowledge of Islam as religion, but also the capacity of the fieldworker to develop emotional empathy with his or her studied community. This process, as I have emphasized in this chapter, requires trust. Anthropologists of Islam should be very aware that the power relationship within the field is more complex than can be expected in other contexts; particularly if the fieldwork is conducted in the west. Informants are very conscious of the political tension existing today and the possibility of exploitation from the mass media. The strong surveillance, profiling and culture of suspicion that is affecting the majority of Muslim communities living in the west or Islamic countries means that informants are very careful to whom they provide access to the community. It is not so uncommon, as I have experienced, that real intelligence gathering may be conducted (through the Internet, collecting the fieldworker's previous writing, political affiliations, collaboration with the mass media and so on).

However, a clear and ethical approach, which transparently not only informs the studied community of the research and project, but also makes them part of it and its implications, can form a strong relationship and help to develop the needed trust. As we have seen, the actions of the anthropologists are evaluated within the political context. Yet the emotional context has its domain as well. The development of empathy and emotional participation in the life of the studied Muslim community can overcome the most difficult situations within fieldwork.

## *NOTES*

1. See, for example, Gold 1958; Gans 1968; Hayano 1979; Adler and Adler 1987; Goffman 1989; Lofland and Lofland 1995.
2. For example, Hunt 1984; Arendell 1997; Devault 1999; Warren 1998 and 2001.
3. For example, Fine and Sandstrom 1988; Gubrium 1988; Diamond 1992.
4. For example, Anderson 1978; Baca Zinn 1979; Zavella 1996.
5. For example, Schwartz and Schwartz 1955; Gans 1968; Karp and Kendall 1982; Zola 1982; Kleinman 1991.
6. Erikson 1967; Cassell 1980; Silverman and Gubrium 1989; Scarce 1994; Van Der Geest 2003; Sen 2004.

7. For instance, Sanjek 1990.
8. For instance, Emerson, Fretz and Shaw 1995.
9. Geertz in a review written in 1982 strongly criticized Said's positions, in particular as far as anthropology was concerned.
10. The gendarmerie is a military body charged with police duties among the civilian population.
11. Indeed, there are rare exceptions, such as Wiktorowicz's (2005) *Radical Islam Rising*.
12. For a similar incident facilitating access through what I can define as a 'test of trust' see Kalir 2006.

# CHAPTER 6

# Beyond the Stereotype: Challenges in Understanding Muslim Identities

## *IDENTITY AND ANTHROPOLOGY*

Identity has fascinated intellectuals, such as philosophers (e.g. Locke 1690/1959 and Hume 1740/1975), psychologists (e.g. James 1890) and sociologists (e.g. Goffman 1959), for centuries. Each discipline, and within it each school and scholar, has provided an interpretation, theory and model. With them, they also provided terminologies that have proliferated into a confusing list. The frustration here is not with this excessive terminology per se, rather, by being used in different contexts and from different disciplines, it has lost its specification. So, 'identity, 'self-identity', 'personal identity, 'self', 'selfhood', 'personhood', 'I', 'me', 'Me' and a plethora of other terms (see Holland 1997) have confused more than clarified.

Sociologists have been exploring the relationship between self, identity and society since the beginning of the nineteenth century[1] with pioneers such as Charles Horton Cooley (1909), George Herbert Mead (1934) and Herbert Blumer (1969). By contrast, the first anthropologists did not show much interest in studying the 'persona'; rather they concentrated their efforts on understanding the symbol, the object and the community seen as an expression of collective identity dictated by cultural processes. In one of the rare articles[2] that analytically and critically discusses the study of identity in anthropology, Sökefeld (1999) has rightly observed that because of the overemphasis on society we have just discussed, anthropologists have denied the relevance that individuality and the personal self have in the study of the 'others'.

He has suggested that social anthropologists took 'Durkheim's concept of "collective representations" ... as justification for the fact that social anthropology gave little attention to the individual, regarding the social as its only object' (1999: 428). According to Sökefeld, this has caused a serious flaw within the anthropological understanding of others' selves,

This certainly applies to understandings of others' selves. In the conceptualization of non-Western selves, the Western self was taken as the starting point and the non-Western self was accordingly characterized as its opposite: unbounded, not integrated, dependent, unable to set itself reflexively apart from others, unable to distinguish between the individual and a role or status that individual occupies, unable to pursue its own goals independently of the goals of a group or community. Effectively, this characterization involved the negation of all the definitional qualities of the self, that is, of those that point to the differentiation of the self from others. We can conclude, then, that by being denied a Western self, anthropology's others were denied a self at all. (1999: 418)

Sökefeld concerns echo Cohen's,

In the past, our concern with groups and categories, that is, with social bases of social relations, has largely ignored the dimensions of the self and self-consciousness, and may therefore be regarded as having dealt with bogus entities. In treating individuals either explicitly or by default as merely socially or culturally driven, ignoring the authorial or 'self-driven' aspects of behaviour, is to render them at best partial, and perhaps more often, as fictitious ciphers of the anthropologist's theoretical invention. (1994: 7)

Indeed, he has reminded us how British social anthropology, by emphasizing social structure, has represented the self of individuals as the direct consequence of the 'structural logic of that individual's social circumstances. If I am a Nuer, then I must think like a Nuer' (Cohen 1995: 1). It is not only an overemphasis on social structure, but also the very idea existing in the 1970s, until recent innovative approaches, that non-western people who share culture would also share consciousness and identity.[3] Yet although I appreciate Cohen and Sökefeld's arguments, I still perceive an unclear definition of self. In particular, in the case of Sökefeld's article, which mentions both self and identity; they tend to blur into each other's domain.

The misleading perception that people form their identities only through social structure and culture has it origin in the old, and now not so frequently discussed, quarrel about the relationship between nurture and nature. Holland (1997), by discussing the lack of interest that anthropologists have had in studying identity and self, has presented the debate in terms of universalists (those who maintain the prominence of nature) versus culturalists (those who maintain the prominence of culture). The 'universalists' argued that, although in the formation of self/identity culture might have some role, it is subordinated to universal biological and natural psychological structures. The 'culturalists' argued the opposite, making self/identity an excusive domain of culture. Culture, according to the latter shapes a person's identity as a bottle shapes the water it contains. Although the main anthropological focus in studying identity has been on culture, the majority of anthropologists have avoided the universalists' and culturalists' extreme viewpoints. Yet in doing so, they have ignored the relevance that individual identity has within societies and the formation of social groups and communities (Cohen 1985).

Within American cultural anthropology, there has been some attempt to address the question of 'self'. Hallowell was one of the first anthropologists to explore this domain (Whittaker 1992). In his ethnographic work on the Ojibwa (1955),[4] which could be considered one of the first structural-functionalist analyses of identity, he suggested a connection between self and social institutions, but recognized that people everywhere are likely to develop an understanding of themselves as physically distinct and separable from others. He argued that self-awareness and self-reflexivity are universal features, however, he also emphasized that other aspects of the self are culturally shaped and cannot be interpreted in terms of a universal perspective.

More recently, another anthropologist has tried to cross the nature–nurture dyad in the study of identity. Obeyesekere (1981) has suggested that symbols play an important role in solving psychodynamic problems and difficulties that people have to deal with. He has argued that people use symbols (the cultural side) to manage the psychological effects (the universal side) they have to face. Nonetheless, the influence that social constructivism has had on anthropology has promoted anthropological analyses of identity and self (often discussed as if they were interchangeable terms) as inconsistent entities. So inconsistent, 'fleeting, fragmentary, and buffeted', to use Holland's words, that 'from the extreme ephemeralist position, daily life, especially in the post-modern era, is a movement from self to self' (Holland 1997: 170).

I agree with Holland's view, since, by reading many anthropological analyses concerning Muslim migrants and their children (see next section), I have found myself thinking of Welsch's words, 'to be healthy today is truly only possible in the form of schizophrenia – if not polyphrenia' (1990: 171). Yet it is not only the representation of Muslims as 'polyphrenic', but also the fact that, as Sökefeld has critically observed, 'In anthropological discourse, the question of identity is almost completely detached from the problem of the self. In the vast body of literature about ethnic identity the self is rarely mentioned, and in writings about the self, a relation between the self and identities is sometimes noted but remains unexplored' (1999: 419). This is not so surprising if we think that social structural theories of identity have been widely (though often implicitly) employed as the theoretical framework for anthropological studies.

We have seen that a major role in the denial of individuality in the formation of identity has been how social scientists during the 1960s understood 'culture'. So, Sökefeld has observed that in anthropology culture has been seen 'not as something ephemeral but ... as a "power" constituted by a system of shared meaning that is effective in shaping social reality' (1999: 427). This, according to him, has prevented some anthropologists recognizing the existence of a *stable and individualistic self*. Indeed, many anthropologists have accepted the idea that self and identity are as unstable and fluid as the cultures that allegedly create them. Sökefeld has suggested that a solution could be achieved by conceiving of 'the self (used here as generic term including "individual", "individuality", "person", etc.) as [a] relatively stable point' (1999: 427). Traditionally, post-modern scholars studying migrants, and in particular Muslim migrants, seem to be keen to deny what Rapport has rightly observed, 'a human-existentialist anthropology which recognizes the radical freedom of the apartness of the individual... Individuals carry with them their own experiential contexts, in short, and human social life is the story of a diversity of individual worlds abutting against one another' (Rapport quoted in Sökefeld 1999: 439).

I have suggested that a full understanding of identity and self (which as I explain in the next section, are not the same thing) can only be reached if we reject that dyad of nature/culture and see culture as a part of nature. Geertz has defined culture as a 'control mechanism – plans, recipes, rules, instructions (what computer engineers call "programs") – for governing behavior' (1973: 44). In a previous version of the same article, he also emphasized that such a 'control mechanism' is achieved by 'the imposition of an arbitrary framework of symbolic meaning upon reality' (1964: 39). In other words, humans without culture could not control their behaviour and would act as ungovernable, chaotic, shapeless, a-meaningful beings (Geertz 1964: 46). Non-humans (animals), though lacking symbols and culture, avoid such chaos because they have natural 'control mechanisms' (i.e. instincts) that substitute for culture. However, I agree with Ingold when he observes that Geertz's conceptualization of culture tends to represent humans as 'suspended in webs of significance [and] puts humans in a kind of free-floating world in which we are ascribing significance to things "out there"' (Ingold 1996: 130). Geertz has presented humans as something different from the rest of nature, as beings resembling mythological fallen angels now trapped between the two dimensions of nature and nurture.

Could we avoid such an abstraction of the Geertzian model of culture and symbols? I argue that this is possible since the issue has been observed through the wrong – I would say – epistemology; indeed, Milton has recently suggested,

> any debate about the naturalness or unnaturalness of cultural phenomena is most accurately seen as a debate about human nature and human experience (often expressed as 'nature and nurture') rather than nature and culture. What confuses the issue, apart from a failure to recognize the different meanings of 'nature', is that human experience and its products are often described as 'culture', while attributes of human nature are often described as 'non-cultural'. (2002: 17)

By agreeing with Ingold who has argued, 'perception involves the whole person, in an active engagement with his or her environment' (1996: 115), Milton has re-considered the role that emotions have in the way in which we relate to our environment. Milton's work on emotions, as well as Damasio's study of consciousness (2000), are central to my understanding of identity.

As we shall see during this chapter, this is very important for a new methodological approach to identity in the case of Muslims. It has been a long-standing tradition to represent Muslim identities through 'difference' and as part of a 'different' cultural domain, which Islam, as religion based on written revelation, has forged. This essentialist vision of Islam, and the culturalist or social structuralist approach to identity privileged in many anthropological studies of Muslim communities, has caused a dangerous differentiation between the western idea (ideological?) of a western self and the western idea (Orientalist?) of Muslim self. This process, of course, is not limited to studies focusing on Muslims, but is the result of a certain discourse of identity and self formed through years of anthropological disinterest in these 'inner' aspects,

> Anthropologists used this dichotomy ['inner' and 'outer'] as an avoidance strategy, arguing that anthropology could deal only with what was empirically manifest (the outer), and must be content to treat anything else (such as the 'inner') as either a matter for imagination (fiction, philosophy), or for specialized scientific investigation (psychology) with a discovery objective different from anthropology's. As genres blur and/ or change, so that it has become proper (if not obligatory) for anthropologists to write reflexively, deconstructively and politically, then, correspondingly, it now seems inadequate to write as if the outer life of symbolic forms, institutions and norms is all there is, or as if an outer life of overt behaviours somehow speaks for itself or is intrinsically meaningful, a social fact somehow independent of the creative consciousness of the individual. (Cohen 1995: 3)

It is the 'creative consciousness' of the individual Muslim that today is trapped into the cage of collective stereotyping of what Muslims should be or how they should behave. During my recent research on Muslim prisoners in Scotland (Marranci 2006c), I interviewed some prison officers and non-Muslim chaplains. From their accounts, it rapidly became clear that they expected the Muslim prisoners to behave in accordance with what the prison officer or the chaplain expected to be 'Muslim behaviour'. Any difference among the Muslim prisoners, who came from several ethnic and national backgrounds as well as different Islamic schools, was not acknowledged. Their individual identity as human beings, and the personal Muslim identity they felt to have, was denied by the assumption that their 'Islamic culture' shaped them in the same way and to the same degree. This is not something affecting only Muslim prisoners in Scotland, and the 'culturalist' assumption is certainly not limited to prison officers and chaplains, but also academics, as we shall see in the next section.

## WHAT MIGHT A MUSLIM BE?

There is no day, at least since September 11, that the mass media have not discussed, argued, framed, stereotyped, deconstructed and re-created Muslim identity. In a certain sense, I can say that there is a highly unsuccessful attempt to profile what a Muslim might be. Of course, the majority of these attempts, from journalists to politicians, from police forces to secret services, are based on social and cultural stereotypes. Indeed, the mass media are often mentioned as the main culprit of the stereotyping process (cf. Poole 2002). This does not mean that the mass media are intentionally creating the increasing stereotypes that dictate what a Muslim should be. Rather it is the process of global information, which forces the mass media to rely on tautological, catching, imaginary depictions of *the* Muslim (or any other category of predefined social identities, e.g. the politician, the pop-star, the drug addict, the paedophile).

Therefore, stereotyping processes have often been related to the description and representation of social identities. Few of us know that the word stereotype derives from a Scottish invention. In 1725, William Ged, a Scottish goldsmith, simplified the printing process by casting a whole page in a single mould, from which a single plate could be produced. From its technical domain, the term passed into abstract usage to indicate a pre-fixed image of an idea. Thus, two related concepts are central to the term stereotype: monolithic structure and production in series. In both the cases, details and personality are lost in favour of fast production and easy manufacture. In the industry of mass global information, these are exactly the necessary elements. The process often becomes rhetorical, or in the worst cases, even a political ideology (i.e. populism). When the definition of identities becomes a political issue, as in the case of Muslims today, the power of labelling, often in the hands of policy-makers, extends to the power of telling people who they are (Bourdieu and Thompson 1991), and what is the correct and socially acceptable way of being, for instance, Muslim. Hence, social cultural identities may dangerously become cages of the personal self. This is particularly evident in the cases of the so-called (or miscalled, cf. Mukadam and Mawani 2006 as well as Marranci 2003b and 2006a) second generations. Indeed, Mukadam and Mawani, have, in my opinion, correctly observed,

> These individuals whose ancestry lies in the Indian subcontinent are still commonly referred to as members of the South Asian diaspora or, worse still, as second-generation immigrants. These labels are unacceptable as they are simply a means of reinforcing differences and go against the vision of full participation and acceptance of all individuals in society irrespective of their ancestry. (2006: 109)

Often these labels also go against the self-definition of who I prefer to refer to as (with an emic definition suggested by some of my respondents) western-born Muslims. Yet the issue is not limited to the question of labelling but also to the quest for identity, which can become the field of a dangerous political battle that Muslims today, particularly when western-born, find themselves in the middle of. The weapon often takes the form of a very simple question, 'Are you British or Muslim?', 'Are you French or Muslim?', 'Are you American or Muslim?' In other words, 'Are you one of us?' This question is not as innocent as it may appear. It is a question of denial, a question of ostracism. In other words, the question, which apparently seems to be a question concerning identity, is in reality questioning political loyalty.

Why do western societies today feel the need to challenge what, in terms of identity, a Muslim might be? The simplest answer is that identity is at the centre of any form of social interaction, and social interactions help us to make sense of how people may behave and relate to each other within communities. The post-September 11 corollary to this answer is that increasingly – terrorist attack after terrorist attack and terrorist plot after terrorist plot – people wish to understand why some others, who are recognized socially and culturally as part of the Muslim community, want to become self-induced martyrs and transform innocent people into forced-martyrs.[5] Although questions about Muslim identities, and how they are changing in a changing world, are certainly legitimate, in this chapter[6] I wish to suggest that the starting points from which many answers are provided are often misleading, if not, in certain cases, flawed – and unfortunately alienating for Muslims.

One of the reasons for this incapacity to develop an approach to Muslim identity that would limit the emphasis on 'differences', 'cultural peculiarity' and 'in-betweenness' is that social scientific interest in identity and Islam is still something recent. Geertz, Gellner and Rabinow, to mention just some of the names we have previously met, were not interested in how Muslims formed their identities, since they were too busy trying to understand how Islam 'creates' Muslims. If we avoid taking into consideration certain proto-academic productions, often within the field of 'anti-terrorism' or 'security studies' as well as 'Middle East studies',[7] we can find the first discussion about Muslim identities within social scientific works on migration. It was during the 1990s that, as a consequence of anthropologists' attempts to understand western-born Muslims, research on identity amplified and fully developed.[8] The question, at that time, was mainly about the effects of integration and assimilation policies. Nonetheless, as we have seen in Chapter 3, events such as the 1988 Rushdie Affair and the 1991 Gulf War redirected the social scientific interest on identity to its political values[9] and the challenge of identity versus loyalty. Although these academic works refer to Muslim identity, they seldom explain how, according to each author, identity should be interpreted. They treat the concept of 'identity' as self-explanatory; in other words, they assume that their readers share the same idea of what identity might be. However, as we shall see below, particularly within the field of anthropology, there is no agreement on how humans develop, form and modify identity. There is, nonetheless, a similarity in these studies. In almost any social scientific study, scholars have privileged the *outside* perspective on identity. In other words, they have mainly analysed what *we do every day when we interact* and use each other's identities in an instrumental way (i.e. to know how to behave). Of course, identity in such a context becomes a matter of differentiation and it has facilitated the interpretation of people's actions as boundary markers.

## *RECONSIDERING SELF AND IDENTITY STARTING FROM CONSCIOUSNESS*

The question 'who am I' is one of the most challenging we can ask. As described above, most studies of identity have approached the topic from an 'outside' perspective. Hence, the study of identity has over-focused on the instrumental use of each other's identities, i.e. identity as social instrument. This seems to suggest that what we socially think of the other becomes *the real* other. Furthermore, in such a context, identity becomes a matter of differentiation facilitating the process of seeing people's actions as boundary makers. Yet, by following Bateson

(2002) we may say that a mistake of logical type has been perpetrated for a long time within the study of identity: because differentiation marks identity in the social world, why should we assume, as many social scientists do, that individuals experience their identity as social differentiation?

It is my contention that this has been, for a long time, a misrepresentation of how personal identity might operate. Unsurprisingly, one of the most quoted books in reference to what some call 'cultural identity' is Frederik Barth's *Ethnic Groups and Boundaries* (1969). Barth's intention was not to develop a theory of identity, but rather to analyse the formation of ethnic groups. Yet the success of his study ensured that the model has also often been misused to define Muslim identities per se, particularly in the case of so-called 'second generations'. But if *personal* identity is not defined by a person's social actions, how is identity formed?

To explain these points, we need to reconsider the concept of identity, and to do so we need to observe a very basic reality that often we forget: in order to feel our identities there is a need to have a *conscious* brain. For a long time the relevance of our bodies in the formation of identity has been neglected because culture and society have been arbitrarily abstracted from nature. It is our brain, or better, its complex neurological system that, as we shall see, enables us to attain consciousness and consequently achieve a long-standing sense of selfhood. According to Damasio, a neuroscientist, evolutionary processes have originated increasingly complex systems of 'selfs', the simplest of which he has called *proto-selves*. All living organisms (even a monocellular paramecium) have *proto-selves*, an unconscious system that is 'a coherent collection of neural patterns which map, moment by moment, the state of the physical structure of the organism in its many dimensions' (2000: 154). Some organisms, however, became more complex than others, and not only have proto-selves but also *consciousness*. Damasio, reminding us that consciousness *is not* monolithic, has suggested the existence of at least two kinds of consciousness: *core consciousness* and *extended consciousness*, which then form two parallel kinds of self, the *core self* and the *autobiographical self*. He has also suggested that the common idea that emotions are subjective feelings should be considered just 'common sense', since in reality emotions are bodily responses which are perceived to *provoke* the feelings. In other words, feelings are derived from a rationalization of emotions.

The result of core consciousness is what Damasio defines as 'the feeling of knowing'; yet, although the core self is formed through a conscious process, we hardly notice it, 'the images that dominate the mental display are those of the things of which you are now conscious' (2000: 172). It is clear that memory has a fundamental role in the formation of the sense of 'self', which, in Damasio's terminology, is represented by the *autobiographical self*. The autobiographical self is formed by two elements, the core self and 'reactivations and display of selected sets of autobiographical memories,' i.e. what Damasio has defined as the *autobiographical memory* (Damasio 2000: 196). He, through convincing clinical examples, has suggested that without autobiographical memories our sense of self (i.e. our sense of past, future and historical-temporal continuity) could not be developed. At the same time, however, without the core self, derived from the core consciousness, 'we would have no knowledge whatsoever of the moment, of the memorized past, or the anticipated future that we also have committed to memory' (2000: 219). Thus, emotions, and the consequent feelings they induce, are the 'engine' of these complex neurological processes that we simply call the 'self'.

For this process to be successful, we need another two elements beyond emotions, feelings and brain: the external world and its inputs (be they natural, social or cultural).[10] Milton has suggested (2002; and Milton and Svasek 2005) that culture can be interpreted as an 'ecological' part of nature, instead of something making human beings different from nature. If this is the case, as I believe, environment has a much more important role and a stronger impact on human beings than social scientists have tended to believe. But in which way do we enter into contact with our environments? Some recent anthropological studies (Ingold 1992; Milton 2002; Milton and Svasek 2005) have argued that emotions are central to the way in which we perceive our surrounding environment. Therefore, as Milton and Svasek (2005) have suggested, we can argue that emotions are ecological rather than a social phenomenon, though social interaction surely raises emotions.

At this point, I can argue that what we call 'self' and 'identity' may not be (as the majority of social scientific theories claim) the sole product of social interaction, though social interaction could provoke changes in them. Yet it is important to recognize that 'self' and 'identity' are not the same. If the self (which we could better refer to as the 'autobiographical self') is a real entity in our neuro-cognitive system, identity isn't. Indeed, Damasio has suggested that identity 'is a delicately shaped machinery of our imagination [which] stakes the probabilities of selection toward the same, historically continuous self' (2000: 225).

In my theory of identity, which I developed in my recent book (Marranci 2006a), I have explained that identity is a process with two functions. On the one hand, it allows human beings to make sense of their autobiographical self, while on the other it allows them to express the autobiographical self through symbols. These symbols communicate personal feelings that, otherwise, could not be externally communicated. Hence, I have concluded that it is *what we feel to be* that determines our personal identity. So, the statement 'I am Muslim' of a hypothetical Mr Hussein is nothing else than the *symbolic communication* of his emotional commitment through which he experiences his autobiographical self. In other words, Mr Hussein has an autobiographical self which he makes sense of through that delicately shaped machinery of his imagination called identity, which he communicates with the symbolic expression 'I am Muslim'. Finally, Mr Hussein is what he feels to be regardless of how others, engaged in countless public discourses surrounding the use of cultural markers, might perceive him.

Now we can observe that human beings live in a sort of tautological circuit: (1) the environment produces stimuli; (2) which produce emotions (the bodily reactions); (3) which human beings perceive and rationalize as feelings; (4) which affect their autobiographical self; (5) which is experienced through the delicately shaped machinery of their imagination (identities); (6) which is affected by the feelings induced by the emotions. What I have described until now is a circuit of causalities based on information both internal and external to the individual. This system aims at maintaining equilibrium between the individuals' internal milieu and their external environments. Psychological as well as psychoanalytic studies tell us that equilibrium between self and identity is essential for a healthy life.

Yet this tautological equilibrium could be disrupted by changes in the surrounding environment. Bateson, during his study of the Iatmul tribe (1936) had occasion to observe cases of 'positive gain', 'various relations among groups and among various types of kin were characterized by interchanges of behaviour such as that the more A exhibited a given behaviour, the more B was likely to exhibit the same behaviour' (Bateson 2002: 98). Bateson called these kinds of relationships *symmetrical changes*. However, he also noticed another pattern in which the behaviour of B although being different from that of A was *complementary* to it. According to Bateson (2000: 323), examples of simple symmetrical changes are armament races, athletic emulation, boxing matches; while examples of complementary changes are dominance–submission, sadism–masochism, spectatorship–exhibitionism. Both symmetrical as well as complementary changes are subject to forms of progressive escalation, which Bateson has called *schismogenesis*. By affecting the relationship between the elements of the circuit, schismogenesis (both symmetrical and complementary) have the power to break down the circular system. It is my contention that to avoid threatening *schismogenetic* processes which may disrupt the tautological mechanism which is our identity, and suffer what has been defined as an identity crisis, human beings have developed what I have called acts of identity (Marranci 2006a). These acts can be expressed through different kinds of actions, from artistic expressions, to particular behaviours, or expressions of rhetoric and ideologies; yet their aim is to counterbalance the *schismogenetic process*. These identity acts try to influence the surrounding environment provoking certain specific emotions, which, consequently, according to the theory explained above, would affect feelings.

## STUDYING MUSLIM IDENTITIES AND THEIR EXPRESSIONS

In the previous sections, we have observed that essentialism and culturalism have characterized the social scientific study of Muslim identities. I have suggested, together with Sökefeld (1999) and Cohen (1994, 1995), that the main issue is how self and identity have been discussed in anthropology during the last thirty years. I think that as anthropologists of Islam we have to pay particular attention, when addressing the issue of Muslims and their identities (particularly in the western context), to what Sökefeld, methodologically, has invited us to consider,

> Our selves and their selves are not necessarily as different as many anthropo-
> logical texts, employing the dichotomy of the self and the other as an a priori
> of ethnography, portray them. After many decades in which difference was
> the paradigm for conceiving of the others' selves, it might be useful to try a
> paradigm of more *similarity*. To allow for such similarity demands an important

methodological reorientation. It requires giving *real importance to the actual individuals we work with while studying 'culture.'* This presupposes not quickly and thoughtlessly subsuming them under some social or cultural category but *representing them, even in the ethnographic text, as individuals*. It is they whom we study, not some superindividual entity. This entity – culture – is only our construction from countless encounters, dialogues, and interactions with actual selves or individuals. (Sökefeld 1999: 431 italics in the original)

If we observe studies on young Muslims, their identities have often been interpreted as 'fluid', 'hybrid' and 'multiple'[11] giving the false impression that western-born Muslims may lack self-determination. Reacting to such overgeneralizations, other more recent studies have tried to recognize the 'creativity' and reaction to the environment that young Muslims show.[12] Yet these studies have based their understanding of identity on implicit or explicit social identity theories or culturalist analysis, missing the vital relationship existing between the autobiographical self, identity and identity acts. The undesired side effect of these approaches is that they end in emphasizing the problems that Muslims living in Islamic countries as well as western-born Muslims have, instead of observing the solutions that they have developed. Furthermore, the reduction of the personal self (i.e. what, following Damasio (2002), I have called autobiographical self) to social structural theories has, in the case of studies concerning western-born Muslims, produced a dangerous – and alienating for the Muslims studied – accepted pathologizing jargon. For instance, in an often quoted and influential study, Archer has employed it by describing young Asian Muslims as 'suffer[ing] from "mixed up" and "confused" identities because of the *"cultural clash"* that results from occupying a *contradictory* location between *conflicting* "majority" and "minority" *cultures* and *identities*' (2001: 82, emphasis added).

By contrast, if we understand identity through the model I have proposed, in which identity is the result of the delicately shaped machinery of our imagination helping to maintain a coherent autobiographical self, we can only affirm that Muslims are not different from any other human beings. If for Gellner (1981), Muslims are Muslims because they have faith in the Qur'an or the saint and for Geertz because of their '(1) system of symbols which acts to (2) establish powerful, pervasive, and long-lasting moods and motivations in them by (3) formulating conceptions of a general order of existence and (4) clothing these conceptions with such an aura of factuality that (5) the moods and motivations seem uniquely realistic' (Geertz 1985: 4), I can now affirm that what makes them Muslim is that they *feel* to be Muslim. Then, and only then, can we observe how they express their 'feeling to be Muslim' through what I have defined as acts of identity. This means that if, for example, almost all Islamic schools of thought consider that a gay person cannot be a Muslim, as anthropologists (Muslim or non) it is the *feeling to be*, its process, its formation, its expression through identity acts which we have to consider and study despite the opinions of others. Only if we start from this basic point, can we successfully observe the network of social interactions, the social structure, and the relationship between the studied individuals and society.

Indeed, I agree with Rapport about 'the universality of the individual as the fount of agency, consciousness, interpretation and creativity in social and cultural life; this by virtue of his or her sole ownership of discrete, corporeal, sense-making apparatuses. Consciousness bounds the (otherwise permeable) individual human body, and is itself a manifestation of that "unique embodiment"' (1997: 6).

Therefore, I wish to suggest that we need to have a paradigm through which the anthropologist of Islam can effectively study Muslims as human beings rather than living symbols of a religion. To do so, we need to observe the *dynamics* of Muslim lives (seen as individual agencies expressed through identity acts) *within* societies. This means taking into consideration the relationship that exists between Muslims and their emotional environment. Such an approach allows us to challenge stereotypes, Orientalisms and essentialisms, which as we have seen, are affecting not only common sense, but also social scientific research. For instance, a study concerning Muslim girls within Scottish secondary education needs to investigate why these girls *feel to be* Muslims, the dynamics of their agencies *within* that particular environment, but combined with the emotional elements of being adolescent and observations of non-Muslim pupils within the same establishment. Then we can move on to observe what I have defined as acts of identity, which are performed in order to maintain a certain coherence between autobiographical self, identity and environment. For this reason, fundamental Islamic rituals, such as the hajj, cannot be seen exclusively as an act performed to respect religious norms. Therefore, the hajj of my friend Ali, although prescribed within the theological doctrines of Islam, becomes something more for the observing anthropologist: a personal identity act within a certain dynamic of autobiographical self, identity and environment. In other words, Ali's hajj is beyond Islam, as religion, and part of that 'feeling to be' which brought him to perform it.

In the same way, we can discuss other identity acts, some of which would take the form of political acts, ideological acts, rhetorical acts and so on. Indeed, it is from this perspective that I have analysed the rhetoric of jihad of some Muslims living in the west. Contemporary political jihad should be understood beyond Islam (as the title of my 2006 book suggests) but within the process of identity affected by a specific *schismogenetic* event, which I have defined as 'the circle of panic' (see Bhabha 1994; Marranci 2006a). For this reason, in my study of jihad, I concluded that some individuals feel to be Muslim because of jihad, and not vice versa. They conduct extreme and irrational violent acts (or use violent rhetoric) because of a certain kind of Islamic interpretation or, as some even believe, because they are Muslims. Yet not all acts of identity are extremist or framed by religious doctrines. Although there are very few studies conducted by anthropologists of Islam, many people who feel to be Muslims have expressed this through, among other things, arts, such as music, cinema, visual arts, sculpture and even comedy. Some of these artistic expressions have become a community-shared identity act, as in the case of the so-called *beur culture* in France.

Beur, or the children and grandchildren of North African immigrants in France, have been at the centre of an artistic movement since the middle of the 1980s. An example is in the so-called *film-beur*, which focuses on the lives of Beurs in the suburban areas of French cities (see Tarr 1993, 1995, 1999; Forbes and Kelly 1995; Austin 1996). Yet it was not only cinema which they decided to use, but also music in the case of raï-Beur (Marranci 2000a, 2000b, 2003a) and a very high number of novelists and writers (see Bonn 2003, Sharpe 2005). Of course, this phenomenon of using arts as act of identity is certainly not confined within the French Beur, but can be found among other children of Muslim immigrants in different parts of the west (see, for instance, Dina and Cullingford 2004).

The overemphasis on 'difference' and 'clash' of cultures, as well as the lack of attention to the active and positive identity acts of Muslims, both living in the west and in other parts of the world, has affected the way in which we, as anthropologists, have (mis)represented Muslim identities. I have suggested that one way to proceed is to reconsider the relationship between individual, identity, society and social structure in order to provide not only analysis and theories but also answers in these difficult times in which some human beings, who *feel to be* Muslims, feel threatened by a fear of others who *feel to be* western, and vice versa. Indeed, this is the circle of panic circulating worldwide within the global village.

## CONCLUSION

In the last twenty years, with the increase of Muslim migration to western countries and the consequent establishment of their families within western societies, the debate surrounding their identity formation, and particularly that of their children, has attracted the attention of not only the academic world but also the mass media. This has opened a debate about the impact that cultural and religious differences would have on the integration, and in some cases such as France, assimilation of Muslim migrants and their children. We have seen that within this framework, different models of identity have been proposed, some of which were emphatically based on culturalist viewpoints. As we have discussed above, some scholars interpreted difference and differentiation as the main element in the formation of Muslim identities. Furthermore, the idea that identities are 'real' essences based on cultural processes has brought some authors to represent, or at least to describe, the identities of western-born Muslims in terms of pathology. Notwithstanding the relevance that difference and differentiation, as well as boundary-making processes, have in social interaction, I have argued that they may not be prominent in the formation of personal identity. Rather, following recent neuroscientific theories (Damasio 2002), I have argued that while the self and the autobiographical self are real, identity is a machinery of personal imagination allowing vital coherence between the individual and his or her environment. Hence, emotions and feelings are central to the development of personal identities.

My explanation of personal identity suggests that to the question 'what is a Muslim?' we cannot answer by only highlighting cultural symbolic elements of reference to Islam as codified religion. Rather, to the question 'what is a Muslim?' we need to answer 'a human being'. Only by acknowledging this simple fact can one observe that the expression 'I'm Muslim' is a proactive engagement with the environment of the autobiographical self, which expresses itself through emotions. In other words, 'I'm Muslim' means 'I feel to be Muslim'. I have suggested that it is by focusing on that 'feel to be' more than the symbolic 'Muslim' that we can understand how Muslim identity, in particular among western-born Muslims is expressed, formed and developed beyond the imposed stereotypes.

## *NOTES*

1. A full discussion of the development of the most important sociological approaches and theories of identity and self cannot be undertaken here for want of space. I suggest reading Gordon 1976; Ashmore and Jussin 1997; Cerulo 1997; Howard 2000; Ellemers, Spears and Doosje 2002.
2. For another interesting critique of the study of identity within anthropology see Holland 1997.
3. Just to mention some examples: Gergen 1968; Dumont 1970; Geertz 1975; Chodorow 1978; Gilligan 1982; Shweder and LeVine 1984; Lykes 1985; Marsella, De Vos and Hsu 1985; Sampson 1985, 1988, 1989; Smith 1985; Holland and Quinn 1987; Triandis 1989.
4. The Ojibwa are a Native American ethnic group located in the upper Great Lakes (i.e. Lakes Superior and Huron) in both Canada and the United States.
5. Indeed, the majority of Islamic scholars have recognized that, despite their religions, victims of terrorism are to be considered martyrs.
6. For more on the concept of jihad and identity you can see Marranci 2006.
7. Just to mention some of the most read: Ye'or 1978, 1984, 1991, 2002; Pipes 1981, 1983, 1997; Kramer 1996, 1998; Akbar 2002; Kressel 2004; Phillips 2006.
8. For anthropological studies discussing first and second generations see Chapter 3 in this book.
9. See, for instance, Nielsen 1985, 1992; Gerholm and Lithman 1988; Lewis and Schnapper 1994; Nonneman, Niblock and Szajkowski 1996; Kepel 1997; Haddad and Esposito 2000; Alsayyad and Castells 2002; Haddad 2002; Werbner 2002.
10. As Ingold (1992, 1996) has suggested, culture could be easily seen as a human-environment relationship.
11. For instance Brah 1979, Mirza 1989, Bhachu 1993, Knott and Khokher 1993.
12. For instance Jacobson 1998, Shaw 1998, Archer 2001, 2002, Roald 2001.

# CHAPTER 7

# The Ummah Paradox

## *MUSLIM COMMUNITIES*

Although certainly not a perfect scientific methodology, Googling words can help to form an idea of how many times a term, or sentence, has been used within the World Wide Web (Cimian and Staab 2004) and so disclosing its popularity. Unsurprisingly, in the case of 'Muslim community', Google suggests about 5,160,000 entries and Google Scholar[1] 8,930 entries. I found it intriguing to compare these results against other research keywords, such as 'Muslim communities' (1,110,000), 'South Asian community' (170,000), 'Arab community' (917,000) and 'Pakistani community' (150,000). What can this Google-exercise tell us? First of all, that after 'Islam' (118,000,000) and 'Muslim' (87,800,000), the keyword 'Muslim community' is certainly the most popular among them within the World Wide Web. Secondly, we can observe that 'Muslim communities', i.e. the plural, is much less popular among cybernauts than the singular form. Finally, we can observe that single geo-ethnic definitions of Muslim communities (South Asian, Pakistani, Arab and so on) have even fewer entries than others existing about Muslim communities in general. The proportion in the case of Google Scholar remains the same, showing the clear preference that scholars have for the singular, all-encompassing, label 'Muslim community'. If we scan a recent book, for instance Wiktorowicz (2005), we meet throughout the text sentences like 'both the Muslim community and the British public in general view movement activists as part of the "lunatic fringe"' (2005: 59). This is a just an example of how the general keyword 'Muslim community' has been freely used, its scientific value unquestioned and transformed into a sort of accepted common sense. Reading newspapers, magazines, watching news reports, blog-reading, surfing websites, scrutinizing forums and chatting the chats, we can be convinced that every school boy knows what 'Muslim community' is and means. Yet try to ask around, even among academics, what 'Muslim community' means and count the different answers, if any. Should we ask: Does there exist something that we can label 'Muslim community' in general or even in specific circumstances (i.e. the British Muslim community')? Is 'Muslim community' nothing else than a cliché?

In my opinion it is essential to the anthropology of Islam that we question and discuss the academic usage of keywords such as 'Muslim community'. Yet I have not come across any critique of (or reflection on) it. The concept is probably so common that it is difficult to achieve the necessary epistemological distance to observe it. Indeed, *lupus in fabula,* I have used it without challenging or questioning its anthropological and sociological value until recently, despite the fact that my ethnographic experiences would have urged me to do so.

In the previous chapters of this book, we have discussed how essentialism can prevent a serious anthropological approach to the study of people *who feel to be Muslims* as well as how they believe, and interpret, Islam. Essentialism, as we have seen, is the main malaise of the anthropologist[2] working on Islam. It induces the representation of a cluster of elements within, in this case, Islam as the essence of it (Hull 1995). As Hasan (2002) has suggested, western scholars are not solely responsible for the widespread use of 'Muslim community'. Muslim theologians, politicians and preachers, during colonialism and subsequent national struggles against it, called upon the idea of a religious collective solidarity through the Qur'anic word 'ummah' (i.e. community of believers) in the hope of a united front for the Islamicization of their societies. Therefore, Hasan has remarked,

> Doubtless, these are important facets, but their significance should not be over-stated to construct a unified Muslim structure of consciousness or a singular Muslim community acting in unison to achieve common goals. Why is it exceptional if some Muslims, falling prey to colonial enumerations and definitions and their own fanciful theories, regarded themselves as an indivisible component of a religious collectivity? (2002: 9)

Furthermore, Salvatore (1997) has pointed out how community leaders, as well as civil servants within governments, have benefited from this generalization. In the case of the former, he has argued, the generic 'Muslim community' has facilitated access to governmental resources; in the case of the latter, the concept has simplified administrative order through categorization and classification.

Nonetheless, the keyword 'Muslim community' has now achieved an emic and etic status which is hardly challengeable through its historical roots. Since we will probably have to work with it, the only solution is to try to clarify how we refer to the concept of Muslim community, or ummah. Two complex elements form this keyword: Muslim + community; neither of them is ever self-defining. They depend upon three essential dimensions: time, place and culture; in other words, context. This means that the idea, or concept, of 'Muslim community' is dynamic and proceeds through stages affected by different environments. Hence, we can speak of a process through which the idea of the ummah is transformed and affected by rhetoric, which goes beyond the mass media and occasional scholarly clichés, in order to become ideology (Eagleton 1991) and ethos. Before we discuss these points further, however, we need to clarify what the term 'community' may mean.

## THE RIDDLE OF THE CONCEPT OF COMMUNITY

Anthropologists, as well as other social scientists, have provided so many definitions of community that Hillery (1955) decided to list those which, according to him, could bring scholars to a much needed agreement. The list was highly unsuccessful; not only have some authors stressed the pointlessness of making it, but many have asked whether, today, we still need the word 'community' at all. For example, Baumann has concluded, 'Hillery researched a grand total of ninety-four meanings attributed to the term by sociologists, and the word appears quite clearly as a common-sense term with no theoretical potential for analytic use' (1996: 14).[3] The concept of community, however, remains central to anthropological studies, or at least it is very difficult to avoid. So, Olwig has observed that there are two main notions of communities seen 'as cultural constructions' (2002: 125): on the one hand, communities have been discussed as 'belonging entities', and on the other as imagined unities based on 'sentiments' (see Appadurai 1996). In the first case, face-to-face-relationships (Strathern 1982; Rapport 1993) enable people to negotiate and shape their identity as a 'community'. In these terms, people have to 'adjust to each other to produce and maintain order and coherence. If such a community is to survive in its valued form, its structure must be organised accordingly, and a strict regime recognised and accepted for its maintenance' (Cohen 1982: 11).

Cohen, however, in a famous essay has moved from an idea of community as embedded in local social structures to one that can act as a symbolic entity (see Cohen 1985). Such a community is not so much rooted in a physical place, as 'in its members' perception of the vitality of its culture. People construct community symbolically, making it a resource and repository of meaning, and referent of their identity' (Cohen 1985: 124). By observing the relationship between social structures, symbols, identities and the formation of boundaries, he has suggested a strongly constructivist approach in which,

[Community] is a largely mental construct, whose 'objective' manifestations in locality or ethnicity give it credibility. It is highly symbolized, with the consequence that its members can invest it with their selves. Its character is sufficiently malleable that it can accommodate all of its members' selves without them feeling their individuality to be overly compromised. Indeed, the gloss of commonality which it paints over its diverse components gives to each of them an additional referent for their identities. (1995: 109)

However, Amit (2002) suggests that even in this revised and attractive conceptualization of community, Cohen has still focused on the central role played by face-to-face relationships, though in this case mediated by symbols instead of acts, kinship and exchanges.

A historian, however, has provided probably the most widely accepted and quoted conceptualization of community. Anderson has suggested that communities do not need any contact among members, not even virtual, since 'community' is part of a collective imagination process, since, he has argued,

the members of even the smallest nation will never know most of their fellow-members, meet them, or even hear of them, yet in the minds of each lives the image of their communion ... it is imagined as a community, because, regardless of the actual inequality and exploitation that may prevail in each, the nation is always conceived as a deep, horizontal comradeship. Ultimately it is this fraternity that makes it possible, over the past two centuries, for so many millions of people, not so much to kill, as willingly to die for such limited imaginings. (1991: 5–7)

Anderson's definition has shifted the idea of community from the one based on interactions mediated through fully encompassing symbols to a community based on 'sentiments' (Appadurai 1996: 8); in other words, a community that needs to generate ideas and beliefs in order to perpetrate itself. This concept of community has opened the door for complex analyses of what have been called 'diasporic and transnational communities' (Clifford 1994; Vetrovec 2001). In his studies of migration and mass media, Appadurai has developed further the insight of Anderson. He has tried to argue that today a complex media network connects the world, enabling people to overcome the concept of nation-state and rethink their lives through the complex circulations of cultural domains. From this point of view, the mass media can create a new genre of community structures, which before were unthinkable. The geographical dimension of place, in this case, should be rearticulated into a new form of locality.

Appadurai has introduced a distinction between what he calls 'locality' and 'neighbourhood' to define a world in which 'locality seems to have lost its onto-logical moorings' (1995: 204). According to Appadurai, 'locality [is] primarily relational and contextual rather than scalar or spatial', while 'neighbourhood ... refers to the actually existing social forms in which locality, as a dimension or value, is variably realized' (1995: 204). In other words, 'neighbourhood' replaces the concept of territorial community. Neighbourhoods 'are contexts, and at the same time require, *and produce* contexts' (1995: 209, emphasis in the original). Yet contexts could be crossed or even shared to produce 'trans-local' neighbourhoods. The result of this is that distinguishing the context of one neighbourhood from another becomes increasingly difficult. Therefore, the 'task of producing locality (as a structure of feeling, a property of social life and an ideology of situated community) is increasingly a struggle' (1995: 213). In the case of the concept of 'home' according to these authors, locality becomes, not a fixed point, but a personal category in which people can move freely.

Nevertheless, there is still a point that these theories seem not to have clarified. Neither Anderson's *'imagined community'*, nor Appadurai's locality, embedded in global dimensions, answers the question of why people, from different national, ethnic and cultural backgrounds are ready, for instance, to sacrifice their lives (Herzfeld 1997), as for example in the case of international violent jihads. To address this question, Herzfeld has developed the concept of 'cultural intimacy'. According to him, cultural means or stereotypes can construct a strong sense of community. So cultural meanings, when shared, can produce a sense of 'cultural intimacy', enabling people to overcome their national and personal differences, and form global communities, as in the case of the ummah.

One point on which all these theories seem to agree, however, is that the act of sharing is the main reason why people form communities. What tends to vary are the explanations for why people decide to share as well as what they share. In the aforementioned studies, another recurrent question is the issue of locality: when the community is beyond physical places, as in the case of the ummah, where do people 'locate' their community? Localizing community, as Appadurai argues, has become difficult. The new media of communication, such as the Internet (Bunt 2003) and 'global' networks open new possibilities to rethink not only space and geographical dimensions but also the role of culture itself (Herzfeld 1997).

I have explained in the previous chapter, and in my previous book (Marranci 2006a), that I consider culture to be part of nature and that I do not see symbols as a *primum movens* through which human beings can assign significance to the external world (Ingold 1996). I suggest that symbols do not lie *outside the individual* but are part of that mechanism that allows us to 'feel' deeply personal, and directly incommunicable, human feelings. Turner (1967) has described symbols as 'storage units' filled with information that not only carry meaning, but also transform human attitudes and behaviour. He described symbols as a 'set of evocative devices for rousing, channelling, and domesticating powerful emotions' (1969: 42–3). Although I agree with Turner's definition, following Damasio, we have to read 'feelings' where Turner speaks of emotions. In other words, symbols are storage units filled with references to stimuli capable of provoking emotions, which induce certain selected feelings. Damasio has told us that emotions have a direct impact on our minds:

> In organisms equipped to sense emotions, that is, to have feelings, emotions also have an impact on the mind, as they occur, in the here and now. But in organisms equipped with consciousness, that is, capable of knowing they have feelings, another level of regulation is reached. Consciousness allows feelings to be known and thus promotes the impact of emotion internally, allows emotions to permeate the thought process through the agency of feelings. (Damasio 2000: 56)

Thus we can argue that symbols also have a direct impact on minds, and they are used (not only among human beings but also among non-humans) to communicate, at an inner level, feelings, which would in other ways be, at the level of direct experience, incommunicable.

## DISCUSSING THE UMMAH

At the beginning of this book, we discussed some of the theological and historical aspects of Islam. We observed that the essential theological element of the Muslim faith is the *shahāda*, the profession of faith. Fundamental to the shahāda is what Muslim scholars call *tawhīd*, the doctrine of the Oneness of God, which claims that everything that exists within the universe has its origin in Allah and will go back unto him. In the Qur'an the term ummah is mentioned sixty times with different, sometimes contrasting, meanings such as the followers of the Prophet, a religious congregation and a minority group within a majority religious community (Hassan 2006).[4] The concept ummah in the Qur'an, moreover, is not restricted to human beings (Sura 6:38) because 'each individual species is an *ummah*, originating from a single source (*umm*). [Yet] Man is the only species within which more than one *ummah* exist' (Al-Ahsan 1992: 12). This is so since the human species, according to the Qur'an, is the only one, after God, characterized by free will, which, inevitably, generates differences.

Nonetheless, we should note that 'ummah' is not the only term employed within the Qur'an, and other Islamic texts, to indicate a 'community'; in Sura 43:23, we find another term: *qaryah* (community). Al-Ahsan (1992) has suggested that there is a substantial difference between how the Qur'an employs and contextualizes the two Arabic terms. Ummah is more a specific term than *qaryah*. As we observe in Sura 2:128, ummah indicates at the same time believing in, and submitting to, God, 'Our Lord, make us submitters to You, and from our descendants let there be a community [*ummah*] of submitters to You. Teach us the rites of our religion, and redeem us. You are the Redeemer, Most Merciful.' Asad has tried to simplify and clarify the discussion on the concept and suggested a straightforward definition: 'a group of living beings having certain characteristics or circumstances in common' (1980: 177).

Muslims, and scholars, tend to agree on the first historical example of Islamic ummah. As we saw in Chapter 2, Muslims decided to start their anno zero from the act of hijra, the migration of Muhammad and his followers from Mecca to Medina in 622 CE. Hijra, in religious terms, means leaving a place to seek freedom of religion, freedom from persecution or, for instance, economic hardship. Summoned as a mediator to resolve feuds among the powerful city tribes, Muhammad established his *ummatul muslimin* (the ummah of Muslims). Through an innovative decision, at least for the Arab tribes of the time, Muhammad resolved the feuds by writing a document; the so-called *Constitution of Medina*, which the majority of Muslim and non-Muslim scholars consider an authentic document.[5] The Constitution has attracted the attention of scholars because of its inclusive characteristics. Indeed, Article 1 reads 'They [people of Medina] are a single community [*ummah*] distinct from (other) people', and Article 25 'The Jews of Banu 'Awf are a community [*ummah*] along with the believers. To the Jews their religion [*dīn*] and to the Muslims their religion...' (*Constitution of Medina* in Watt 1956: 221–5). Watt has suggested that the above article of the Constitution includes within the concept of ummah all 'believers' in one God, instead of restricting it to the community of Muslims. It is clear that within the general ummah, based on civil society and civil rules, others, based on religious and moral values as well as religious rules, existed.

Another historical fact, which Watt has rightly highlighted in his study, is the challenge that the conceptualization of ummah presented to the traditional Arab understanding of society and identity. So, Watt has reminded, 'the political thinking of the Arabs of Muhammad's time had at its centre the conception of the tribe. The tribe was essentially a group based on blood-kinship' (1956: 238). Although some authors (see for instance Mandaville 2001: 69–82) have argued that the ummah is nothing else than an extended concept of tribe, the majority agree with Watt that the new concept of ummah had, and still has, challenged the pillar of the tribal system: loyalty to the members on the basis of kinship ties. According to Al-Ahsan (1992), the distinction between loyalty towards people and loyalty to God is expressed in the Qur'an by the differentiation between the terms, both meaning 'community', *qawm* (i.e. group of people whose loyalty is to each other) and *ummah* (i.e. people whose loyalty is only to Allah).

Can we explain, as some historians of Islam (e.g. Nieuwenhuijze 1959), anthropologists (e.g. Gellner 1994) and political scientists (e.g. Kramer 1996) have, the use of ummah among contemporary Muslims only, or mainly, through its theological and historical values? My answer, forged by the experience of being an anthropologist, is certainly negative. We need to go beyond, but at the same time be aware of, the historical and theological trajectories of this complex concept. Yet we cannot derive our anthropological and sociological analysis from those, though noble, references. Indeed, Nieuwenhuijze's Islamicist study (1959) and Gellner's socio-political theory are good examples of the almost unavoidable fallacies we may fall victim to if the easy path of historical, theological and historical analogies tempt us.

Nieuwenhuijze, after a thick and informative, theological and historical debate on the concept of ummah tried to jump to sociological conclusions about the consequences that this Islamic concept might have for contemporary Muslims, so we are taught that,

> The *ummah* is the unique principle of social identity valid in Islam, it makes for the only Islamic Community, of which any Muslim is a member simply by virtue of being Muslim. This necessitates expansiveness in the way this community is realized. It also promoted elements that can become significant for experiencing the unity of this community. (1959: 19, italics in the original)

I am confident that, having reached this point in my book, the reader is able to spot the trouble of such essentialism: the ummah exists beyond the Muslim, as if it were a person; even worse, it becomes 'the unique principle of social identity valid in Islam'. Yet people do not speak a language because the language, historically, exists in itself, but rather they use the language that they need or have actively learnt; they even manipulate it and modify it to express themselves and their autobiographical self through their processes of identity.

Similarly, Muslims are not part of the ummah because the ummah exists in itself beyond their physical and mental realities, but because they use it, and transform it through their feelings of being Muslim. To have an ummah, you need a mind; whatever 'ummah' might mean (and we will see that it has as many meanings as the minds who conceptualize it), it cannot exist beyond the mental processes that we call mind. The case of Gellner, a sophisticated scholar influenced more by European historicism and philosophical idealism than anthropological theories, shows how tempting it can be to deny the essence of the individual to affirm the essence of culture.[6] Therefore Kamali's criticism of Gellner's understanding, and misuse, of the concept of ummah sounds particularly appropriate,

> Ernest Gellner (1994) claims that civil society cannot arise in Muslim communities because the unique and exclusive sacralization of one faith makes pluralism impossible (1994: 195). There are several problems with this proposition. He mixes the religious notion of umma, which is the concept of a religious community in relation to its Messenger, namely the Prophet, with the peoples residing in different Muslim countries. For him, the citizens of Egypt, Iran and Iraq are just different bits and pieces of the umma. This use of the notion of umma as a homogeneous phenomenon referring to the entire 'Muslim world' neglects the reality of different cultural and institutional arrangements in the various 'Muslim' societies. He fails to take into account in his discussion the sociocultural and even economic diversity of different Muslim countries. (Kamali 2001: 464)

As we have seen in the previous chapters of this book, Gellner has interpreted Muslim societies believing in a paradox: that Islam forges the Muslim's mind. In other words, there is a real Islam and real Muslims. Discussion of the issue of authenticity (who and what is the real Muslim), which may be legitimate within the emic discourse of the community, is not an appropriate practice within the anthropology of Islam.

Other social scientists, however, have avoided such essentialism and analysed the ummah through some of the community theories we have discussed above. Hassan (2006), after describing the ummah sociologically as a 'transformative concept', which can adapt to the different social instances according to the social actor's needs, has argued that the a-ethnic and a-national characteristic of ummah facilitated its emancipation from territorial dimensions. This, he has suggested, has transformed, over time, the theological and historical concept of ummah into a 'state of mind, a form of social consciousness or an imagined community' (2006: 312). Therefore, Hassan has argued that to understand the concept of ummah from a sociological viewpoint we need to take into consideration two analytical perspectives: ummah as community and ummah as collective identity. If, according to Hassan, the ummah as community is a clear by-product of the human capacity of 'imagining communities', the ummah as collective identity, 'is grounded in the socialization process in human societies' and the formation of cultural boundaries (2006: 314).

After the collapse of the Ottoman Empire in 1924 and the subsequent development of Islamic nationalism influenced by European nationalistic ideologies, as well as increasing migration toward the west, the question as to whether a community could exist without a nation or a defined boundary was raised. The advent of the Internet, however, has provided, according to some scholars, that sense of communality and belonging through a virtual – but not for this reason less real – network (see Roy 1996, 2002). Mandaville can thus claim, 'we can speak of the Internet as allowing Muslims to create a new form of imagined community, or reimagined umma' (1999: 24). Nonetheless, despite the Internet and a certain romanticized rhetoric of the ummah (see the last section of this chapter), which seems also to have affected some scholars, divisions and conflicts among Muslims as well as Muslim states persist.[7] Khan, indeed, has suggested that the concept of ummah is mainly symbolic within the British Muslim community when compared to the 'day-to-day issues they face as ordinary citizens' (2000: 38).

During my research, I have often observed rhetorical conceptualizations of ummah, in which the unity of Muslims has been exalted. Yet, despite this rhetoric, Muslim communities are not free from national divisions, sectarian discriminations and even racism. Nonetheless, my respondents could not acknowledge the paradox they offered.[8] This ummah paradox, which, as I have emphasized in this chapter, goes beyond historical and textual contradictions, has raised the question, as Schmidt has highlighted, of 'how people go about transforming and vitalizing imagination into transnational community practice, for example through what political scientist Thomas Faist calls "generalized forms of reciprocity and diffuse forms of solidarity"'[9] (Schmidt 2005: 577). Cohen (1985) has answered suggesting that 'community' is nothing else than a mental structure, in which the symbols are fundamental to solidarity mechanisms and a sense of belonging, which then form identity. In the next section, starting from some interesting insights provided by Hetherington (1998) and Maffesoli (1996),[10] I shall provide a new reading of the contemporary conceptualization of ummah.

## THE UMMAH: A COMMUNITY OF FEELINGS?

When I met Ali, who is thirty years old and of Algerian origin, chatting in London Central Mosque with some of his friends, I was invited to sit with them while waiting for the familiar invocation of the *adhān* (call to prayer). Their conversation topic focused on the recent conflict between Hezbollah and Israeli forces (July 2006), which left Lebanon in rubble. One of Ali's friends pointed out that the suffering of the Lebanese Muslims had to be the suffering of all the ummah. The others reinforced the idea that only through the ummah could Muslims maintain their *iman'* intact during such hard challenges. When I asked how they understood the concept of ummah, they agreed with Ali's explanation,

> You have to feel part of ummah; you have to feel the brothers that even you do not know because he is you and you are him. There is a unity that is basically emotional; it is something that goes beyond just the concept in itself. I would say that the ummah connects people through the shared experience of being Muslim.

Ali has a degree in psychology and unsurprisingly he provided a quite sophisticated answer. Nonetheless, other Muslims, though using different, sometimes less sophisticated terms, have described the ummah as a sharing of empathy and emotions. The ummah becomes visible and 'activated' in its 'trans-ethnic' and 'trans-national' ethos during particular emotional events.[11]

Hence, we can acknowledge that emotions and feelings are central to the conceptualization of the ummah. Nevertheless, academic studies have overlooked this aspect of the contemporary use of ummah in favour of more traditional symbolic determinism within the studies of community. However, there has been some attempt in developing a theory of community to avoid such symbolic determinism. Hetherington's work (1998) has provided a framework for a sociological and anthropological understanding of community that re-establishes the centrality of feelings and emotions in the process of identification and community formation. In developing his theory, Hetherington has modified Maffesoli's understanding of 'emotional communities' (1996) as well as Schmalenbach's definition of *Bund* (1922).

Maffesoli has suggested that grouping and identification are not based on rationality and 'its modes of identification and organisation' (1996: 52), but rather on the expression of sentiments, feelings and the capacity of sharing them, through 'affectual forms of sociation' (1996: 52). He has argued that the source of ethic within the community is not a product of the rational but rather of the expressive and emotional. Hetherington has used Maffesoli's argument to show how people who are not in a predominant social position can identify with those in the group who are in subaltern conditions, through what he has called 'a politic of metonymy',

> One becomes authentic, has an identity that is real and valuable by identifying with that (or who) which is marginalized within society. The politics of difference is not only a politics where those in a subaltern position begin to speak for themselves and challenge the way they are represented as the other within society, it is also a politic of metonymy in which those not in a subaltern position identify with one or more such positions as means of valorizing their own identity as real and significant. (Hetherington 1998: 71)

If we observe how, and in particular when, Muslims refer to the ummah, Hetherington's conclusion appears pertinent to the function, and the *raison d'être*, of the contemporary ummah.

Yet we need to introduce another element, the *Bund* (or communion), in order to clarify how emotions and feelings are at the centre of the ummah. Hetherington has explained the historical development of the term Bund and its, mostly unknown, usage within sociology, and concludes that mutual sentiments and feelings make it 'a fully conscious phenomenon' (Hetherington 1998: 89). Hetherington's Bund differs from Weber's idea that being part of a group is an unconscious fact because it is a fundamental need of the individual (1968). The Bund, Hetherington has told us, is a space in which energy and charisma tend to be defused and become part of a collective ideologization of feelings. I would add to Hetherington's argument that the Bund is part of the process of the formation of the autobiographical self, expressed as we have seen, through personal identity.[12]

Hetherington's final observation of the community of emotions[13] and the Bund is particularly relevant to understand why within the ummah, despite finding charismatic people (i.e. those who have baraka; see Marranci 2006a), they do not become objects of adoration. This is because, as Hetherington has explained,

> Among emotional communities ... a generalisation of charisma within groups seeking to disperse this 'substance' in the form of 'energy' or 'commitment' to all members of the Bund will probably be favoured over charismatic leaders. Charisma in this more general sense is likely to be perceived as the basis of authentic unmediated interpersonal relationships, expressed through the performativity of the occasion as well as within a Bund rather than through adoration of a leader. Such emphatic relations come to be seen as unmediated and direct, based purely in feeling (1994: 94).

Indeed, charisma within the contemporary rhetoric of ummah is diffuse and not centralized. It is more a question of recognized spiritual power, i.e. *baraka*, than rational analysis of ideas and actions.

## CONCLUSION

In this chapter, we have started questioning the label 'Muslim community'. Despite a widespread use within both the mass media and the academic world, no real effort has been made to clarify its use. The impression is that, like other successful keywords such as identity, self, nationalism and fundamentalism, the usage has made it appear self-defining. Just a very brief look at how anthropologists have addressed the concept of 'community' shows that this is not the case. The majority of anthropologists today have suggested that communities form through shared symbols that allow an imagined space of communality. Some of them have also pointed out that the Internet, and more generally the globalized mass media, has increasingly facilitated this process. The concept of ummah (i.e. community of believers) has been explained and analysed from different viewpoints: theological, historical, sociological and anthropological. While the theological approach has highlighted the different ideas of ummah within the Islamic sources, the historical approach has explored the first experiences of the Muslim community, in particular the case of Medina, in reference to the theological conceptualization of ummah. The majority of anthropologists have based their understanding of ummah on the emic interpretations provided during ethnographic research (see, for instance, Lukens-Bull 2005), while sociologists have preferred to focus on the aspects of social belonging to the group and social identities. Yet none of these approaches have been free from essentialism.

One of the reasons for this essentialism is the lack of attention to the divisions, religious sectarianism and even racism existing among Muslims. This leads to a paradox: Muslims acknowledge the divisions, but do not see them as a factual denial of the ummah beyond a general religious rhetoric. Social scientists also have evidence that a certain collectivity and sense of belonging is visible among Muslims, in particular during times of crisis, such as the Rushdie Affair or the more recent Danish Cartoons Affair. In order to avoid essentialism but at the same time explain this trans-national, trans-ethnic and often trans-sectarian (Sunni versus Shi'a) sense of belonging, I have suggested that we need to reconsider the role that emotions and feelings have in it.

Notwithstanding the visible antagonisms existing among Muslims, a vivid rhetoric of a single, united, ummah is, from an emic viewpoint, acknowledged. Evidence of global reactions to local incidents involving offences to Islam, its Prophet or Muslims in general confirms that, in certain circumstances, Muslims are able to put aside differences in order to find a unity behind the concept of ummah, instead of regrouping around a single charismatic leader. Maffesoli (1996) has suggested that communities are not based on rational, but rather emotional processes producing a sense of ethos, which can be shared among members who are connected not merely through physicality but by empathy. If we observe how Muslims discuss and represent the conceptualization of the ummah, it is not difficult to recognize a strong similarity to Maffesoli's 'community of emotions'. However, since I agree with Damasio's theory of emotions (Chapter 5, this book), I have suggested that emotions are a reaction to the environment, and it is the feelings which may be shared in the form of ethos. Hence, I prefer to speak of community of feelings.

We have also observed that Hetherington (1998) has suggested that certain communities could be understood through the concept of Bund. Within the Bund, charisma is not localized (i.e. a single charismatic leader or a charismatic group), rather charisma is diffused in the form of 'power' and 'energy'. Again, we can observe a similarity between the Bund and the ummah. Although today no Muslim recognizes the existence of a charismatic leader representing the ummah, charisma is diffused through the concept of *baraka*, which could be seen as the 'power' or 'energy' discussed by Hetherington. Baraka, indeed, is a special transfer of divine energy between Allah and a person, who then can even charge an object with it. Although, as I have shown in another book (Marranci 2006a), there are different interpretations as to what exactly baraka is, who can achieve it and how, Muslims recognize that some people within the ummah possess baraka.

Therefore, the ummah paradox is resolved if we consider the ummah as: (1) a community of feelings, (2) based on a religious Bund, (3) characterized by a shared basic ethos (i.e. belief in the shahāda and tawhīd), (4) expressed through a diffused charisma. Indeed, although different forms of sectarianism exist among Muslims, they can be considered as part of an internal dynamic,[14] which, however, does not contradict or deny the shared, and fundamental, basic ethos. Whenever, as in the case of the Rushdie Affair, Palestinian Intifada, Danish Cartoons Affair and other less known or minor incidents, the ummah is threatened by external forces, the shared ethos is, or seems to be, that the internal dynamic is suspended in favour of a visible unity.

## *NOTES*

1. Google Scholar is a Google research engine providing results based on academic journals, papers and books.
2. Or any other social scientists working within a qualitative methodology.
3. Also Macfarlane 1977; Cohen 1985; Lustiger-Thaler 1994; Guijt and Shah 1998.
4. Also Nieuwenhuijze 1959; von Grunebaum 1961, 1962; Denny 1975; Giannakis 1983; Rahman 1984; Dallal 1995.
5. You can read Watt 1956 for an extensive discussion of the constitution.
6. See the previous chapter in this book for my view on the culture/nature debate.
7. Also Eickelman and Piscatori 1996. For a critique of the ummah as post-national entity, see Grillo, Riccio and Salih 2000.
8. For an example involving exogamic marriages within some Muslim communities see Marranci 2006b.
9. Quote from Faist 2004: 21–2.
10. I have to notice that Maffesoli's work and much of Hetherington's efforts to revitalize 1920s–1930s German sociological studies of community have remained totally unknown to the majority of anthropologists of Islam.
11. See, for instance, the recent case of the Danish Cartoons Affair as well as the previously discussed Rushdie Affair and the support given to the different outbreaks of the Palestinian intifada.
12. I wish to recall here that, in the previous chapter, we observed how identity is a machinery of our imagination aiming towards a sense of stable self.
13. Yet following my theory of identity, I suggest that we have to speak of a community of feelings.
14. This internal dynamic, which I call diatribe systems, does include, among other actions, violence.

# CHAPTER 8

# The Dynamics of Gender in Islam

## *GENDER IN ISLAM = WOMEN IN ISLAM?*

Muslim women have attracted the attention of the West for as long as Western scholars have encountered Islam. The mysterious and exotic image of the harem mixed with the fear of powerful Muslim armies reaching Vienna, the door of Europe. Today, we may think that the morbid curiosity about Muslim women, seen as different, mysterious and in particular, complacent victims of the sexualized, disproportionately virile oppression of the 'Moslem man' is confined to eroticized romantic novels and travel journals within specialized shelves of European libraries. Today, to satisfy our judgmental curiosity about Islam and its female believers, we do not have the Christian polemicist caricature of Islam that Voltaire offered in his *Mahomet* (1736/1905). Rather, we have a by-product of our imagined, yet still much romanticized, idea of a civilized superiority in which white Western men and women alienate themselves within the illusion of possessing secular-based rights of gender equality. The morbid curiosity is alive still, centuries after Voltaire's *Mahomet* and thousands more books on Islam and women; as I understood during my rambling within an airport.

A delay of my flight bestowed some unwanted time upon me. I decided to perform the usual pilgrimage among the monotonous airport gadget shops and newsagents. While scanning some shelves busy with various magazines, the cover of a *National Geographic* issue attracted my attention. A too-familiar picture of a young woman with deep green eyes exalted by the delicate framework of a red scarf was, on the right-hand side, compared with a prematurely aged, unhealthy face which unemotionally surfaced from a deep blue *burqu'*. The title on the cover emphatically announced, 'A Life Revealed'. Although I needed some time to appreciate the similarity between the two faces, it was clear that the same woman owned both, though, indeed, diachronically. The two portraits of the same woman seemingly wished to emphasize the degenerative effects that the Taliban's regime had on the young and beautiful woman whom the photographer met for the first time in Afghanistan during the Russian occupation.

'Why such a cover?' I wondered. The answer could be found in a controversial war. The American Afghan War had failed in the task of capturing or killing Osama bin Laden – the anchorman of the Hindu Kush much loved by extremists worldwide – and had also missed the infamous one-eyed Mullah Omar. Yet the US administration could still claim something positive out of an unconvincing military campaign; they had freed Afghan women from the burqu', the epitomic symbol of 'Islamic' oppression. Much ink has been spent in magazines describing the oppression of Afghan women *because* they were forced to wear the burqu', which had become, in the collective mass mediated unconscious, a symbol of Islam itself. The *National Geographic*'s cover demonstrated the fetishized western desire to lift the burqu' and disclose the mysterious feminine Other. In this instance, however, it is not the unveiling of the eroticized eastern beauty of the condemned, but much dreamt of harem, to the curious western white man (or woman, why not?), but rather the exposure of an aged and weathered face of a woman who had too many children and too little food. Doubtless, while some western women would generously offer their expensive makeup to cover up the marks of a different life in a different place, the *National Geographic*'s photographer, from his androcentric camera lens, had emphasized a Western (stereotyped) viewpoint about what a western woman and man would be concerned with: her wrinkles.

If the fantastic world of *Thousand and One Nights* inspired the imagination of the Europeans, late nineteenth-century colonialism employed a misrepresentation of the Islamic discourse on gender in order to assert its colonialist rights over Muslim societies. So, Ahmed has observed,

> Thus the reorganized [colonial] narrative, with its new focus on women, appears to have been a compound created out of a coalescence between the old narrative of Islam ... (which Edward Said's *Orientalism* details) and the broad, all-purpose narrative of colonial domination regarding the inferiority, in relation to European culture, of all Other cultures and societies, a narrative that saw vigorous development over the course of the nineteenth century. (1992: 150)

The morbid, yet eroticized (though paternalistic) curiosity about Muslim women has filled the imaginations of first European and then American popular culture. Indeed, as Said (1978) has shown, the Orientalists' voyeurism of both artists and scholars – though sometimes latent – manifested itself in the form of power control. The popular and Orientalist interest in gender and Islam is certainly not recent. Anthropology, as well as other disciplines in the social sciences, provided colonial theories with Orientalist views of Middle Eastern women, both Muslims and non.[1] However, while Europe was observing the women of the 'Others', European women were observing their own position within mainly androcentric societies. With socialist movements spreading, western feminist arguments became increasingly known and successful. Of course, feminism, as an ideology and political discourse, crossed the European frontier to reach the 'third world' and the colonized territories. This, as we shall see, would change both the way in which western feminist scholars observed Muslim women as well as how Muslim women scholars addressed the issue of gender in the Islamic world.

French ethnographies, in particular dealing with Northern Africa, had paid some attention to the role of gender among Arab and Berber tribes. Gender, in this case, was part of the study of kinship; often relegated to the topic of marriage. Islam was of little or no interest to the French ethnographer. As we have seen in the previous chapters, something, however, changed with Anglo-American anthropologists, such as Geertz (1968), Gellner (1981) and Gilsenan (1982). In this case, an essentialist view of Islam became the key through which to understand Middle Eastern and South Asian societies, which now they identified as 'Muslim' (Varisco 2005). Yet any reader approaching these classic anthropological works on Islam could only learn that Islam is just business for men. Varisco (2005: 47) has noticed about Geertz's *Islam Observed*, 'I am confused by the lack of direct references to Muslim informants in a study that purports to "observe" Islam... In the village alleyways Geertz may have talked to men with the likely names of Muhammed and 'Ali, but in *Islam Observed* the individual Muslims encountered are mostly icons.' Yet, in these famous studies, Muslim women are not even icons; they are just ghosts. Some male anthropologists' studies tend to silence the voices of Muslim women.

Since the middle of the 1970s, feminist scholars of both Muslim and non-Muslim origin started to gender Islam. The studies mainly addressed gender and Islam in the MENA regions (see Beck and Keddie 1978; Keddie 1991; Ahmed 1992; Tucker 1993) focusing on two main aspects: the conditions and status of Muslim women in Islam. These studies, however, immediately became a battleground between those who accused Islam – as religion – of fostering gender inequalities and being oppressive towards women, and those – in particular Muslim feminists – who blamed local cultural traditions for the disadvantages and discriminations and exalted 'real' Islam as the solution. The latter focused on the economic rights that Muslim women enjoyed within Islam, while the former focused on dress codes, and in particular the 'veil', as strong evidence of the patriarchal oppression of Islam on women. One of the first Muslim scholars to write a successful study of gender in Islam was the Moroccan sociologist Mernissi.

In 1975, Mernissi's *Beyond the Veil* became the successful matrix for future feminist studies of gender in Islam. Despite the subtitle 'Male-Female dynamics', Mernissi focused only on women, basing her analysis on ethnographic studies she conducted with Moroccan women. She has not discussed the dynamics among genders within Moroccan society, but rather the impact that the discourse of sexuality in Islam has on Muslim women. The central topic of her book is sophisticated, but extremely monolithic. Mernissi focused on 'the traditional Muslim view of women and their place in the social order' (Mernissi 1975: 1). She suggested the latter depends upon the attitude of the 'Muslim mind' towards sexuality and *sharī'a*, which she has presented as a means of moral control. Indeed, we can read, 'the link in the *Muslim mind* [emphasis added] between sexuality and the sharī'a has shaped the legal and ideological history of the Muslim family structure and consequentially of the relation between the sexes' (1975: xv). The main argument is that men use Islam to control women's dangerous sexuality and impose patriarchal structures, of which Muslim women are responsible for the propagation and transmission (Roald 2001). Mernissi's Feminist–Freudian approach to Islam and gender has certainly shown some attractive insights, but also evident weakness. Her analyses suffer from, I would say, Freudian reductionism. Mernissi has reduced Islam, as a religious system, to an inverted chastity belt, protecting the men from the temptation of a dangerous and uncontrolled female sexuality. This idea has found some support among other feminist scholars such as Hussain (1984) and Sabbah (1984). Nonetheless, the most flawed aspect of Mernissi's argument is the idea that 'a Muslim mind', forged by the rules and ethos of Islam, can exist. This essentialist argument is certainly not new, as we can easily trace it back to Orientalistic viewpoints such as those expressed by Baring (1908).

During the 1980s, a new generation of feminist Muslim scholars paid particular attention to the topic of gender, colonialism and Islam, as in the case of Bodman and Tohidi (1998) and, in particular, Ahmed (1992). Partially rejecting the previous Freudian sexual-centric analysis and criticism, these new studies employed a post-modern and, often Fanonian, anti-colonial approach. Ahmed, in her book *Women and Gender in Islam*, has offered an interesting social and historical discussion and analysis of women in the Middle East. Ahmed has shown a very different approach from that advocated by Mernissi. She has recognized that Islamic societies did oppress women and continue to do so, but at the same time has rejected colonialist and Orientalist views of Islam. Ahmed has argued, 'the political uses of the idea that Islam oppressed women and noting that what patriarchal colonialists identified as the source and main forms of women's oppression in Islamic society was based on a vague and inaccurate understanding of Muslim societies' (1992: 160). Her criticism did not stop at the Orientalist and colonial heritage, but strongly extended to Western feminist ideas of Islam, 'critical of the practice and beliefs of the men of their societies with respect to themselves acquiesced in and indeed promoted the European male's representations of the Other men and the cultures of the Other men and joined, *in the name of feminism*, in the attack on the veil and the practices generally of Muslim societies' (1992: 243 italics added). Ahmed, indeed, has suggested that the western view of gender in Islam and the western paternalistic attitude towards women in Islam could in reality cover an attempt to strip Muslim women not just of their veils but rather of their culture and Muslim identity.

Therefore, Ahmed's book is something more than a study of gender and women in Islam – and indeed very little could be found about gender – but a rather critical analysis of the threats that Muslim women will encounter when developing their own strategies for emancipation. Ahmed explains these threats as, on the one hand, an attractive Islamist revision of Islam, and on the other, a European feminism ready to profess the same colonial superiority over Muslim women which patriarchy does. Ahmed has suggested that Muslim women should reclaim both the right to have their own Arab and Islamic identity and the right to interpret Islam in such a way that it can empower their voices in a political and social male-dominated space. Notwithstanding the validity of Ahmed's argument and the political elements that she has introduced in the discourse of gender and Islam, we should notice again that gender, in her work, means just women. She, like Mernissi before her, has missed an important opportunity to discuss the dynamics between genders within Muslim societies, both historically as well as socially. Many studies focusing on gender and Islam are in reality analyses derived from the ideologies of feminist movements within certain specific social, political and historical contexts (Baron 1994; Chatty and Rabo 1997). Anthropologists working on gender in Muslim societies have preferred to discuss it as part of localized ethnography. Thus, during the 1980s, the focus would remain on Muslim women living in the Middle East or other Islamic countries.[3] Muslim women living in western countries have not attracted anthropological interest until recently.

Sofie Roald (2001) is one of the first anthropologists to offer an interesting view inside the different understandings of gender existing among western Muslim communities. Her book *Women in Islam*, although mainly based on the opinions of Islamic scholars and leaders of Islamic movements, discloses what feminists have ideologically omitted: the male perspective. Roald's book seeks to appeal to both Muslims and non-Muslims, and addresses specific theological questions, such as the different positions on marriage, divorce, dress code and even female circumcision. Yet Roald's main aim is to show the cultural impact, in particular when Western, on interpretations of Islam. In her conclusions she observes,

> In the present study I have applied a model of two oppositional cultural patterns; the 'Arab cultural base pattern' and the 'Western cultural patterns'. I broadly defined these two cultural patterns as the patriarchal versus the equality pattern respectively. Within these cultural ideas there are local variations which I have taken into consideration when necessary. The 'normative field' in which the process of interpretation of social issues in the Islamic sources takes place lies between these two poles. (2001: 294)

Roald explores the impact that contact with the 'west' has on the interpretation of Islamic sources as far gender is concerned. She observes that the Manichaean division of the discourse of gender between the 'patriarchal' Arab pattern and the allegedly 'equal' western pattern raises some questions. Consequently, she suggests a very different approach from the traditional Islamic feminist discourse on gender. Avoiding a useless essentialist approach to Islam, Roald presents the theological discourse of Islam and gender through her informants' interpretations. Despite this anti-essentialist approach, for Roald, although the male scholar's voice is represented, gender in Islam remains very much 'women in Islam'. Therefore, Roald's study still has something in common with the traditional feminist ones. The main interest of these authors, despite being anthropologists, has been the Islam–women relationship seen as mediated through different degrees of male patriarchy. Patriarchy itself has been interpreted as a vertical relationship, in which the woman is merely the oppressed object.

This constant omission of gender from ethnographic studies of Islam, has, in more recent times, brought some anthropologists to argue that the study of gender 'must be central to an anthropology of Islam' (Tapper and Tapper 1987). Some recent ethnographies, such as Okkenhaug and Flaskerud (2005) and Droeber (2005), have framed the discussion on gender starting from ethnographic fieldwork. In these cases, the voices of ordinary Muslims have been considered and analysed. Islam and gender, in other words, are observed through the practice of everyday life.

Droeber's book, *Dreaming of Change, Young Middle-Class Women and Social Transformation in Jordan*, has observed the dynamics of gender and social change of young Jordanian women coming from a middle-class family background. In her ethnography, the dynamics of gender and the negotiations taking place between her male and female respondents are visible. In the Introduction, she states,

> What I am interested in are young women's everyday experiences and how these shape and are shaped by their social environment. This view already indicates my answer ... about the impact of religion on women's lives. It is generally not an 'either/or', but often a combination of repression and empowerment, and always a clear 'it depends', i.e. namely on time, place, and circumstances. (2005: 8)

The overall picture is very different from the preceding studies, in which the focus was on the relationship between Islam and women. In Droeber's book the idea of negotiations and the young women's 'constant involvement in the processes of bargaining with the prevailing notions of gender and power' (2005: 308) allows the reader to observe the entangled network – of which Islam is only one of the elements – which forms the social discourse of gender. Yet, even Droeber seems to relate gender solely to Muslim 'women'. Although she has a chapter with an intriguing subsection, 'Femininity and Masculinity in Jordan', the subsection still discusses women and only very few words are spent on masculinity.

It seems safe to argue that to date 'gender in Islam' has meant nothing else than 'women in Islam'. Surely we cannot deny that a certain traditional androcentric bias has prevented male anthropologists, especially during the 1970s and 1980s, from observing the active role that Muslim women had, and have, in their societies and in interpreting Islam. However, it is also true that feminist anthropologists, who ideologically have focused on Muslim women as the victims of Islam, have overlooked the fact that gender also includes masculinity. We can only agree with Okkenhaug and Flaskerud that 'men and masculinity in the Middle East are still almost non-existing research areas' (2005: 2). In other words, studies on gender in Islam have suffered from a generalized, when not politicized, reductionist understanding of both gender and Islam.[4]

So many years of essentialist approaches to gender among Muslims have caused a simplification of the dynamics of gender in Islamic societies and Muslim communities, in which relationships between Muslim men and women can be understood only through the dominance–submission model. This negative reductionism suggests that Muslim men – all of them? – are an active and oppressive force empowered by Islam, while women are passive, submissive and disempowered by Islam. Shankland has emblematically offered us an extreme example of this dominance–submission model,

> A girl is also controlled first of all by parents. When she marries she becomes the responsibility of her husband. She remains under his control until she becomes a widow, when she may enjoy a greater degree of freedom. At any time, though, she remains constrained by male relatives and the other men of the settlement, all of whom feel the right to control her behaviour. (2003: 54)

Shankland is an anthropologist of the 'Gellnerian school'. Yet he has gone even farther than Gellner in his essentialist views of Islam. For instance, Shankland has invited other anthropologists and social scientists to consider his insight (diplomatically hidden in a short note) 'that there is something *within Islamic faith* which assumes the axiomatic inferiority, or at least separation, of women from men (and therefore the power to run society)' (2003: 316, emphasis added). Shankland, in other words, has suggested that Islam, as a religion, imposes the dynamics of dominance–submission between the genders, and such dynamics dictate the power structure of Muslim societies. Surely, his extreme essentialist understanding of Islam has facilitated his extremely flawed, if not today anachronistic, view of gender among Sunni Muslims. Even more relevant here is his incapacity to recognize, as an anthropologist, the relationship between genders in Muslim societies as complex networks of different dynamics, involving culture, identity, environment and emotions, not just religion. Shankland, however, is not the only anthropologist to have overlooked such dynamics; others have transformed the male Muslim voices of their informants into the voice of Islam. Consequently, Islam has been reduced in their analysis into a sort of dangerous 'cultural Viagra'.

## ISLAM, GENDER AND MIGRATION

We have observed that gender among Muslim societies has been studied mainly within Islamic countries. Indeed, interest in gender and Muslim migration is relatively recent. This should be of no surprise since, as we saw in chapters 3 and 4, migration has been considered for a long time a male business. With the exponential increase of Muslim women migrating towards the West – as refugees, economic migrants, family regrouping – the 1990s saw migrant Muslim women shifting from being considered an academic 'curiosity' to a topic worth researching in anthropology and sociology. Nonetheless, the field of migration studies was not immune to the androcentric views that had to be deconstructed within the field of Middle Eastern studies. For instance, despite being the mid 1990s, Clifford had to reaffirm the centrality of gender in immigration studies by arguing, 'diasporic experiences are always gendered. But there is a tendency for theoretical accounts of diasporas and diaspora cultures to hide this fact, to talk of travel and displacement in unmarked ways, thus normalizing male experiences' (1994: 313). Women, according to him, retain a particular position within the immigrant family; they propagate the cultural traditions of their families. Because of immigration, however, some of them may achieve an economic and social freedom outside their families.

Other scholars have suggested that the act of migrating to a western country could become a proactive element in the emancipation of Muslim women. For instance, Abdulrahim (1993) has observed that migration may induce fundamental changes in the 'traditional cultural codes' of Muslim women:

Instead of the traditional method of taking refuge with relatives or neighbours, young women had the opportunity to turn to a German women's centre. These

women, in the majority of cases, return to the family household, but a small
and increasing number of exceptions are significant. Taking refuge outside
the community, even if temporarily, indicates that an alternative to family
organisation now exists for women. By using it as a threat, young women have
increased their power in a conflict situation. (1993: 70)

These positive examples emphasize the advantages that Muslim women and their
daughters can have from the experience of immigrating into western countries.
Yet they show only one side of the coin. The decision to use supports outside the
family network is often the only option left in the context of migration because of
the disruption to the extended support networks of friends and family these Muslim
women have in their countries of origin. Although some Muslim women can indeed
find the experience of migration as 'liberating', others struggle with it.

I had occasion in Northern Ireland to interview a Muslim woman who had
suffered domestic abuse. She had no other members of her family in Belfast, and
had no choice other than to ask for support from the 'women's refuge'. However,
she described her need 'to beg for a place where to stay' as 'humiliating, degrading
and upsetting'. The reason she felt distressed asking for help from unknown women
was because, as she put it, 'only prostitutes in my country end in these institutions.
I mean, I have a good family and good friends back home (homeland) who would
have supported and helped me during those difficult times. But here I had no choice
other than ending in the women's refuge.'

Nonetheless, Lutz (1991) has argued that since the colonial representation of
Middle Eastern Muslim women as passive was so deep-rooted, it was increasingly
difficult to avoid reproducing the stereotype while studying Muslim migrant women.
However, Lutz has identified another risk in the study of Muslim women in the
west, the fact that 'the Western woman serves as counterpoint: as the standard for
measuring women elsewhere' (Lutz 1991: 2). This issue has become particularly
visible in the case of French research on gender and migration.

French scholars, such as Lacoste-Dujardin (2000), Souilamas (2000) and
Tribalat (1995), have suggested that migration is axiomatically positive for the
emancipation of Muslim women,

emancipation is more relevant to daughters and especially the older daughters in
a family, although even the younger children, both boys and girls, may benefit
by being brought up by an emancipated mother, more able to stimulate them in
their studies and to incite them to social success. (Lacoste-Dujardin 2000: 66)

Lacoste-Dujardin (2000) has interpreted as positive the disempowerment of the
figure of the father that immigration often produces. The Muslim father often
became unable to remain the breadwinner of the family as the Qur'an dictates,
finding himself dependent on his wife or even children. Lacoste-Dujardin has, to
use Lutz's observation, based her feminist analysis on a predominant ethnocentric
idea of 'woman', failing to observe that Muslim migrant women and their daughters
may possess or have developed different ideas of 'emancipation' from that prevalent

in post-1968 France. What would have been interesting to study, and what has still not been researched, is how Muslim migrant women react to the western feminist idea of emancipation.

However, we should remember that gender is not only a useful analytic concept, as it can also become a powerful political discourse. We may consider the 1979 Iranian revolution as one of the most prominent examples. Iranian women with their black *chādor*, which would finally trap them, represented the symbol of that revolution which asked for an equal, homogenized society under the guide of the Ayatollah, the only true Shi'a guide towards Islam. Yet in France, Muslim women found themselves at the centre of another political battle, that of the 'assimilation' of the younger generations. The *ḥijāb* (headscarf) has recently acquired the status of a counter-hegemonic symbol that wishes to deny the imposed homogeneity of French secularism. Fifteen years after the 'headscarf affair' (Dayan-Herzbrun 2000) the French government has enforced a controversial law banning all readily visible religious symbols, aiming to prevent female Muslim students from wearing their ḥijābs. Many Muslim women in France perceive the legislation as anti-democratic. Thus a considerable number of Muslim women in France, as well as in the rest of the world, fiercely opposed the government's legislation and their protest reached an international audience (Thomas 2005; Brems 2006).

The ḥijāb has been often misunderstood as a symbol of Islamic oppression, which must be removed in order to allow Muslim women to achieve full emancipation and, in this case, to become a French citizen. It is therefore unsurprising that Lacoste-Dujardin, like many other French anthropologists, has suggested that girls and boys of Muslim origin could be transformed into French citizens upholding the French values of *laicïté* only if their mothers became emancipated, preferably through divorce, from their families, since, for Mernissi and Lacoste-Dujardin, patriarchy is an oppressive, superimposed structure which Muslim men are able to impose because of Islam. If in Shankland's dramatic hyperbole, Muslim women are gifts to be exchanged between Muslim men, in the works of many French scholars, such as Lacoste-Dujardin, Muslim women need to be rescued, 'unveiled', and so be empowered by the French *laicïté* (secularism).

The tendency of sociology and anthropology is often to focus on 'issues', facilitating a constant emphasis on the difficulties and problems of the population studied. This increases the risk that scholars may present individuals, or a particular category within the studied society, as passively under the control of undetermined sociocultural forces. Lutz has urged anthropologists to 'look at them [immigrant women] as newcomers, needing time to adjust to both differences and similarities in the host societies life-styles' (1991: 23). Muslim migrant women are capable of negotiating between their Islamic and cultural values and the values of their host societies. A new generation of anthropologists, such as the Italo-Moroccan anthropologist Ruba Salih has recognized this dynamic.

Salih, who has conducted an anthropological study concerning Moroccan immigrant women living in Italy (2000), argues that, 'immigrant women contextually negotiate the boundaries of inclusion and exclusion of Self and Other, according to the diverse and sometimes intersecting hegemonic discourses that they may face in different places and phases of their lives' (2000: 323). She emphasizes the abilities of Muslim immigrant women to renegotiate new boundaries instead of passively assimilating within the host 'Western' models. She reminds us that Muslim immigrant women actively take part not only in their families, but also in their host societies. While the majority of French scholars we have discussed seem to interpret Islam as an obstacle to assimilation, Salih argues that Muslim immigrant women integrate Islam into their complex negotiation processes, which involve not only their host societies but also their former homelands. Basch, Glick Schiller and Szanton (1994) have argued that immigrants are part of 'deterritorialized nation-states' (i.e. a state that 'stretches beyond its geographical boundaries') so that 'the nation's people may live anywhere in the world and still not live outside the state [and by extension] wherever its people go, their state goes too' (1994: 269). However, Smith (1999) has criticized Basch's idea of 'deterritorialized nation-states', arguing that it might affect the concept of diaspora. Smith has reminded us that, despite the available communication technology, in their host countries Muslim immigrant women may still experience displacement.

Avoiding the radicalism of Basch et al. (1994), Salih, in another article (2001), suggests that Moroccan immigrant women are plurinational subjects. This highlights the fact that Muslim women experience 'embeddedness with multiple hegemonic structures operating at more than one national level which conditions their potential to move, their identities and their transnational activities in a gendered way' (2001: 669). It is precisely because Muslim immigrant women are 'plurinational' that they cannot be politically passive subjects as some have suggested. Indeed, far from being passive 'repeaters' of men's discourses, Muslim immigrant women develop their own political and religious views.

Islam has a central role in the lives of the majority of Muslim migrant women who, having lost the support of the extended network of friends and family that they enjoyed before migration, have to meet other Muslim women coming from different countries which have divergent cultural and religious norms. Sisterhood is often mediated through the concept of *ummah*, as I observed in the case of Northern Ireland and Scotland (Marranci 2003b, 2007). Indeed, the Islamic rhetoric smoothes possible conflicts by emphasizing common understandings. Women's groups, partially similar in their activities to those existing in Islamic countries, are promoted and organized. Sometimes, the relationships between main male-dominated mosques and these women's groups are not easy, as the case of Al-Nisa Women's Group might exemplify.

In 1998, the same year as the Good Friday Agreement, Mrs Khan and some Pakistani women established the Al-Nisa Women's Group in Belfast. During one of my conversations with Mrs Khan, she explained why they decided to form this organization, which would have an important impact on the integration of Muslim women within Northern Ireland,

Twenty-seven years ago there were few Muslims in Northern Ireland and even fewer women. Moreover, no women were involved in the activities of the mosque. They did not have any influence. Even though they were very active

- more than men I have to say - we did not have any woman on the [mosque's] committee. So we needed to do something to educate Muslim women in an Islamic way. Well, three years ago we organized Al-Nisa thanks to the funds that the government and NICEM had provided. We are now a charity organization with our charity number. Of course, men were not very happy about this organization and our independence and freedom, even though all our activities and actions were completely Islamic!

Muslim migrant women have actively tried to fight the isolation they were subjected to because of the particular Northern Irish political environment and the strong patriarchal structure of the Pakistani and Bangladeshi Muslim communities.

The women's efforts to become an active part of Northern Irish society led to increased tension with local mosque leaders. The fact that the Al-Nisa Women's Group was ostracized by the Belfast Islamic Centre highlights the difficulty of integrating Muslim women into the male majority. Because of their irreconcilable differences, the collaboration between the Al-Nisa Women's Group and the BIC broke down in the summer of 2002. The mosque committee banned Al-Nisa Women's Group not only from using the BIC logo, but also the mosque premises. Despite the male-dominated mosque shunning them, the Al-Nisa Women's Group did not disappear. One of the women's aid organizations in Belfast, dealing with refugees, offered a meeting space and office to them. This generous donation resulted from the trans-community support network that had developed over the years. While both Muslim migrant women and Muslim migrant men claim to have 'Islamic' identities, the formation of their respective identities originates from different processes and experiences of their environment, which, as we have seen in Chapter 5 of this book, influence their identities.

## THE LOST MASCULINITY: A NEED FOR RESEARCH

The majority of works and studies that we have reviewed have discussed gender as if 'gender' meant 'femininity'. Studies of masculinity in the context of Muslim societies are surprisingly rare (for exceptions, see Ghoussoub and Sinclair-Web 2000 and Lahoucine 2006) despite the attention that gender studies have paid to masculinity in other societies and cultures. Even less, as we will discuss later, has been written concerning Muslim gays and lesbians. One of the reasons for this lack of attention to masculinity and homosexuality in Islam could be found in the fact that gender has not been understood as dynamics between subjects. In a contemporary anthropological approach to Muslim lives, we cannot reduce gender to femininity, since it is only through the observation and analysis of the relationships between the genders which we can achieve a full picture.

So, let us go back to my ethnographic example in Belfast and try to include masculinity within the analysis. The main issue at hand is why the al-Nisa group was, in reality, banned from the local mosque. The key to understanding it can be found in a particular event that took place during the General Meeting in which the ban was decided, when the Al-Nisa Women's Group found itself at the centre of a heated discussion. The qualifier 'heated' is indeed appropriate, for during the meeting, a young Muslim man attempted to set fire to that year's controversial annual report issued by the Al-Nisa Women's Group. This hostile action was instigated by the transcript of a speech given by the president of the Al-Nisa Women's Group at a conference on the topic of women in Northern Ireland. The controversy surrounded the following statement: 'As women, let us not forget that other equally strong elements make up our identities. Some of us are disabled, old, young, *lesbian or bisexual*, rich, poor and so on'. Clearly, the majority of the men at the mosque found the reference to homosexuality inappropriate and unacceptable. Yet this was not just because orthodox interpretations of Islam have forbidden homosexuality. The migration experience, as we have discussed before, challenges the main symbol of masculinity. Pels (2000) has suggested that Muslim migrant men suffer disempowerment within their family because of unemployment or underpaid jobs, which effectively reduce the possibility of their being the family breadwinner. Some may think that this might be just an economic issue, but the fact is that Islamic law requires Muslim men to support their families financially. Unemployment or, more often, their husbands' underpaid jobs 'force' Muslim women to experience role reversal economically speaking. In other words, there is a dramatic inversion of the Islamic precepts structuring the traditional Muslim family. Moreover, the majority of my respondents in Belfast highlighted how living in a non-Muslim country could expose Muslims to 'western bad influences and illnesses' of which the most dangerous was, indeed, homosexuality.

The president of Al-Nisa's reference to homosexuality challenged two main aspects of the Muslim men's masculinity: first their capacity to control their families and give a good Muslim education to their children, and secondly, the power to control the mosque space as mainly a wholly male space. The printed statement referring to homosexuality, and in particular to lesbians, challenged the image of a masculine Islam. The fact that the Muslim community was well aware that some of their members were gays and lesbians, though officially they did not 'come out', increased the will of the majority of committee members to ban the Al-Nisa Women's Group, seen as a subversive and disruptive feminine element. Without paying attention to the relationship between genders, as well as the symbolic and identity values the community attributes to its understanding of gender, I would not have been able to explain this ethnographic example fully.

## THE DYNAMICS OF HONOUR

Masculinity is not the only element that anthropologists and sociologists studying Islam have overlooked. Although the feminist scholars we discussed at the beginning of this chapter have focused on patriarchy as well as the male representation and stereotypes of Muslim women (see Mernissi 1975; Hussain 1984; Sabah 1984; Ahmed 1992; Roald 2001; Droeber 2005), we know very little, or nothing, about Muslim women's stereotypes concerning Muslim men. Anthropologists studying

Islam have interpreted the honour/shame complex[5] (Peristiany 1965; Wikan 1984; Akpinar 2003) as mainly based on the male patriarchal control of the women of the family. A noticeable exception is the seminal study of Abu-Lughod (1986). By studying the concept of honour among Egyptian Bedouins, Abu-Lughod has observed that in that society women hold codified 'honour' rules to which men (at least if they want to achieve a successful marriage) must conform:

> Women claim, for instance, that 'real men' control all their dependents and beat their wives when the wives do stupid things. One woman, whose daughter was about to marry one of the most respected men in the camp, said, 'my daughter wants a man whose eyes are open – not someone nice... No, she wants someone who will order her around'... One old woman told me, 'when a man is really something [manly] he pays no heed to women.' 'A man who listens to his wife when she tells him what to do is a fool' said a young woman ... many agreed adding 'if a man is fool, a woman rides him like a donkey'. (1986: 89, 95)

During my research, I started to wonder whether Muslim migrant women could have similar 'honour rules' and formed stereotypes concerning the idea of the 'real' Muslim man (see Marranci 2006a). I have found that certainly the discourse of honour and shame in Islam could not be limited to the male gender. As in other aspects of gender we have discussed, a full understanding can only be reached if the relationships between the genders are understood as dynamics. Muslim women as well as Muslim men can be affected by the behaviour of their relatives. Stewart (1994) has observed that honour is a bipartite system; the concept would be relevant to both the honour acknowledged and the acknowledger. As for communication, the individuals taking part in the social interaction should share the rules on which honour is granted or withdrawn. In the case of honour/shame, it is true that in a majority of cases Muslim women have the unwanted power to dishonour their male relatives by breaking the Islamic norms of modesty, in particular through sexual behaviours. If the Muslim woman 'brings shame' on her family, the male relatives have to re-establish their jeopardized honour through symbolic, or in the worst cases real physical punishment (Akpinar 2003).

However, since anthropologists have greatly overlooked masculinity in Islam, it is very difficult to find studies which tell us what may happen if it is a male relative who 'brings shame to the family' and in what instances shame is brought by a man. Although more studies in different Muslim societies are needed, having studied Muslim migration in Europe, I have come across some situations in which the honour/shame process saw Muslim men in the position of the one who shames the family. To illustrate, I will offer an ethnographic example I collected in Ireland.

Saida is a 37-year-old Egyptian woman living in Dublin who married a 43-year-old Egyptian man, Eyad, convinced that he could find fortune in Europe as a businessman. He sold his little shop in Cairo and transferred his wife and two daughters to Dublin. Eyad was known in his neighbourhood to be a good Muslim who cared for his family and went to the jum'a every Friday. Saida was not so happy about her husband's move. She was very worried about the education of their daughters and the influence that a non-Muslim country might have on them. Her husband opened the shop that he dreamt of and started to build up a successful business. He also began to enjoy the life of Dublin, mixing with non-Muslim friends and patronizing pubs. Very soon afterwards, he drank alcohol, though was never drunk, and avoided the mosque. He still defined himself a Muslim, but decided to stop practising. Saida was particularly concerned about her husband's new behaviour and tried to convince him to 'go back to Islam'. Although he promised her many times that he would resume practising at the beginning of each Ramaḍan, he never did. Meanwhile, back in Egypt, Saida's family became aware of the problems she was facing with her husband and one of Saida's brothers decided to approach his brother-in-law's family, whose father was very religious.

Saida, who used to go to the mosque regularly, in particular for the weekly Muslim Women's Circle, was made aware of the gossip concerning her husband. Some Muslim women blamed her for the non-Islamic behaviour of her husband. Gossip about Saida's daughters, who at that time were aged fifteen and seventeen, also started to spread among the Egyptian community. Of course, the behaviour of Saida's husband had affected the reputation of Saida and her daughters; in other words, it had affected Saida's 'honour' as a good Muslim woman, expressed in the function of wife and mother. During one of our interviews, she was very distressed and told me that she was planning to divorce and go back to her family in Egypt, 'How can I feel proud of my husband when he is even unable to achieve respect from his own children?' She stated, 'He has not even the respect of his family in Egypt. He could have money now, but he has lost his Muslim identity and brought shame to everybody, in particular to me and his daughters, who, Inshallah, I hope will still find a good Muslim husband, despite the reputation of their own father.' She then concluded, 'My divorce is justified; I have an Islamic dignity, I am a Muslim woman and I will not compromise any longer'.

Eyad did not bring shame to his family by disrupting the Islamic rules of modesty, something that, according to the Qur'an, not only Muslim women should respect but Muslim men also. By failing to be the 'good Muslim', the responsible Muslim father and husband, and indulging in overtly 'western' behaviours, Eyad had 'brought shame' to his family. The community had noticed that he stopped practising Islam, and this disrupted the reputation that his wife and daughters had enjoyed before.

It is clear that Muslim women have formed a certain model of masculinity, which, like the Muslim men's feminine ideal, is based on Islamic values. There is a relationship between the dynamics of honour and shame between the genders. Both men and women are considered, though in different roles, the guardians of the religion. Honour is not only linked to a respect for gender roles among the members of the family and expected moral behaviours, but femininity and masculinity are charged and embedded with a sanctity which makes them responsible for each other's *dīn*. If this is correct, as I think (yet more research is needed on this subject), it means that the western concept of patriarchy is not useful to a correct analysis of gender in Islam and new approaches, going beyond classic feminist ideologies, are needed.

## THE LAST TABOO: THE NON-HETEROSEXUAL MUSLIMS

If the sexual behaviours of a member of a Muslim family can jeopardize the status, if not the unity, of his or her family,[6] non-heterosexual sexual behaviours are considered – as two non-heterosexual Muslims told me – the most shameful and threatening of all family sins. I met Afra in London while attending a meeting discussing young Muslims and their future. Afra is among the few Muslim women of the group who does not wear a ḥijāb. Furthermore, her haircut, short and punky, vividly contrasted with the few other Muslim women who did not veil, but still had long hair. Afra was neither South Asian nor Arab, but both. Her father was from Lebanon, her mother from Pakistan, and she was born in England. As she explained, 'I have to make sense of many different family traditions, by which sometimes I am confused. This is the reason for which I feel very comfortable to define myself Muslim, though many of them [Muslims] would reject my identity as hypocritical and blasphemous.' The reason the other Muslims might reject her identity became clear to me when she straightforwardly told me, 'I am a Muslim lesbian, you know.'

Afra discovered her non-heterosexuality in her final years of secondary school. At that time, she used to wear the ḥijāb and attend the Muslim women's group of her local mosque. Her mother was particularly religious. She had educated Afra to respect Islam and its practices, such as prayers and Ramaḍan. When Afra felt attracted to some of her female friends, she understood the possible consequences of her sexual orientation. Her first reaction was to increase her practice of Islam to 'avoid temptations'. At nineteen years old, she even considered getting married, but her father was against the idea, since he wished her to finish her studies first. When she began university, she met another woman with whom she started a relationship. Afra went through a crisis of identity, since being Muslim was very important for her. Today Afra, now twenty-five years old, has resolved her non-heterosexual Muslim identity by accepting herself as she is, 'I'm a creature of God, and sexual instincts are part of the human being. God created me in this way, so why should I stop being Muslim? I want to be Muslim, but I have to accept that I can only be a non-heterosexual one.' If Afra has accepted the fact that she is a non-heterosexual Muslim, her mother has not. However, her father, who tended to be more secular in his approach to Islam, commented on her coming out in these words, 'Well, I have still to thank Allah. When you told us you needed to speak to us about a very serious matter, I thought it was about drugs!' By contrast, her mother has not accepted Afra's non-heterosexuality, and the relationship between them was still tense the day I met Afra. To come out, at least with her parents and friends, has helped Afra to avoid the compartmentalization of her identity and life.

Not all non-heterosexual Muslims, however, decide to 'come out' and admit their sexual orientation. Some, like Amjad, a 35-year-old Moroccan living in Scotland, have to cope with a 'double life'. Amjad left Morocco ten years ago and since then he has lived in both England and Scotland. Although Amjad was not 'mosque-going', he respected Islam and defined himself as Muslim. He knew very early in life that he was 'different' and claimed that 'things were even more difficult

in Morocco. People called me the "bint" the girl, because they saw I was different.'
The fact that Amjad was visibly effeminate exposed him to jokes and even physical
attacks. 'I think that my parents knew what was wrong with me. I mean, that I felt
more like a girl.' He told me, 'So, they arranged a marriage which was supposed to
resolve my problem, because Muslim men have to marry and marriage is the main
door of adulthood and, like circumcision, makes you visibly a man.' He married a
cousin, who was five years older than he was. He did not tell her about his sexual
orientation and decided to migrate to Europe to find a job. He left his wife behind
and he usually visits her during the holidays. In Scotland, by contrast, he has non-
heterosexual relationships. Amjad has clearly divided his life into two different
identity spaces. Indeed, as Boellstorff (2005a) has concluded in his research,

> whether *gay* Muslims uphold heteronormativity (e.g., by seeing their homo-
> sexual desires as sinful, marrying heterosexual, or stating that they plan to
> marry) or destabilize it on some level (e.g., by their homosexual desires as
> God given or saying that they will not marry heterosexually), to date no point
> of commensurability between the 'languages' of Islam and *gay* subjectivity
> has been reached. Yet *gay* lives exist and are lived every day; what exists is
> a habitation, not a resolution, of incommensurability. [Yet] This simultaneous
> habitation of the categories *gay* and Muslim is subconsciously incomplete.
> (2005a: 582–3)

Homosexuality has been the most overlooked topic of gender studies within
Muslim societies. Schmiduke has observed,

> The investigation of homosexual practices in Islamic civilization has until
> recently been a closed subject of enquiry. Seeing the history of homosexuality
> as a marginal field, if not an embarrassing and distasteful subject of study,
> Western scholars of Islam and Middle East have either ignored it altogether,
> treated it in occasional footnote or, at worst, misrepresented and judged it on
> the basis of their personal moral convictions. Scarcely any attempt was made
> to go beyond observing overt homosexual behaviour to analyse the social and
> cultural forms of such homosexual activities, whether they were patterned by
> age, gender or class, how they functioned or affected individuals and society
> at large, and what might be the causes of the various forms of homosexuality
> practices. Even among gay historians, the study of the homosexual practices of
> the Middle East was long neglected. (1999: 261)

The lack of information and studies on the topic has brought some of my students
to ask me whether gay and lesbian Muslims ever existed in the history of Islam. So
many of them are surprised when they discover that medieval Christian polemics
represented Islam not only as an overtly sexualized and immodest religion,[7] but also
as a religion tolerant towards – if not inviting to – homosexuality (Daniel 1993).
  This was because, in the Middle Ages, within Arab societies non-heterosexual
behaviours, in particular involving young people, commonly appeared in novels

and poems. Murray and Rose (1997) have provided some historical examples from different provinces of the Ottoman Empire. They seem to suggest that passive non-heterosexual relationships during the teenage years would not have affected the honour of the future adult men. It was considered a form of 'education', which was somewhat similar to how ancient Greeks saw the practice of pederasty. However, if the non-heterosexual behaviour continued beyond the teenage years, people regarded it as a syndrome (Rosenthal 1991) that was very difficult to cure.

Nonetheless, the orthodox interpretations of Islam agree that the Qur'an (through the story of Lot) has condemned non-heterosexual relationships; the sunna condemns it in even harsher terms. Confusion, however, surrounds the correct punishment. Some ḥadiths show the Prophet to be almost tolerant to homoerotic desires; while in others he is described as being very harsh in his request for punishment, which in some cases involved stoning both the culprits to death (Pellat 1992).These differences have marked the divergences on the matter expressed by the different Islamic Schools. Hence, the legislation available in different Islamic countries (Sofer 1992) varies in the level of severity of the punishment. Yet, as I have observed during my research, not all heterosexual Muslims consider non-heterosexual relationships as grievous sins against Islam. Many, in particular living in the west, perceive non-heterosexual Muslims as suffering from identity and sexuality problems – in the best case, a contradiction to be reconciled through Islam.[8]

During the mid 1990s, as Schmiduke (1999) has emphasized in her review article, the study of non-heterosexual Muslims started from historical and literature based research,

> Among the first publications in the field was Bruce W. Dunne's outline of an agenda for historical research on homosexuality in the Middle East (Dunne 1990). It was followed by *Sexuality and eroticism among males in Moslem societies*, a collection edited by Arno Schmitt and Jehodea Sofer (1992), consisting primarily of personal accounts by Western travellers of their disappointing sexual encounters with Arabs and Iranians. In his subsequent *Bio-bibliography of male-male sexuality and eroticism in Muslim societies* (1995), Arno Schmitt provided a wealth of references to Islamic and Western primary and secondary sources dealing with homosexuality and homoeroticism in Islamic civilization. (1999: 260)

In more recent publications, still within the field of history and literature, we find Wright and Rowson (1997) and Murray and Roscoe (1997). The latter publication includes a section entitled *'anthropological studies'*, which discusses non-heterosexual behaviour in some Muslim societies such as Iraq and Indonesia. Unfortunately, the authors have only summarized the studies, the chapters are very short and the analysis still stems from the historical and literary approaches of the previous sections.

Nonetheless, these first studies have increased anthropologists' interest in the study of non-heterosexual Muslims. For example, since 1999, Boellstorff has conducted fieldwork in Indonesia on non-heterosexual Muslims and written interesting ethnographies (1999, 2003, 2004a, 2004b, 2004c, 2005a, 2005b) discussing the relationships that his respondents had with their Muslim non-heterosexual identities. Even more recent is the anthropological study of non-heterosexual ethnic minorities in the west. One of the first scholars to address the subject among the British South Asian community is the anthropologist Kawale (2003). Although Kawale has discussed not only first and second generations of South Asian gays and lesbians but also bisexuals (indeed a novelty), she has, however, focused only on ethnicity. The majority of Kawale's informants might have been Muslims, since they were of Pakistani or Middle Eastern origin, but the difficult relations between religion, ethnicity and non-heterosexual identities have not been explored.

Thus, the researches of Yip (2004a, 2004b, 2004c) and Siraj (2006) are innovative in this respect. In observing Muslim non-heterosexual social interactions with family and peers, Islam, seen as part of the identity formation, becomes the central topic of Yip's and Siraj's analyses. Yip's in-depth study has highlighted the difficulties of the process of combining the two identities. He has observed that non-heterosexual Muslims acknowledge that the Qur'an and ḥadiths reject non-heterosexual relationships; yet the majority have little knowledge of theological arguments. Yip has also found that the majority of non-heterosexual Muslims still practise their religion, though they tend to compartmentalize their lives so as to avoid a possible crisis of identity. Indeed, what Murray and Rose (1997) described in their historical investigation is still a strong argument among contemporary Muslim communities, both in the west and the Islamic world: 'non-heterosexuality is a western disease'. Yet Yip has emphasized how the Muslim communities explain this 'western disease' as the result of an intense exposure to western values, such as individualism and secularism. By contrast, Yip has found that many non-heterosexual Muslims explain their sexual preference as inevitable, since God created them with such a sexual orientation. This has led some of them to reinterpret the Islamic texts in such a way that non-heterosexuality is, if not justified, at least tolerated or not punished.

Yip (2004c) has also emphasized how families of non-heterosexual Muslims see marriage as the most effective 'cure' for their children's sexual preferences. Some non-heterosexual Muslims have given in to pressure to get married. In her study, Siraj has presented an extreme example in which a non-heterosexual Muslim remained married for thirteen years to a woman whom he neither loved nor sexually desired (Siraj 2006: 210–11). Nevertheless, non-heterosexual Muslims living in the west have to face challenges and rejection from not only the Muslim community but also western, white non-heterosexuals. In his research, Yip has shown that the wider non-heterosexual community regard non-heterosexual Muslims as exotic and find their religiosity contradictory. Kawale (2003) and more recently Siraj (2006) have discussed the relevance that support groups have for non-heterosexual Muslims. Indeed, recently social support groups, such as Al-Fatiha and Al-Habaib in London, mainly formed by South Asians, have been active in challenging the orthodox interpretation of non-heterosexuality in Islam.

# CONCLUSION

Islamic texts, in common with those of many other religions, have discussed the relationship between the genders and the position of women and men within their families and societies. Nonetheless, since Islamic texts can only be interpreted, we have found that there exist different opinions on gender in Islam. Although, when we leave aside the theological debate, and we explore the first studies of Muslim societies (see Geertz 1968; Gellner 1981; Gilsenan 1982) we find evidence of a disinterest towards the study of gender, and the 'veil' soon became the symbol of often futile debates about the alleged oppression of women by Islam, instead of by Muslims. During the 1970s, feminist scholars, both Muslim and non, applied feminist analysis to different aspects of the life of women in Islam. Though some ethnographic studies were included within their discussions (see, for instance, Mernissi 1975) the Qur'an and the ḥadiths were still seen as the main sources for explaining the behaviour of Muslim men towards Muslim women. Many of these studies, by essentializing gender in Islam, have overlooked other important aspects of gender, such as masculinity. Yet feminist scholars have, until recently,[9] sacrificed relevant subjective elements such as emotions and the identity formation of Muslim women to a discussion of Islam as a patriarchal power.

This approach has also affected the first studies of gender in Islam in a migration context. French scholars have been among the first to study this topic (Tribalat 1995; Souilamas 2000; Lacoste-Dujardin 2002). Yet two elements affected their analysis. First, they accepted the main western feminist viewpoint that Islam, as religion, empowers men who then oppress Muslim women. So, the disempowerment of Muslim migrant men, particularly in their role as the breadwinner father, has, according to these French scholars, the positive side effect of emancipating, often through divorce, Muslim migrant women and their children. As Lutz (1991) has suggested, these ethnocentric views are based on the idea that western processes of female emancipation should be universal. Secondly, Mozzo-Counil (1994), a social worker who conducted an ethnographic study of North African Muslim women in France, has emphasized in her interesting, though almost unknown study the relevance that emotions, feelings and memories have in understanding gender and Islam. Mozzo-Counil's book focuses on the human aspect, disclosing the emotions and thought processes these women went through. The sentiments of these women as well as their complex psychological relationships with their own bodies *become* part of Mozzo-Counil's narration and argument. She has reminded the anthropologist that, 'the Maghribi women of the first generation communicate through their bodies, the cry of their suffering bodies, the joy of their dancing bodies' and through them the experience of their immigration (1994: 9, translation from French is mine). Indeed, some of Mozzo-Counil's respondents have suffered depression and isolation because of immigration. Yet the emancipation of some of them has only worsened their social and economic position, instead of improving their lives. Mozzo-Counil could present a more complex picture of the lives of Muslim women because she recognized the relevance that women's networks played in the pre-migration lives of these women and the impossibility of re-creating those models of solidarity that her informants enjoyed in their homeland. So, for instance, Ganguly has recognized that women's memory plays an important role in making sense of their migration:

> The recollections of the past serve as the active ideological terrain on which people represent themselves to themselves. The past acquires a more marked salience with subjects for whom categories of the present have been made unusually unstable or unpredictable as a consequence of the displacement enforced by postcolonial and migrant circumstances. (Ganguly 1997: 29–30)

This also means considering that both Muslim men and women, both heterosexual and non, are today part of a complex network of local and global dimensions (Featherstone, Lash and Featherstone 1995).

However, if the study of gender in Islam focusing on women has increasingly developed in different directions, this is not the case for the study of masculinity. Social scientists, and in particular anthropologists, have for many years overlooked the relevance that the study of masculinity has to the understanding of the dynamics of genders in Islam. Gender, in other words, has meant only the study of women. Only recently, under the influence of gender studies, have social scientists started to answer the question: 'What does it mean to be a Muslim man?' (Lahoucine 2006) As in the case of Muslim women, these studies have, again, focused primarily on the Middle East and other Muslim societies. More studies are required in the field of migration, in which, as Pels (2000) has demonstrated, different and difficult social contexts challenge masculine Muslim identities. Yet the most overlooked topic within gender studies in Islam has certainly been the study of non-heterosexual Muslims. Non-heterosexual practices in Islamic countries attracted the attention of medieval Christian polemicists, who used them to demonstrate the licentiousness of Islam. Yet it was only at the end of the 1990s that anthropologists started extensive fieldwork on the topic. Even more recent is the sociological and anthropological research on non-heterosexual Muslims in the west. However, topics such as the relationship between non-heterosexual Muslims and the mainstream non-heterosexual community are still at a pioneering level.

Further research is certainly needed. Though, from a critical analysis of some relevant examples of the available research on gender and Islam, we can observe that for a contemporary anthropological approach it is fundamental to observe the *dynamics* of gender. This means taking into consideration how femininity *and* masculinity are understood within the social cultural context, and, in contrast to the more traditional approaches, the role that the dynamics among genders play in shaping, through identities, Islam.

## *NOTES*

1. For critical discussions of gender and colonialism, see Fee 1974; Rogers 1978; Etienne and Leacock 1980; Ahmed 1992.

2. For an interesting criticism of Mernissi's approach see Varisco 2005: 81–113.

3. For an extended bibliography: Kimball and von Schlegel 1997.

4. The list of panels and the titles of presented papers during international conferences on Middle East, or Islam, confirm this trend.

5. The honour and shame theory suggests that in certain societies men's honour depends on their ability to control women's sexuality. Extreme attempts to control and regulate the sexuality of the family's women can lead to some men performing honour killings in the hope of re-establishing their forfeited honour.

6. In some disgraceful circumstances this can extend to the lives of some of its members, such as in the case of honour killings.

7. For a discussion of medieval representations of Muhammad as a licentious prophet, see Roded 2006.

8. For similar findings, see also Kawale 2003; Yip 2004a, 2004b, 2004c; Boellstorff 2005; Siraj 2006.

9. For an interesting study which takes into consideration emotions, identities and personality, see the interesting contemporary approach of Miriam Cooke (2001) to the life of Muslim women.

## CHAPTER 9

# Conclusion

## *ELENCHOS II*

STUDENT: After this journey through anthropological studies on Islam and Muslims, what have we learnt?

ANTHROPOLOGIST: That there are as many methodologies, theories and ideas on what Islam might be, what Muslim societies are, and how fieldwork should be conducted, as there are anthropologists debating them.

STU: A common project would surely be useful, in particular today, with all this turmoil surrounding Islam and the Muslim world.

ANT: I don't think we can reach an agreement about what the anthropology of Islam might be. I have only suggested that we need to reconsider how we study Muslims to avoid recurrent essentialisms.

STU: Like the one about women in Islam?

ANT: Yes, this is a good example that we have discussed before. Many studies, though sometimes not openly, continue to ask whether Islam oppresses Muslim women or not.

STU: Don't you think this is a question anthropologists may answer?

ANT: This is just a faulty question, and trying to answer it would provide a faulty answer. Unfortunately, we have no shortage of faulty reasoning on Islam.

STU: What do you mean by faulty reasoning?

ANT: We can only learn Islam through the people who practise it or discuss it, or through books, which, however, somebody should read and understand. Indeed, I learned how Muslims pray for the first time from Abd al-Kader, the salesman, the Qur'an and ḥadiths from Abd al Hādī, the imam, and the rest from different books I have read, but understood through the use of my mind. An abstract Islam does not exist. Muslims, through the faculties common to any human mind, provide interpretations, explanations, accounts and descriptions. What I have called discourses.

STU: So, you agree with el-Zein that Islam should be contextualized or it does not exist.

ANT: I have argued that what we call Islam is a map of these discourses. This is different from saying that Islam does not exist without a determined context. At least it exists as cognitive map in the minds of those who feel to be Muslims.

STU: So are anthropologists studying the map or Muslims? Sometimes it seems that they focus on Islam, others on Muslims societies, but then again, some present it as shaped by Islam as doctrine. It is not clear what the anthropology of Islam is studying. I have the impression that it is floating between total relativism and total essentialism.

ANT: For decades, anthropologists did not try to discuss the complexity of studying Islam. In many cases, the solution was to divide the field in two: the little traditions of the Sufis and the great traditions of the Ulemas. Some influential scholars, such as Geertz and Gellner, have definitely mistaken the map for the territory. Also, we have to notice that the study of Islam has been subjected to a thematization led more by ideological and political interests than by purely academic ones. These are what Abu-Lughod has referred to as 'zones of theorizing'.

STU: I'm surprised, Doc. Anthropologists conduct fieldwork, stay with people and take part in their lives. So how could they confuse the map with the territory?

ANT: Because some of them observed the territory through another powerful discourse, the discourse of culture, and others among them ended up essentializing it.

STU: Well, culture is fundamental to anthropological studies. I don't think we can avoid discussing it.

ANT: Everything depends on how we define culture, and I am very convinced that the recent research suggesting that culture is a part of nature, and not an exception, is on the right track. But, in any case, if you essentialize culture, you end up stripping human beings of their basic universal elements. So, the Muslim is reduced to a vehicle of expression for symbols forming the culture.

STU: Maybe it is for this reason that reading classic anthropological studies of Islam, I have not found the voices behind the anthropologist's voices.

ANT: Essentialism may blind even the most skilled and sophisticated anthropologist. Geertz, Gellner and Mernissi, for example, wanted to understand Islam, and not what they saw as just a product of it, the Muslims.

STU: Why did anthropological methodologies, such as fieldwork and participant observation, not prevent this?

ANT: Anthropological fieldwork, like any other methodology, has its history. Time changes many things, and studies are the offspring of the intellectual environment in which they developed. The studies you have mentioned are sons and daughters of the 1960s and 1970s. Anthropologists who decided to study Muslim societies needed to establish and reaffirm their identity within the discipline, since it was challenged by two powerful fields of studies, the traditional Islamic studies and, more recently, Middle East studies. In the process of exalting culture and making it the Holy Grail of the discipline, some anthropologists, finding refuge solely in symbolic interpretations, submerged informants' emotions, ideas and sense of self. I have suggested that we need to reconsider how emotions and feelings are part of fieldwork.

STU: Students in anthropology are still taught fieldwork methodologies as if they would research Muslim societies only in Islamic countries. I want to study Muslims in the west, but there are not many possibilities to learn from the experiences of other anthropologists or from handbooks.

ANT: Unfortunately, this is true. However, today we have to overcome the idea of exotic fieldwork and 'home' fieldwork. Today we cannot understand Islam and Muslims without taking into consideration the global dimensions. In certain cases, fieldwork can be only trans-local, whereas in others we have to pay attention to the networks linking the communities within Islamic and western countries. Yet in many universities, we are still discussing and teaching fieldwork as anthropologists in the 1970s did.

STU: I came across your blog and also the blogs of people who were part of your research. Is it not strange to see comments on your research and memories about you made public by your informants during fieldwork?

ANT: After September 11, we have to face the fact that the anthropologists of Islam and their research are more and more public. The expansion of the Internet, forum and blog, not only challenges us with exciting new possibilities, but also with an unprecedented visibility to our future informants and respondents. The power relationship between the anthropologist and the informant, or the studied community, should be reconsidered.

STU: Like identity?

ANT: I strongly think that identity is at the centre of anthropological research on Muslim and Islam today. I do not want to say that this is the blueprint that we miss, but surely is a gravitational centre of many contemporary studies.

STU: Why?

ANT: During the 1980s, as we have seen, many anthropologists considered the identity, for instance, of Muslim migrants and their children as shaped by cultural differences. So, while the parents had to pass, say, from culture A to culture B, their children, born in culture B but educated within culture A, had to resolve the A/B dichotomy or their in-between identity.

STU: Surely, the children suffered a crisis of identity.

ANT: I think that we should be very careful lest we continue the pathologization of western-born Muslims. First of all, we should not consider any culture as a monolithic reality. Western culture in itself does not exist, it is just another map of discourses. Second, cultures, in the west or any Islamic country, are affected by globalization. People do not live in A or B, but in an environment shaped by multi-contexts. Third, we cannot impose a culture upon some people only because they were born in a certain context or within certain religious traditions.

STU: So, can we study Muslim identity avoiding the risk of essentialism?

ANT: I think so. It is important to acknowledge how each person defines himself or herself. Yet it is also true that I hardly ever found Muslims saying 'I am not a Muslim', even though they did not respect the code of conduct that people expect Muslims to respect, such as not drinking alcohol. 'Are they Muslims?' I have been often asked. Of course they are, because they feel to be Muslim.

Identity is an imaginary machinery that makes sense of and provides a sense of unity to the autobiographical self. It is a process affected by emotions and feelings, by the relationship with environment. Anthropologists should focus more on the *feeling to be*, how it is formed, and the ways in which it is expressed and maintained.

STU: But it seems that anthropologists studying Muslims, particularly in the west, have focused on some aspects but not others. For example, I have been surprised at the number of studies on Islam and gender. Just out of curiosity, I noticed that in Google Scholar 'Muslim women' has 9,100 entries, 'Muslim men' 2,500, 'veil and Islam' 8,690, 'hijab and Islam' 1,540, while there is no mention of any study mentioning men's clothing, as part of identity, or masculinity as a research topic.

ANT: Well, here again is the thematization that I was referring to before. We have seen that Orientalists, in their novels, paintings and scholarly research, found the theme of femininity and women in Islam extremely ero-exotic. Colonialism reinforced the myth of North Africa, East Asia and Indian women as erotic mystery, between veil and seduction. Anthropologists, during the 1960s and 1970s, were not immune from these Orientalist influences, as Rabinow's *Reflections on Fieldwork in Morocco* can show.

STU: But feminist anthropologists have tried to deconstruct these Orientalist views.

ANT: Yes they did; but again some still ended in the trap of essentialism. The symbols, such as the ḥijāb, became the focus. Many of these anthropologists, finally, found themselves entangled in a political, sometimes ideological, diatribe about whether it is right or wrong to ban the veil or ḥijāb. The focus of gender in Islam, or better the dynamics among genders within Muslim communities, has remained largely overlooked. So, I think that as anthropologists of Islam we need to refocus on the dynamics of gender, which include, of course, the over-neglected aspect of masculinity.

STU: Once, while surfing the Internet for research, I came across a website called Imaan[1] organized by gay and lesbian Muslims. However, I have not found much academic research on this topic.

ANT: The research available is very recent. This is a quite difficult topic, since many Muslims reject the fact that some of their co-religionists can be non-heterosexual and still claim that they are Muslim. The majority of Muslims tend to interpret non-heterosexuality as a sort of disease, often of western origins. Therefore, it is important for a contemporary anthropology of Islam to focus on identity as the 'feeling to be'. If a non-heterosexual personal *feels* to be Muslim, it is from this *feeling* that we, as anthropologists, should start despite the fact that other Muslims may deny Muslim gay identity as such.

STU: So, if we cannot study Islam in itself, but rather the different discourses of those who feel to be Muslims, how can we speak of a Muslim community? The ummah does not exist; it is just a religious category!

ANT: Ask any Arab Muslim if he or she considers a Bangladeshi Muslim a brother or sister, and surely the answer will be a wholehearted yes. Yet, ask Mr Iqbal, or Afra, his wife, if they consider Bilal, the Bangladeshi owner of the Indian restaurant on the corner, a brother in Islam, and they may say that he is not. The reason? Although Bilal does not drink, he sells and serves alcohol. For the Salafi couple, Bilal is not just a bad Muslim, but a hypocrite, worse than a non-Muslim. During my research, I have collected much evidence of theological, ethnic and racial divisions within the same local Muslim community. Scholars have often employed the terms 'Muslim community' and 'ummah' as we might use nation. However, the ummah, as a real entity does not exist...

STU: Then, is the ummah just a theological utopia?

ANT: Well, the point is that in certain circumstances we have some evidence that, despite the divisions and sectarianism, Muslims are able to act as one community, without the need of a recognized leader. You have probably read about the Rushdie Affair, and surely you have seen on TV the global protests against the French ban on Islamic scarves and the more recent Danish Cartoon Controversy.

STU: Yes, there has been an incredible mass protest by Muslims all over the world. Also there was a boycott of Danish products, I remember that a Muslim friend of mine told me that he used to receive text messages inviting the ummah to the boycott.

ANT: So, there is a sense of unity, of belonging, which, however, is not expressed through a single charismatic leader. For this reason, I have suggested that the *ummah* is (1) a community of feelings, (2) based on a religious Bund, (3) characterized by a shared basic ethos (i.e. belief in the shahāda and tawhīd), (4) expressed through a diffused charisma.

STU: This has been a journey through opinions about what Muslims and Islam might be. Yet, at the end, I still do not know what the anthropologist of Islam is.

ANT: There is no blueprint or paradigm, but only open trajectories.

## OPEN TRAJECTORIES

Gilsenan (1990) has described the reactions, at the end of the 1960s, of his fellow anthropologists when he selected the Middle East as a fieldwork location and Islam as research. His research was considered eccentric at best, or not 'real' anthropology at worst. At the time, some of his colleagues saw the study of urban Islam as a part of Islamic studies. Being one of the three main monotheistic religions, which have canonized theologies and written revelations, Islam was less attractive for anthropologists than tribal, oral traditions. So, following Redfield's popular classification between 'great traditions' and 'little traditions' (1956: 70), the very few anthropologists studying Muslim societies found refuge in the villages, among Sufi saints, members of *ṭuruq* (pl. of *ṭarīqa*, Sufi order), kinships and folklore. Classical studies, such as Geertz (1968) and Gellner (1981), explained Muslim societies as developing from the tension between the two traditions, in which the great tradition, based on scripturalism, led to fundamentalist visions of Islam

(Zubaida 2003). However, the division between little and great traditions, as a typology of Islam, and the focus on Islam as a cultural symbolic system able to shape Muslim life facilitated essentialism in the anthropological study of Islam, which was unusual within anthropology of religion (see Chapter 3).

If the 'exotic' studies of Muslim communities suffered from essentialist views which interpreted the social structure and political organization of Muslim societies as a direct result of theological aspects, more recent studies of Muslims in the west suffer from essentialist views which interpret Muslim identity as a by-product of Islam, as religion (see Chapter 4). Throughout *The Anthropology of Islam*, we have observed that essentialism has affected how Muslim societies and communities have been studied. Some anthropologists have tried, during the last thirty years, to question how we, as anthropologists, research, analyse and represent Islam. El-Zein (1977) directly addressed his criticism against the theological and, from a different standpoint, the anthropological views rejecting that 'The concept of Islam thus defined the nature of the subject matter and its appropriate modes of interpretation or explanation' (1977: 227). Asad (1986a) has rejected el-Zein's position that 'Islam as an analytical category dissolves' (el-Zein 1977: 252) and proposed that Islam should be studied as a tradition, with the consequence that 'there clearly is not, nor can there be, such a thing as a universally acceptable account of a living tradition. Any representation of tradition is contestable' (Asad 1986a: 16).

El-Zein and Asad wrote their essays in an attempt to spark a discussion aimed at clarifying a field of research that was developing without clear directions. Yet during the 1980s some Muslim anthropologists (see, for instance, Mahroof 1981 and Ahmed 1986) embarked upon the project of formulating an Islamic anthropology. In other words, if the anthropology of Islam developed from the experience of fieldwork within Muslim societies, Islamic anthropology started as a blueprint. However I have shown that in the efforts to characterize the new field with a distinctive identity from western anthropology, Ahmed's project became phagocytized by its theological emphasis. Lukens-Bull (1999), finally, has suggested that we have to start from where Muslims start Islam. Although he has argued that anthropologists have to observe the 'how' of Muslim submission and practice to respect God's will, I still feel that this does not provide a paradigm for the anthropology of Islam. Others, like Donnan (2002) have tried to suggest that whatever Muslims say about Islam is Islam. However, is this self-definition epistemologically satisfactory? Take the example of the concept of ummah (Chapter 7), should an anthropologist just stop at an emic definition? I think that emic definitions are the base of etic analysis, and not the other way around. Finally, Varisco (2005), at the end of a timely and challenging critical review of the 'classic' literature on the anthropology of Islam, has adopted a definitely anti-essentialist position. He has rightly reminded us that a definition of Islam would have little value for anthropologists, since it is what Muslims do and explaining why they do things differently that is relevant. Culture, Varisco has emphasized, is at the centre of the anthropological study, since 'anthropologists inevitably must go beyond the ethnographic context observed to a broader comparative understanding of how every given human act relates to the potential for specifically human interaction' (2005: 162).

In *The Anthropology of Islam*, we have observed some of the trajectories that anthropologists studying Islam have followed and developed. Some of them derived from a specific approach to fieldwork (Chapter 5) and ethnography, others start from philosophical and political instances, like the feminist studies of gender and Islam (Chapter 8), and yet others from social issues, as in the case of migration (Chapter 4). Yet all these studies, consciously or by default, point towards two fundamental aspects: identity and community. Nonetheless, few of these studies ever clarified how they defined these two concepts. They are often considered self-evident or just common sense (chapters 6 and 7). Expressions such as 'Muslim community', 'ummah', 'Muslim minority' and 'Muslim generations', to mention just some, are overused within academic works. The main reason for this is the formation of a 'jargon', a certain number of keywords, which simplify, through generalization, the necessity of reflection on the context. Very few anthropologists, I am sure, will be ready to persevere in arguing that there may exist something called Muslim community, ummah or Muslim minority.

The genesis of *The Anthropology of Islam* rests not in the attempt to assert what the anthropology of Islam should be, but rather in an effort aimed at starting a reflexive debate among scholars and students. I have suggested, throughout this book, that we, anthropologists, should study human beings rather than just adjectives. This can appear to be a futile or obvious statement. Yet throughout the chapters of this book, readers can find evidence of the level of abstraction, generalization and essentialization existing even in recent studies concerning Islam and Muslims. The adjectives – being religious, national, ethnic – often came first. After September 11, the war on terror (which, like any war, could only be a war on people), the consequent destabilization of not only political equilibrium, but also interfaith relationships, raises new challenges to the anthropological study of Islam. Indeed, our studies are inevitably political even when just ethnographic; they may become part – despite the intention of the researcher (see Chapter 7) – of the uncontrolled mosaic of stereotypes and rhetoric addressing the wrong question: 'what went wrong with Islam?' or even 'what is wrong with Islam?' For instance, the attempt to answer the question 'what is wrong with Islam?' has prevented the development of gender studies on Islam capable of observing the existing dynamics between expression of gender and sexuality (Chapter 8). One the one hand, Muslim women were sometimes reduced to their wardrobe, while on the other, Muslim non-heterosexual identities were neglected, since they remained highly opposed and unrecognized within orthodox Islam. So, the anthropology of Islam cannot only be based on what we can learn from Muslims (Donnan 2002) or from what the majority of Muslims say about Islam within specific contexts (el-Zein 1977), or else we risk neglecting those experiences of Islam that are in contradiction with mainstream interpretations. It is my contention, as I have explained throughout this book, that the starting point to avoid social scientifically unproductive essentialism is to go beyond symbolic reductionism.

I have argued that human identity is related to the self and environment, through emotions and feelings. Yet, the discussion about emotions and feelings has had no real debate within the anthropological study of Muslims. By contrast, I believe that a person is not Muslim because of reading the Qur'an, following the different Islamic theological instances, or because of being born Muslim, but rather because a person *feels to be Muslim*. It is this feeling – as a product of the relationship between emotions and environment – that the anthropology of Islam can contribute to the understanding of the different dynamics of Muslim life. Indeed, starting from this view, which is just another open trajectory, we can reconsider Islam not as *a tradition*, but rather as a map of discourses derived from the different ways of feeling to be Muslim.

## NOTES

1. The organization website is http://www.imaan.org.uk/

# Glossary

**adhān**: Muslim call to prayer.

**al-ḥajar al-aswad**: The Black Stone embedded in the south-eastern corner of the *ka'ba*. The origin of the stone is debated but Muslims believe it is a divine meteorite, which fell at the feet of Adam and Eve.

**al-Jabhah al-Islāmiyah lil-Inqādh**: The Islamic Salvation Front, the most important Islamist movement in Algeria which won the first turn of parliamentary elections in 1991, forcing the Algerian army to stop the elections. The consequence was one of the most bloodthirsty civil wars of modern times.

**al-jum'a**: Congregational prayers, of which the most important for Muslims is the *yawm al-jum'a*, the Friday prayer which is introduced by a sermon.

**al-salām 'alaykum**: 'Peace be upon you'. This is the usual greeting among Muslims.

**arkāna al-islam**: The five pillars of Islam.

**āyat**: The Arabic word means 'sign' and it used to refer to the verses of the Qur'an. Muslims believe that each word of the Qur'an is a 'sign' of God (i.e. a miracle).

**burqu'**: A Muslim woman's outfit that is very common among certain Afghan tribes (e.g. Pashtun). It has become particularly well known since the Taliban imposed it on all Afghan women.

**chābi**: Very popular urban musical genre in Algeria. The texts of the songs, often in Algerian or Moroccan dialects, often narrate the suffering of migration, love and marginalization.

**chādor**: A Persian word indicating a Muslim female garment, used in particular in Iran after the revolution. It is composed of a full-length semi-circle of fabric open down the front. Women have to throw it over their head and hold it shut in front by the hands.

**dīn**: Semitic word often translated as 'religion'. In the Qur'an, Islam itself is often described as dīn. In other words it is linked to the idea of submission to God and respect of the *sharī'a*.

**dunyā**: Another word that is very difficult to translate into English. Often used by Arab Muslims as translation of the word 'secularism', it indicates, in opposition to the realm of the spirit, the realm of the material world.

**dustur al-medinah**: The Constitution of Medina, one of the first known constitutions. The constitution regulated the relationships among the community living under Muhammad's leadership in Medina.

**fatwā**: A word meaning legal opinion or view. The term became common in western mass media usage after Ayatollah Khomeini's death sentence against Rushdie. Yet, legally speaking, Khomeini's sentence was not, from an Islamic legal viewpoint, a fatwā.

**ghusl**: A complete ritual shower to be performed before a prayer to purify a person from major body impurity.

**hijra**: Indicates the migration towards Medina that Muhammad performed to save the new religion and its followers from persecution. Officially this started the Muslim calendar so that hijra also means Islamic year.

**ḥadith**: The sayings of the Prophet transmitted by his followers through a chain of narration. Depending on how trustworthy the chain is considered, the *ḥadith* may be considered *ṣaḥīḥ* (sound), *ḥasan* (fair), *ḍaʿīf* (weak) or *saqīm* (infirm, i.e. false).

**ḥajj**: The pilgrimage to Mecca that Muslims have to perform at least once in their lives. During the ḥajj, the pilgrims re-enact Abraham's and his wife's actions.

**ḥijāb**: Traditional and widespread Muslim headscarf.

**ifṭār**: Indicates the ritual of breaking the fast during *ramāḍan*. Normally this is performed by eating three dates and drinking some water or milk.

**ijmāʿ**: The consensus of the scholars in Islamic jurisprudence.

**iḥrām**: The word has two meanings: (1) the state of sacredness that Muslims enter into during the ḥajj, (2) the special garments that Muslim men dress in, symbolically marking the link between the ḥajj and the final journey after death. Indeed, a Muslim who has performed the ḥajj will be buried in his *iḥrām*.

**ijtihād**: The individual legal opinion of a scholar, who starting from previous laws and past events exercises an independent judgement. The opposite of *ijtihād* is *taqlīd*, imitation.

**īmān'**: Indicates faith and right belief. The word is also associated with what a person feels in his/her heart about Islam in contrast with what he or she actually says.

**isnād**: The chain of narrators of the actions and sayings of Muhammad. The *isnād* is used to validate or question the trustworthiness of an *ḥadith*.

**id al-adhā**: The feast of the sacrifice to remember the story of Isaac. It also marks the end of ḥajj.

**ʿīd al-fiṭr**: The feast of breaking the ramāḍan fast.

**ʿidda**: The legal Islamic waiting period that follows a woman's divorce or the death of her husband before she can marry again. Normally the length of time is equivalent to three menstrual cycles.

**jāhillyya**: Pre-Islamic times that were affected by idolatry.

**jamarah**: The stone pillars representing the devil at which pilgrims throw small stones at the start of id al-adhā. *Jimar* refers to the small pebbles that pilgrims collect. There are three pillars, known as the greatest, the middle and the smallest. They are in Mina and face the direction of Mecca.

**kaʿba**: A cube-shaped building at the centre of the Holy Mosque, the kaʿba is the holiest structure in Islam and some Muslims consider it to be the centre of the world. The kaʿba is the qibla, the direction in which Muslims perform prayer.

**khilāf**: Head of the Islamic community.

**khitān**: Circumcision.

**laylat-al-Qadr**: The Night of Power or the Night of Decree. This is the most important night in the Islamic year, and it is celebrated during the 26th and 27th of the month of *ramāḍan*. The night celebrates Allah's revelation of the Qur'an to Muhammad (see Sura *al-Qadr* 97).

**madhāhib**: A word meaning 'schools of thought'. The four main Sunni schools are the *ḥanafīs*, *mālikis*, *shāfi'īs*, and *ḥanbalīs*, which have been named after their founders.

**mahr**: The gift, often a considerable amount of money, that a groom has to pay to his future spouse.

**nikāh**: Contract which makes the marriage valid.

**qibla**: Direction of the prayer toward the *ka'ba*.

**rak'a**: A full cycle of standing–bowing–prostrating–standing forming the Muslim prayer (*ṣalāt*).

**ramāḍan**: The month of the fast, and the holiest month of the Islamic calendar.

**rasūl**: Messenger, envoy, apostle.

**shahāda**: The Muslim profession of faith.

**shahīd**: Derived from the verb 'to witness', it indicates a person who sacrifices his life for Islam (i.e. martyr).

**sharī'a**: Islamic law

**shaykh**: Title of a Muslim religious leader and scholar.

**sīrah:** Biography and stories related to the Prophet and part of the sunna.

**sunna**: The narrated tradition of the actions and sayings of the Prophet. It is composed of *sīrahs* and *ḥadith*. Before Islam, the sunna referred to the traditions of the tribe.

**ṣāhib**: The word means 'friend' and normally indicates Muhammad's companions.

**ṣalāt al-janazah**: Special prayer (*ṣalāt*) performed during funerals.

**ṣalāt**: Prayer. The Muslim prayer is performed at specific times of the day marked by the position of the Sun. These times are called *ṣalāt al-fajr* (morning prayer), *ṣalāt al-'aṣr* (midday prayer), *ṣalāt al-maghrib* (sunset prayer) and *ṣalāt al-'isha'* (night prayer). The Muslim prayer consists of certain specific movements coordinated with recitation of the Qur'an and sentences exalting Allah.

**sawm**: The word means 'fasting', and the most important fast for Muslims is that of the *ramāḍan* month.

**tajwīd**: The rules guiding the proper recitation of the Qur'an.

**tawhīd**: The absolute oneness of God.

**thobe:** Traditional Islamic tunic.

**talāq**: Islamic divorce.

**tawāf:** Ritual that is part of the *ḥajj* consisting of walking around the *ka'ba* seven times.

**ummah**: The community of all Muslims and believers in one God.

**wuqūf**: The act of standing on the Plain of 'Arafa. It is considered one of the most important parts of *the ḥajj*.

**Zakāt**: Means both 'purification' and 'growth' and refers to the amount of money that all adult Muslims, financially able, have to pay to support specific categories of people, who may also be non-Muslims.

# References

Abadan-Unat, N. (1977), 'Implications of migration on emancipation and pseudo-emancipation of Turkish women', *International Migration Review* 11(1): 31–57.

Abbas, T. (ed.) (2005), *Muslim Britain: Communities under Pressure*, London: Zed Books.

Abdulrahim, D. (1993), 'Defining Gender in a Second Exile: Palestinian Women in West Berlin', in G. Buijs (ed.), *Migrant Women*, Oxford: Berg, pp. 55–82.

Abu-Lughod, L. (1986), *Veiled Sentiments: Honor and Poetry in a Bedouin Society*, Berkeley: University of California Press.

Abu-Lughod, L. (1989), 'Zones of Theory in the Anthropology of the Arab World', *Annual Review of Anthropology* 8: 267–306.

Adler, P. A. and Adler, P. (1987), *Membership Roles in Fieldwork Research*, Newbury Park, CA: Sage.

Afshar, H. (1989), 'Education: Hopes, Expectations, and Achievements of Muslim Women in West Yorkshire', *Gender and Education* 1(3): 261–72.

Ahmed, A. S. (1984), 'Defining Islamic Anthropology', *Rain* 65: 2–4.

Ahmed, A. S. (1986), *Toward Islamic Anthropology: Definition, Dogma and Directions*, Herndon, VA: International Institute of Islamic thought.

Ahmed, A. S. (1988), *Discovering Islam: Making Sense of Muslim History and Society*, London: Routledge.

Ahmed, A. S. (2002), *Discovering Islam: Making Sense of Muslim History and Society,* revised edition, New York: Routledge.

Ahmed, L. (1992), *Women and Gender in Islam*, New Haven and London: Yale University Press.

Ahsan, M. M. (1998), 'Teaching Islam to Pupils in British Schools', *Muslim Educational Quarterly* 6(1): 6–14.

Akbar, M. J. (2002), *The Shade of Swords: Jihad and the Conflict between Islam and Christianity*, London: Routledge.

Akpinar, A. (2003), 'The Honour/Shame Complex Revisited: Violence against Women in the Migration Context', *Women's Studies International Forum* 26(5): 425–42.

Akre, J. (1974), 'Emigration Impact on a Turkish Village: a Personal Account', *Migration News* 6: 17–19.

Al-Ahsan, A. (1992), *Ummah or Nation? Identity Crisis in Contemporary Muslim Society,* London: Islamic Foundation.

Aldrich, H. (1981), 'Business Development and Self-Segregation: Asian Enterprise in Three British Cities', in C. Peach, V. Robinson, and S. Smith (eds), *Ethnic Segregation in Cities*, London: Croom Helm, pp.170–92.

AlSayyad, N. and Castells, M. (2002), *Muslim Europe or Euro-Islam: Culture and citizenship in the age of globalization*, Lanham: United Press of America.

Amit, V. (ed.) (2002), *Realizing Community, Concepts, Social Relationships and Sentiments*, New York: Routledge.

Anderson, B. (1991), *Imagined Communities: Reflections on the Origin and Spread of Nationalism*, London and New York: Verso.

Anderson, E. (1978), *A Place on the Corner*, Chicago: University of Chicago Press.

Anderson, J. W. (1984), 'Conjuring with Ibn Khaldun: From an Anthropological Point of View', in B. B. Lawrence (ed.), *Ibn Khaldun and Islamic Ideology*, Leiden: Brill, pp. 111–12.

Andezian, S. (1988), 'Migrant Muslim women in France', in T. Gerholm and Y. G. Lithman (eds), *The New Islamic Presence in Western Europe*, London and New York: Mansell Publishing Ltd, pp. 196–204.

Anwar, M. (1976), *Between Two Cultures: A study of the Relationships between Generations in the Asian community in Britain*, London: Community Council.

Anwar, M. (1979), *The Myth of Return: Pakistanis in Britain,* London: Heinemann.

Anwar, M. (1982), *Young Muslims in a Multi-Cultural Society: Their Educational Needs and Policy Implications*, London: The Islamic Foundation.

Anwar, M. (1984), 'Employment patterns of Muslims in Western Europe', *Journal: Institute of Muslim Minority Affairs* 5(1): 99–122.

Anwar, M. (1990), 'Muslims in Britain: some recent developments', *Journal: Institute of Muslim Minority Affairs* 11, (2) 347–61.

Appadurai, A. (1995), 'The Production of Locality', in R. Fardon (ed.), *Counterworks: Managing the Diversity of Knowledge,* London: Routledge, pp. 204–25.

Appadurai, A. (1996), *Modernity at large. Cultural dimensions of globalization,* Minneapolis: University of Minnesota Press.

Archer, L. (2001), '"Muslim Brothers, Black Lads, Traditional Asian": British Muslim Young Men's Constructions of Race, Religion and Masculinity', *Feminism & Psychology*, 11(1): 79–105.

Archer, L. (2002), 'Change, Culture and Tradition: British Muslim Pupils Talk about Muslim Girls' post-16 "Choice"', *Race, Ethnicity, and Education* 5(4): 359–76.

Arendell, T. (1997), 'Reflections on the Researcher-Researched Relationship: A Woman Interviewing Men', *Qualitative Sociology* 20(3): 341–68.

Armstrong, K. (2002), *Islam: A Short History*, revised edition, New York: Modern Library.

Aronowitz, A. (1998), 'Acculturation and Delinquency Among Second-Generation Turkish Youths in Berlin', *Migration* 4: 5–36.

Asad, M. (1980), *The Message of the Quran,* Gibraltar: Dar al-Andalus.

Asad, T. (1986a), 'The Concept of Cultural Translation in British Social Anthropology' in J. Clifford, and G. Marcus (eds), *Writing Culture: the Poetic and Politics of Ethnography*, Berkeley: University of California Press, pp. 141–64.

Asad, T. (1986b), *The Idea of an Anthropology of Islam*, Washington DC: Centre for Contemporary Arab Studies.

Asad, T. (1990), 'Ethnography, Literature, and Politics: Some Readings and Uses of Salman Rushdie's *The Satanic Verses*', *Cultural Anthropology* 5(3): 239–69.

Ashmore, D. R. and Jussin, L. (eds) (1997), *Self and Identity*, New York and Oxford: Oxford University Press.

Austin, G. (1996), 'Beur Cinema', in *Contemporary French Cinema: An Introduction*, Manchester and New York: Manchester University Press, pp. 42–6.

Baca Zinn, M. (1979), 'Field Research in Minority Communities: Ethical, Methodological, and Political Observations by an Insider', *Social Problems* 27: 209–19.

Barclay, H. (1969), 'The Perpetuation of Muslim Tradition in the Canadian North', *Muslim World* 59: 64–73.

Baring, E. (Earl of Cromer) (1908), *Modern Egypt*, New York: Macmillan.

Baron, B. (1994), *The Women's Awakening in Egypt: Culture, Society, and the Press*, New Haven, CT, London: Yale University Press.

Barth, F. (1969), *Ethnic Groups and Boundaries: The Social Organisation of Cultural Difference*, Oslo: Universitetsforlaget.

Barton, S. (1986), *The Bengali Muslims of Bradford*, Leeds: University of Leeds.

Basch, L., Glick Schiller, N. and Szanton C. (1994), *Nations Unbound: Transnational Projects, Postcolonial Predicaments and Deterritorialized Nation-States*, New York: Gordon and Breach.

Basit, T. N. (1997), '"I Want more Freedom, but not too Much": British Girls and the Dynamism of Family Values', *Gender and Education* 9(4): 425–39.

Bateson, G. (1936), *Naven: a Survey of the Problems Suggested by a Composite Picture of the Culture of a New Guinea Tribe Drawn from Three Points of View*, Cambridge: Cambridge University Press.

Bateson, G. (2000), *Steps to an Ecology of Mind: Collected Essays in Anthropology, Psychiatry, Evolution, and Epistemology*, Chicago: University of Chicago Press.

Bateson, G. (2002), *Mind and Nature: A Necessary Unity*, New Jersey: Hampton Press.

Bauman, Z. (1996), 'On Communitarians and Human Freedom: Or, How to Square the Circle', *Theory Culture Society* 13: 79–90.

Ba-Yunus, L. and Ahmad, F. (1985), *Islamic Sociology: an Introduction*, Cambridge: The Islamic Academy.

Beck, L. and Keddie, N. (eds) (1978), *Women in the Muslim World*, Cambridge: Harvard University Press.

Becker, J. (1993), *Gamelan Stories: Tantrism, Islam, and Aesthetics in Central Java*, Tempe: Arizona State University.

Beeman, W. O. (2004), 'U.S. Anti-Terrorist Message Won't Fly in Islamic World', in R. J. González (ed.), *Anthropologists in the Public Sphere*, Austin: University of Texas Press.

Betty, A. (1999), 'On Ethnographic Experience: Formative and Informative (Nias, Indonesia)' in C. W. Watson (ed.), *Being There: Fieldwork in Anthropology*, London: Pluto Press, pp. 74–97.

Bhabha, H. (1994), *The Location of Culture*, London and New York: Routledge.

Bhachu, P. (1993), 'Identities Constructed and Reconstructed: Representations of Asian Women in Britain', in G. Buijs (ed.), *Migrant Women: Crossing Boundaries and Changing Identity*, Oxford: Berg, pp. 99–118.

Bhatti, F. M. (1981), 'Turkish Cypriots in London', *Research Papers: Muslims in Europe* 11, Birmingham: Centre for the Study of Islam and Christian-Muslim Relations, pp. 1–20.

Bloch, M. and Parry, J. (1982), *Death and the Regeneration of Life*, Cambridge: Cambridge University Press.

Blumer, H. (1969), *Symbolic Interactionism: Perspective and Method*, Berkeley: University of California Press.

Boase, A. M. (1989),'Review of Ahmed 1986', *Arabia: the Islamic World Review* 6: 65.

Bodman, H. and Tohidi, N. (eds) (1998), *Women in Muslim societies: Diversity within unity*, Colorado: Lynne Rienner Publishers.

Boellstorff, T. (1999), 'The Perfect Path: Gay Men, Marriage, Indonesia', *GLQ: A Journal of Gay and Lesbian Studies* 5(4): 475–510.

Boellstorff, T. (2003), 'Dubbing Culture: Indonesian Gay and Lesbian Subjectivities and Ethnography in an Already Globalized World', *American Ethnologist* 30(2): 225–42.

Boellstorff, T. (2004a), 'The Emergence of Political Homophobia in Indonesia: Masculinity and National Belonging', *Ethnos* 69(4): 465–86.

Boellstorff, T. (2004b), 'Playing Back the Nation: *Waria*, Indonesian Transvestites', *Cultural Anthropology* 19(2): 159–95.

Boellstorff, T. (2004c), 'Zines and Zones of Desire: Mass Mediated Love, National Romance, and Sexual Citizenship in Gay Indonesia', *Journal of Asian Studies* 63(2): 367–402.

Boellstorff, T. (2005a), 'Between Religion and Desire: Being Muslim and *Gay* in Indonesia', *Anthropologist* 107(4): 575–85.

Boellstorff, T. (2005b), *The Gay Archipelago: Sexuality and Nation in Indonesia*, Princeton: Princeton University Press.

Bonn, de C. (2003), *Migrations des identités et des textes entre l'Algérie et la France, dans les littératures des deux rives*, Paris: L'Harmatan.

Bourdieu, P. (1960), *Algeria*, Cambridge: Cambridge University Press.

Bourdieu, P. and Thompson, J. B. (eds) (1991), *Language and symbolic power*, Cambridge: Harvard University Press.

Bowen, J. R. (2007) *Why French Do not Like Headscarves*, Princeton and Oxford: Princeton University Press.

Bowie, F. (2000), *The Anthropology of Religion*, Oxford: Blackwell.

Brah, A. (1979), 'Inter-Generational and Inter-Ethnic Perceptions: A Comparative Study of South Asian and English Adolescents in Southall', unpublished Ph.D. Thesis, University of Bristol.

Brems, E. (2006), 'Diversity in the Classroom: The Headscarf Controversy in European Schools', *Peace and Change* 31(1): 117–31.

Brown, D. W. (2003), *A New Introduction to Islam*, Malden, MA: Blackwell.

Buitelaar, M. (1993), *Fasting and Feasting in Morocco: Women's Participation in Ramadan*, Oxford: Berg.

Bujra, A. S. (1971), *The Politics of Stratification: A Study of Political Change in a South Arabian Town*, Oxford: Clarendon.

Bunt, G. R. (2003), *Islam in the Digital Age*, London, Sterling and Virginia: Pluto Press.

Burton, J. (1994), *An Introduction to the Hadith*, Edinburgh: Edinburgh University Press.

Cassell, J. (1980), 'Ethical Principles for Conducting Fieldwork', *American Anthropologist* 82: 28–41.

Cerulo, K. A. (1997), 'Identity Construction: New Issues, New Directions', *Annual Review of Sociology* 23: 385–409.

Chatty, D. and Rabo, A. (1997), 'Formal and Informal Women's Groups in the Middle East', in D. Chatty and A. Rabo (eds), *Organizing Women: Formal and Informal Women's Groups in the Middle East*, Oxford: Berg, pp. 1–22.

Chelkowski, P. J. (ed.) (1989), *Ta'ziyeh. Ritual and Drama in Iran*, New York: New York University Press.

Chodorow, N. (1978), *The Reproduction of Mothering: Psychoanalysis and the Sociology of Gender,* Berkeley: University of California Press.

Chon, R. (1994), *Frontiers of Identity; the British and the Others*, London: Longman.

Cimian, P. Staab, S. (2004), 'Learning by Googling', *Acm Sigkdd Explorations Newsletter* 6(2): 24–33.

Clifford, J. (1983), 'On Ethnographic Authority', *Representations* 1: 118–46.

Clifford, J. (1988), *The Predicament of Culture: Twentieth Century Ethnography, Literature and Art*, London: Harvard University Press.

Clifford, J. (1994), 'Diasporas', *Cultural Anthropology* 9 (3): 302–38.

Clifford, J. and Marcus, G. (eds) (1986), *Writing Culture: the Poetic and Politics of Ethnography*, Berkeley: University of California Press.

Cohen, A. P. (1982), 'Belonging: The Experience of Culture', in A. P. Cohen (ed.), *Belonging: Identity and Social Organization in British Rural Cultures*, Manchester: University Press, pp. 1–17.

Cohen, A. P. (1985), *The Symbolic Construction of Community,* London and New York: Tavistock Publications.

Cohen, A. P. (1994), *Self Consciousness: An Alternative Anthropology of Identity*, London: Routledge.

Cohen, A. P. (1995), 'Introduction', in P. Cohen, and N. Rapport (eds), *Questions of Consciousness*, Florence, KY: Routledge, pp. 1–20.

Cooke, M. (2001), *Women Claim Islam*, London: Routledge.

Cooley, C. H. (1909), *Social Organization: A Study of the Large Mind,* Glencoe, IL: Free Press

Crapanzano, V. (1973), *The Hamadsha: A Study in Moroccan Ethnopsychiatry,* Berkeley: University of California Press.

Crapanzano, V. (1980), *Tuhami: Portrait of a Moroccan,* Chicago: University Press.

D'Alisera, J. (1999), 'Field of Dreams: the Anthropologist Far Away at Home', *Anthropology and Humanism* 24(1): 5–19.

Dahya, Z. (1965), 'Pakistani Wives in Britain', *Race* 6(4): 311–21.

Dahya, Z. (1972), 'Pakistanis in England', *New Community* 2(3): 25–33.

Dahya, Z. (1973), 'Pakistanis in Britain: Transients or Settlers?', *Race* 14(3): 241–77.

Dahya, Z. (1974), 'The Nature of Pakistani Ethnicity in Industrial Cities in Britain', in A. Cohen (ed.), *Urban Ethnicity,* London, Tavistock, pp. 77–118.

Dallal, A.S. (1995), "Ummah" in J. Esposito et al. (eds), *The Oxford Encyclopaedia of the Modern Islamic World* (Vol. II). New York: Oxford University Press.

Damasio, A. R. (1999), *The Feeling of What Happens: Body and Emotion in the Making of Consciousness,* New York: Harcourt Brace.

Damasio, A. R. (2000), *The Feeling of What Happens: Body, Emotion and the Making of Consciousness,* London: Vintage.

Damasio, A. R. (2002), 'How the Brain Creates the Mind', *Scientific American* 281(6): 112–17.

Daniel, N. (1993), *Islam and the West: The Making of an Image,* Edinburgh: Edinburgh University Press.

Dayan-Herzbrun, S. (2000), 'The Issue of the Islamic Headscarf', in J. Freedman and C. Tarr (eds), *Women, Immigration and Identities in France,* Oxford and New York: Berg, pp. 69–82.

Denny, F.M. (1975), 'The Meaning of Ummah in the Quran', *History of Religions* 15(1): 35–70.

Devault, M. L. (1999), 'Talking and Listening from Women's Standpoint: Feminist Strategies for Interviewing and Analysis', *Social Problems* 37: 96–116.

Diamond (1992), *Making Gray Gold: Narratives of Nursing Home Care,* Chicago: University of Chicago Press.

Dien, M. I. (2004), *Islamic Law,* Edinburgh: Edinburgh University Press.

Dina, I and Cullingford, C. (2004), 'Boyzone and Bhangra: The Place of Popular and Minority Cultures', *Race Ethnicity and Education* 7(3): 307–320.

Donnan, H. (2002), *Interpreting Islam,* London: Sage.

Droeber, J. (2005), *Dreaming of Change: Young Middle-Class Women and Social Transformation in Jordan,* Laden and Boston: Brill.

Dumont, L. (1970), *Homo hierarchicus,* Chicago: University of Chicago Press.

Durkheim, E. (1915), *The Elementary Forms of Religious Life,* London: George Allen & Unwin.

Dwyer, C. (2000), 'Negotiating Diasporic Identities: Young British South Asian Muslim Women', *Women's Studies International Forum* 23(4): 457–86.

Dwyer, K. (1982), *Moroccan Dialogues: Anthropology in Question,* Baltimore: Johns Hopkins University Press.

Eagleton, T. (1991), *Ideology: An Introduction*, London: Verso.

Edwards, D. B. (1991), 'Review of Discovering Islam: Making Sense of Muslim History and Society', *International Journal of Middle East Studies* 23(2): 270–3.

Eickelman, D. F. (1976), *Moroccan Islam*, Austin: University of Texas Press.

Eickelman, D. F. (1981a), *The Middle East and Central Asia: an Anthropological Approach*, New Jersey: Prentice Hall.

Eickelman, D. F. (1981b), 'A Search for the Anthropology of Islam: Abdul Hamid El-Zein', *International Journal of Middle Eastern Studies* 13: 361–5.

Eickelman, D. F. (1982), 'Muslim Society' (review), *Man* (n.s.) 17: 571–2.

Eickelman, D. F. (1990), 'Knowing One Another: Shaping an Islamic Anthropology', (review), *American Anthropologist* 92(1): 240–1.

Eickelman, D. F. and Piscatori, J. (1996), *Muslim Politics*. Princeton: Princeton University Press.

Elkholy, A. (1984), 'Toward an Islamic Anthropology', *Muslim Education Quarterly* 1: 2.

Ellemers, N, Spears, R, and Doosje, B. (2002), 'Self and Social Identity', *Annual Review of Psychology* 53: 161–86.

el-Zein, A. H. (1977), 'Beyond Ideology and Theology: the Search for the Anthropology of Islam', *Annual Review of Anthropology* 6: 227–54.

Emerson, R. M., Fretz, R.L. and Shaw, L.L. (1995), *Writing Ethnographic Fieldnotes*, Chicago and London: University of Chicago Press.

Erikson, T. (1967), 'A Comment on Disguised Observation in Sociology', *Social Problems* 12: 366–73.

Ernst, C. W. (2004), *Rethinking Islam in the Contemporary Word*, Edinburgh: Edinburgh University Press.

Esposito, J. L. (1988), *Islam, the Straight Path*, Oxford: Oxford University Press.

Esposito, J. L. (ed.) (1995), *The Oxford Encyclopaedia of the Modern Islamic World*, Vol. 2, New York: Oxford University Press.

Etienne, M. and Leacock, E. (1980), 'Introduction', in M. Etienne and E. Leacock (eds), *Women and Colonization: Anthropological Perspectives*, New York: Praeger Publishers, pp. 1–24.

Evans-Pritchard, E. E. (1940), *The Nuer*, Oxford: Calarendon Press.

Evans-Pritchard, E. E. (1949), *The Sanusi of Cyrenaica*, Oxford: Clarendon Press.

Evergeti, V. (1999), 'Negotiations of Identity: The Case of a Muslim Minority Village in Greece', unpublished PhD thesis, Department of Sociology, Manchester University.

Evergeti, V. (2004), 'Trust and Social Capital in the Field: Reflections from an Interactionist Ethnography in Minority Communities in Greece', in R. Edwards (ed.), *Social Capital in the Field*, Families and Social Capital Working Papers Series. Available online at http://www.lsbu.ac.uk/families/workingpapers/familieswp10.pdf

Evergeti, V. (2006), 'Boundary Formation and Identity Expression in Everyday Interactions: Muslim Minorities in Greece', in J. Stacul, C. Moutsou and H. Kopnina (eds), *Crossing European Boundaries: Beyond Conventional Geographical Boundaries*, Oxford: Berghahn Books, pp. 176–96.

Ewing, K. P. (1994), 'Dreams from a Saint: Anthropological Atheism and the Temptation to Believe', *American Anthropologist* 96(3): 571–83.

Faist, T. (2004), 'The Transnational Turn in Migration Research: Perspectives for the Study of Politics and Polity', in M. Povrzankovic (ed.), *Transnational Spaces: Disciplinary Perspectives*, Malmö: Malmy University, pp. 11–45.

Featherstone, M., Lash, S. and Robertson, R. (eds) (1995), *Global Modernities*, London: Sage.

Fee, E. (1974), 'The Sexual Politics of Victorian Social Anthropology', in M Hartman and L. Banner (eds), *Clio's Consciousness Raised*, New York: Harper Torch Books, pp. 86–102.

Fernea, R. and Malarkey, J. M. (1975), 'Anthropology of the Middle East and Northern Africa: A Critical Assessment', *Annual Review of Anthropology* 4: 183–206.

Fine, G. A. and Sandstrom, K.L. (1988), *Knowing Children: Participant Observation with Minors*, Newbury Park, CA: Sage.

Flaubert, G. (1972), *Flaubert in Egypt: A Sensibility on Tour*, Boston: Little Brown.

Forbes, J. and Kelly, M. (eds) (1995), 'Beur Culture', in *French Cultural Studies: An Introduction*, Oxford: Oxford University Press, pp. 269–72.

Ganguly, K. (1992), 'Migrant Identities: Personal Memory and the Construction of the Selfhood', *Cultural Studies* 6(1): 27–50.

Gans, H. J. (1968), 'The Participant-Observer As Human Being: Observations on the Personal Aspects of Field Work', in H. S. Becker, B. Geer, D. Riesman, and R. S. Weiss (eds), *Institutions and the Person*, Chicago: Aldine, pp. 300–17.

Gardner, K. and Shukur, A. (1994), '"I'm Bengali, I'm Asian, and I'm Living Here"; the Changing Identity of British Bengalis', in R. Ballard (ed.), *Desh Pardesh: The South Asian Presence in Britain*, London: Hurst, pp. 142–64.

Gardner, K. and Shukur, A. (1999), 'Location and Relocation: Home the "Field" and Anthropological Ethics (Sylhet, Bangladesh)', in C. W. Watson (ed.), *Being There: Fieldwork in Anthropology,* London: Pluto Press, pp. 49–71.

Geaves, R. (1995), *Muslims in Leeds, community religions,* project research papers no. 10, Leeds: University of Leeds.

Geaves, R. (2005), 'The Dangers of Essentialism: South Asian Communities in Britain and the "World Religions" Approach to the Study of Religions', *Contemporary South Asia* 14(1): 75–90.

Geertz, C. (1960), *Religion of Java*, Chicago: Chicago University Press.

Geertz, C. (1964), 'The Transition to Humanity', in S. Tax (ed.), *Horizons of Anthropology*, Chicago: Aldine, pp. 37–48.

Geertz, C. (1968), *Islam Observed*, New Haven and London: Yale University Press.

Geertz, C. (1973), 'Deep Play: Notes on the Balinese Cockfight', in C. Geertz, *The Interpretation of Cultures*, New York, NY: Basic Books, pp. 412–54.

Geertz, C. (1975), 'On the Nature of Anthropological Understanding', *American Scientist* 63: 47–53.

Geertz, C. (1982), 'Conjuring with Islam', *The New York Review of Books* 29(9): 28.

Geertz, C. (1985), 'Religion as a Cultural System', in M. Banton (ed.), *Anthropological Approaches to the Study of Religion*, London: Travistock, pp. 1–46.

Geertz, C. (1988), *Works and Lives: the Anthropologist As Author,* Stanford: Stanford University Press.

Geertz, C. (1993), 'Religion as a Cultural System', in C. Geertz (ed.), *The Interpretation of Cultures: Selected Essays*, London: Fontana, pp. 87–125.

Geertz, C. (1995), *After the Fact. Two Countries, Four Decades, One Anthropologist,* Cambridge, Mass.: Harvard University Press.

Geest, S. van der (2003), 'Confidentiality and Pseudonyms', *Anthropology Today* 19(1): 14–18.

Gellner, E. (1981), *Muslim Society*, Cambridge: Cambridge University Press.

Gellner, E. (1994), *Conditions of Liberty, Civil Society and its Rivals*, London: Hamish Hamilton.

Gennep, A. van (1909/1960), *The Rites of Passage*, Chicago: University of Chicago Press.

Gergen, K. J. (1968), 'Personal Consistency and the Presentation of Self', in C. Gordon and K. J. Gergen (eds), *The Self in Social Interaction: Classic and Contemporary Perspectives*, New York: Wiley, pp. 17–56.

Gerholm, T. and Lithman, Y. (eds) (1988), *The New Islamic Presence in Europe*, London: Mansell.

Ghoussoub, M. and Sinclair-Web, E. (eds) (2000), *Imagined Masculinity: Male Identity and Culture in the Modern Middle East*, London: Saqi Books.

Giannakis, E. (1983), 'The concept of Ummah', *Graeco-Arabica* 2: 99–111.

Gilligan, C. (1986), 'Remapping the Moral Domain: New Images of the Self in Relationship', in T. C. Heller, M. Sosna, and D. E. Wellbery (eds), *Reconstructing Individualism: Autonomy Individuality and the Self, Western Thought*, Stanford, CA: Stanford University Press, pp. 237–52.

Gilsenan, M. (1973), *Saint and Sufi in Modern Egypt: An Essay in the Sociology of Religion,* Oxford: Clarendon.

Gilsenan, M. (1982), *Recognizing Islam: Religion and Society in the Modern Middle East*, London: I. B. Tauris.

Gilsenan, M. (1990), 'Very Like a Camel: The Appearance of an Anthropologist's Middle East', in R. Fardon (ed.), *Localizing Strategies: Regional Traditions of Ethnographic Writing*, Edinburgh and Washington: Scottish Academic Press, Smithsonian Institution Press, pp. 222–39.

Glebe, G. (1990), 'Segregation and Migration of the Second Generation of Guestworker Minorities in Dusseldorf', *Espace, Populations, Sociétés* 2: 257–78.

Goffman, E. (1959), *The Presentation of Self in Everyday Life,* Garden City, NY: Doubleday.

Goffman, E. (1989), 'On Fieldwork', *Journal of Contemporary Ethnography* 18: 123–32.

Gold, R. L. (1958), 'Roles in sociological field observations', *Social Forces* 36: 123–32.

Goldziher, I. (1971), *Muslim Studies*, London: George Allen & Unwin.

González, R. J. (ed.) (2004), *Anthropologists in the Public Sphere*, Austin: University of Texas Press.

Gordon, C. (1976), 'Development of Evaluated Role Identities', *Annual Review of Sociology* 2: 405–33.

Grillo, R.D., Riccio, B. and Salih, R. (2000), 'Introduction', in Grillo, R.D., Riccio, B. and Salih, R., *Here or There? Contrasting Experiences of Transnationalism: Moroccans and Senegalese in Italy*, Falmer: CDE Working Paper, pp. 3–24.

Grillo, R.D., Riccio, B. and Salih, R. (2003), 'Cultural essentialism and cultural anxiety', *Anthropological Theory* 3(2): 157–173.

Grunebaum, G. von (1955), *Medieval Islam: A Study in Cultural Orientalism*, Chicago: Chicago University Press.

Grunebaum, G. von (1961), 'Nationalism and Cultural Trends in the Arab Near East', Studica Islamica 14: 121–53.

Grunebaum, G. von (1962), *Modern Islam: The Search for Cultural Identity*, Berkeley: University of California Press.

Gubrium, J. F. (1988), *Analyzing Field Reality*, Newbury Park, CA: Sage.

Guijt, I. and Shah, M. K. (1998), *The Myth of Community*. London: Intermediate Technology Publications.

Haddad, Y. and Esposito, J. (eds) (2000), *Muslims on the Americanization Path?* New York: Oxford University Press.

Haddad, Y. Y and Qurqmazi, I. (2000), 'Muslims in the West: a select bibliography', *Islam and Christian-Muslim Relations,* 11(1): 5–49.

Haddad, Y. Y and Qurqmazi, I. (ed.) (2002), *Muslims in the West: from Sojourners to Citizens*, Oxford & New York: Oxford University Press.

Hallaq, W. B. (1999), 'The Authenticity of Prophetic Hadith: A Pseudo-Problem', *Studia Islamica* 89: 75–90.

Halliday, F. (1995), 'Islam is in Danger: Authority, Rushdie and the Struggle for the Migrant Soul', in J. Hippler and A. Lueg (eds), *The Next Threat: Western perceptions of Islam*, London: Pluto, pp. 71–81.

Hallowell, A. I. (1955), *Culture and Experience*, Philadelphia: University of Pennsylvania Press.

Halstead, M. (1988), *Education, Justice and Cultural Diversity: an Examination of the Honeyford Affair 1984–85*, London: Falmer.

Hammoudi, A. (1980), 'Segmentary, Social Stratification, Political Power and Sainthood: Reflections on Gellner's Theses', *Economy and Society* 9: 279–303.

Hannerz, U. (2003), 'Macro-scenarios. Anthropology and the Debate over Contemporary and Future Worlds', *Social Anthropology* 11(2): 69–187.

Hart, D. K (1988), 'Review of Ahmed 1986', *Middle East Studies Association Bulletin* 15: 1–2.

Hasan, M, (2002), *Islam in the Subcontinent: Muslims in a Plural Society*, Delhi: Manohar.

Hassan, R. (2006), 'Globalisation's Challenge to the Islamic Ummah', *American Journal of Social Sciences*, 34(2): 311–23.

Haw, K. F. (1994), 'Muslim girls' schools and conflict of interests?', *Gender and Education* 6: 63–74.

Hayano, D. (1979), 'Auto-ethnography: Paradigms, Problems, and Prospects', *Human Organization* 38: 99–104.

Hefner, R. (1987), 'The Political Economy of Islamic Conversion in Modern East Java', in W. R. Roff (ed.), *Islam and the Political Economy of Meaning*, London: Croom Helm, pp. 53–78.

Heglnad, M, E. (2004),'Zip In and Zip Out Fieldwork', *Iranian Studies* 37(4): 575–83.

Herbert L. B and Tohidi, N. (eds) (1998), *Women in Muslim Societies: Diversity within Unity*, Boulder: Lynner Rienner.

Herbrechtsmeier, W. (1993), 'Buddhism and the Definition of Religion: One More Time', *Journal for the Scientific Study of Religion*, 32(1): 1–17.

Herzfeld (1997), *Cultural Intimacy: Social Politics in the Nation State*, New York and London: Routledge.

Hetherington, K. (1994), 'The Contemporary Significance of Schmalenbach's Concept of the Bund', *Sociological Review* 42: 1–25.

Hetherington, K. (1998), *Expressions of Identity: Space, Performance, Politics*, London: Sage.

Hewer, C. (1992), 'Muslim Teacher Training in Britain', *Muslim Education Quarterly* 10: 21–34.

Hewer, C. (1996), 'The Education of Muslims in Birmingham', *Cycnos* 13(2): 101–8.

Hillery, G.A (1955), 'Definitions of Community: Areas of Agreement', *Rural Sociology*, 20: 86–118.

Holland, D. and Quinn, N. (1987), *Cultural models in language and thought*, Cambridge: University Press.

Holland, D. and Quinn, N. (1997), 'Selves as Cultured, as Called by an Anthropologist who Lacks a Soul', in D. R. Ashmore and L. Jussim (eds), *Self and Identity*, New York and Oxford: Oxford University Press, pp. 160–90.

Howard, J.A. (2000), 'Social Psychology of Identities', *Annual Review of Sociology* 26: 367–93.

Hull, J. (1995), 'Religion as a Series of Religions: a Comment on the SCAA Model Syllabuses', *World Religions in Education*, London: Shap, pp. 11–16.

Hume, D. (1740/1975), *Treatise of Human Nature*, Oxford: Clarendon Press.

Hunt, J. (1984), 'The Development of Rapport through the Negotiation of Gender in Field Work Among Police', *Human Organization* 45: 283–96.

Hussain, F. (ed.) (1984), *Muslim Women*, London: Croom Helm.

Ingold, T. (1992), 'Culture and the Perception of the Environment', in E. Croll and D. Parkin (eds), *Bush Base: Forest Farm*, London: Routledge, pp. 14–32.

Ingold, T. (1996), 'Against the Motion', in T. Ingold (ed.), *Key Debates in Anthropology*, London: Routledge, pp. 112–18.

Jacobson, J. (1998), *Islam in Transition: Religion and Identity among British Pakistani Youth*, London and New York: Routledge.

James, W. (1890), *Principles of Psychology*, New York: Holt.

Kalir, B. (2006), 'The Field of Work and the Work of Field: Conceptualising an Anthropological Research Engagement', *Social Anthropology* 14(2): 235–46.

Kamali, M. (2001), 'Civil Society and Islam: a Sociological Perspective', *Archive of European Sociology* 53(3): 457–82.

Karp, I. and Kendall, M.B. (1982), 'Reflexivity in field work', in P. F. Secord (ed.), *Explaining Human Behaviour: Consciousness, Human Action and Social Structure*, Beverly Hills. CA: Sage, pp. 250–69.

Kawale, R. (2003), 'A Kiss is Just a Kiss... Or Is It? South Asian Lesbian and Bisexual Women and the Construction of Space', in N. Puwar and P. Raghuram (eds), *South Asian Women in the Diaspora*, Oxford: Berg, pp. 179–98.

Keddie, N. (1991), 'Problems in the Study of Middle Eastern Women', *International Journal of Middle Eastern Studies* 10: 225–40.

Kepel, G. (1997), *Allah in the West: Islamic Movements in America and Europe*, California: Stanford University Press.

Khan, Z. (2000), 'Muslim Presence in Europe: the British Dimension–Identity, Integration and Community Activism', *Current Sociology*, 48(4): 29–43.

Kimball, M. R. and von Schlegell, B.R. (eds) (1997), *Muslim Women throughout the World: a bibliography*, Boulder: Lynne Rienner Publishers.

Kleinman, S. (1991), 'Fieldworker's feelings: what we feel, who we are, how we analyze', in W. B. Shaffir and R. A. Stebbins (eds), *Experiencing Fieldwork*, Newbury Park, CA: Sage, pp. 184–95.

Knott, K. and Khokher, S. (1993), 'The relationship between religion and ethnicity in the experience of young Muslim women in Bradford', *New Community* 19: 593–610.

Korzybski, A. (1948), *Science and Sanity: An Introduction to Non-Aristotelian Systems and General Semantics*, Lakeville CT: The International Non-Aristotelian Publishing Co.

Kramer, M. (1996), *Arab Awakening and Islamic Revival: The Politics of Ideas in the Middle East*, New Brunswick, NJ: Transaction Publishers

Kramer, M. (1998), 'The Salience of Islamic Antisemitism', www.ict.org.il/articles/ (accessed 1 May 2006).

Kressel, N. (2004), 'The Urgent Need to Study Islamic anti-Semitism', *The Chronicle Review*, http//chronicle.com/free/v50/i27/27b01401.htm (accessed 31 May 2006).

Krieger-Krynicki, A. (1988), 'The Second-Generation: the Children of Muslim Immigrants in France', in T. Gerholm and Y.G. Kuthman (eds), *The New Islamic Presence in Western Europe*, London and New York: Mansell Publishing Ltd, pp. 123–32.

Kritzeck, J. (1964), *Peter the Venerable and Islam*, Princeton NJ: Princeton University Press.

Kunin, S. (2002), *Religion: Modern Theories*, Edinburgh: Edinburgh University Press.

Lacoste-Dujardin, C. (2000), 'Maghribi families in France', in J. Freedman and C. Tarr (eds), *Women, Immigration and Identities in France*, Oxford: Berg, pp. 57–69.

Lahoucine, O. (ed.) (2006), *Islamic Masculinities*, London: Zed Books.

Lewis, B. and Schnapper, D. (eds) (1994), *Muslims in Europe*, London: Pinter.

Lewis, P. (1994), *Islamic Britain: Religion, Politics and Identity Among British Muslims*, London: I.B. Tauris.

Little, A. Mabey, C. and Whitaker, G. (1968), 'The Education of Immigrant Pupils in Inner London Primary Schools', *Race* 9(4): 439–52.

Locke, J. (1690/1959), *An Essay Concerning Human Understanding*, New York: Dover.

Lofland, J. and Lofland, L.H. (1995), *Analyzing Social Settings: A Guide to Qualitative Observation and Analysis*, Belmont, CA: Wadsworth.

Lukens-Bull, R. A. (1996), 'Metaphorical Aspects of Indonesian Islamic Discourse about Development', in R. A. Lukens-Bull (ed.), *Intellectual Development in Indonesian Islam*, Tempe: Arizona State University, Chapter 8.

Lukens-Bull, R. A. (1999), 'Between Texts and Practice: Considerations in the Anthropology of Islam', *Marburg Journal of Religion* 4(2): 1–10

Lukens-Bull, R. A. (2005), *A Peaceful Jihad*, New York: Palgrave Macmillan.

Lustiger-Thaler, H. (1994), 'Community and Social Practices: the Contingency of Everyday Life', in V. Amit-talai and H. Lustiger-Thaler (eds), *Urban Lives: Fragmentation and Resistance*, New York: McClelland & Stewart Inc., pp. 20–44.

Lutz, H. (1991), *Migrant Women of 'Islamic Background': Images and Self-Images*, Amsterdam: MERA.

Lykes, M. B. (1985), 'Gender and Individualistic vs. Collectivist Bases for Notions About the Self', in A. J. Stewart and M. B. Lykes (eds), *Gender and Personality: Current Perspectives on Theory and Research*, Durham NC: Duke University Press, pp. 268–95.

Macfarlane, A. (1977), 'History, Anthropology, and the Study of Communities', *Social History* 5: 631–52.

Maffesoli, M. (1996), *The Time of the Tribes*, London: Sage.

Magnarella, P. J (1986), 'Anthropological Fieldwork, Key Informants, and Human Bonds', *Anthropology Humanism Quartely* 11(2): 33–7.

Mahroof, M. (1981), 'Elements for an Islamic Anthropology', in *Social and Natural Sciences: the Islamic perspective*, Jaddah: KAA University & Hodder & Stoughton, pp. 15–23.

Malinowski, B. (1922/1978), *Argonauts of the Western Pacific*, London: Routledge and Kegan Paul.

Mamdani, M. (2002), 'Good Muslim, Bad Muslim: A Political Perspective on Culture and Terrorism', *American Anthropologist* 104(3): 766–75.

Mandaville, P. (1999) 'Digital Islam: Changing the Boundaries of Religious Knowledge?' *ISIM Newsletter* 2(1): 2–47.

Mandaville, P. (2001), *Trasnational Muslim politic – Reimagining the umma*, New York, London: Routledge.

Marcus, G. (1995), 'Ethnography in/of the World System: the Emergence of Multi-Sited Ethnography', *Annual Review of Anthropology* 24: 95–117.

Marcus, G. and Fisher, M. (1986), *Anthropology as Cultural Critique: An Experimental Movement in the Human Sciences*, Chicago: University of Chicago Press.

Marranci, G. (2000a), 'A Complex Identity and its Musical Representation: Beurs and Raï Music in Paris', *Music & Anthropology* 5, [http://www.muspe.unibo.it/period/ma], (accessed 21 November 2005).

Marranci, G. (2000b), 'La Musique Raï: Entre Métissage et World Music Moderne', *Cahiers de musiques traditionnelles* 13: 137–150.

Marranci, G. (2003a), *'The Adhan among the Bells: Studying Muslim Identity in Northern Ireland'*, unpublished PhD Thesis, Belfast: The Queen's University of Belfast.

Marranci, G. (2003b), 'Pop-Raï: From Local Tradition to Globalisation', in G. Plastino (ed.), *Mediterranean Mosaic*, London and New York: Routledge, pp. 101–20.

Marranci, G. (2004), 'South Asian Muslims in Northern Ireland: Their Islamic Identity, and the Aftermath of 11th of September', in T. Abbas (ed.), *South Asian Muslims in Britain, Post September 11th*, London: Zed Books, pp. 222–34.

Marranci, G. (2005), 'Pakistanis in Northern Ireland in the Aftermath of September 11', in T. Abbas (ed.) *Muslim Britain: Communities under Pressure*, London: Zed Books, pp. 222–33.

Marranci, G. (2006a), *Jihad Beyond Islam*, Oxford: Berg.

Marranci, G. (2006b), 'Muslim Marriages in Northern Ireland', in B. Waldis and R. Byron (eds), *Migration and Marriage; Heterogamy and Homogamy in a Changing World*, Munster and London: LIT Verlag, pp. 40–66.

Marranci, G. (2006c), *Muslims inside: Muslim identity formation and experience of Islam within HM Scottish Prisons*, unpublished report, Aberdeen: University of Aberdeen.

Marranci, G. (2006d), 'The Transmission of Islamic Heritage in Northern Ireland', in M. Nic Craith and U. Kockel (eds), *Cultural Heritages as Reflexive Traditions*, London, New York: Palgrave Macmillan, pp. 138–57.

Marranci, G. (2007), 'Migration and the Construction of Muslim Women's Identity in Northern Ireland', in C. Aitchison, P. Hopkins, and M. Kwan, (eds), *Geographies of Muslim Identities: Representations of Diaspora, Gender and Belonging*, London and New York: Ashgate, pp. 79–92.

Marsella, A., De Vos, G. and Hsu, E. L. K. (eds) (1988), *Culture and Self*, London: Tavistock.

Matin-Asgari, A. (2004), 'Islamic Studies and the Spirit of Max Weber: A Critique of Cultural Essentialism', *Critical Middle Eastern Studies* 13(3): 293–312.

May, H. E. (1997), 'Socratic Ignorance and the Therapeutic Aim of the Elenchos', *Apeiron* 30(4): 37–50.

Mdaghri, D. A. (1975), 'Cultural action amongst Maghrebi migrants in Europe', *Migration News* 5: 16–22.

Mead, G. H. (1934), *Mind, Self, and Society*, Chicago: University of Chicago Press.

Mernissi, F. (1975), *Beyond the Veil: Male–Female Dynamics in a Modern Muslim Society*, New York: Schenkman Publishing Company.

Metcalf, B. D. (ed.) (1996), *Making Muslim Space in Northern America and Europe*, Berkeley: University of California Press.

Mildenberger, M. (1982), 'What Place for Europe's Muslims? Integration or Segregation?', Research Papers: Muslims in Europe, No 13, Birmingham: Centre for the Study of Islam and Christian-Muslim Relations.

Milton, K. (2002), *Loving Nature*, London: Routledge.

Milton, K. and Svasek, M. (eds) (2005), *Mixed Emotions: Anthropological Studies of Feelings*, Oxford: Berg.

Mirza, K. (1989), 'The Silent Cry: Second Generation Bradford Muslim Women Speak', Research Papers: Muslims in Europe, No 43, Birmingham: CISC, Selly Oak Colleges.

Modood, T. (1998), 'Anti-Essentialism, Multiculturalism and the "Recognition" of Religious Groups', *Journal of Political Philosophy* 6: 378–99.

Modood, T. (1990), 'The British Asian Muslims and the Rushdie affair', *The Political Quarterly* 62(2): 143–60.

Momen, M. (1985), *An Introduction to Shi'i Islam*, New Haven and London: Yale University Press.

Morris, B. (2005), *Anthropology and Religion: A Critical Introduction*, New York: Cambridge University Press.

Morrison, B. (1987), *Anthropological Studies of Religion: an Introductory Text*, Cambridge: Cambridge University Press.

Mozzo-Counil, F. (1994), *Femmes maghrébines en France*, Paris: Chronique Social.

Mukadam, A. and Mawani, S. (2006), 'Post-Diasporic Communities: a New Generation', in S. Coleman and P. Collins (eds), *Locating the Field, Space, Place and Context in Anthropology*, Oxford and New York: Berg, pp. 105–27.

Munson, H. (1993), *Religion and Power in Morocco*, New Haven: Yale University Press.

Munson, H. (1995), 'Segmentation: Reality or Myth?', *The Journal of the Royal Anthropological Institute* 1(4): 821–9.

Murray, S and Rose, W. (1997), *Islamic Homosexuality: Culture, History and Literature*, New York and London: New York University Press.

Naser, S. H. (2002), *Islam: Religion, History, and Civilization*. San Francisco, CA: Harper San Francisco.

Newton, E. (1993), 'My Best Informant's Dress: the Erotic Equation of Fieldwork', *Cultural Anthropology* 8(1): 3–23.

Ney. M. (2003), *Religion, the Basics*, London: Routledge.

Nielsen, J. S. (1981), 'Muslims in Europe: An Overview', Research Papers: Muslims in Europe, No 12, Birmingham: Centre for the Study of Islam and Christian-Muslim Relations.

Nielsen, J. (1985), *Muslims in Britain: An Annotated Bibliography 1960–84*, Coventry: University of Warwick, Centre for Research in Ethnic Relations.

Nielsen, J. (1987), 'Muslims in Britain: searching for an identity?', *New Community* 1(3): 384–94.

Nielsen, J. (1992), *Muslims in Western Europe*, Edinburgh: Edinburgh University Press.

Nieuwenhuijze, C. A. O. van (1959), 'The Ummah: An Analytical Approach', *Studia Islamica* 10: 5–22.

Nigosian, S. A. (2004), *Islam: Its History, Teaching, and Practices*, Bloomington and Indianapolis: Indiana University Press.

Nonneman, G., Niblock, T. and Szajkowski, B. (eds) (1997), *Muslim Communities in the New Europe*, Reading: Ithaca Press.

Nourse, J. W. (2002), 'Who's Exploiting Whom? Agency, Fieldwork and Representation Among the Lauje of Indonesia', *Anthropology and Humanism* 27(1): 27–42.

Obeyesekere, G. (1981), *Medusa's Hair: An Essay on Personal Symbols and Religious Experience*, Chicago: University of Chicago Press.

Okkenhaug, M. and Flaskerud, I. (eds) (2005), *Gender, Religion and Change in the Middle East*, Oxford: Berg.

Olwig, K. F (2002), 'The Ethnographic Field Revisited. Towards a Study of Common and Not So Common Fields of Belonging', in V. Amit (ed.), *Realizing Community, Concepts, Social Relationships, and Sentiments*, New York: Routledge, pp. 106–24.

Passaro, J. (1997), '"You Can't Take the Subway to the Field!": Village Epistemologies in the Global Village', in A. Gupta and J. Ferguson (eds), *Anthropological Locations: Boundaries and Grounds of a Field Science*, Berkeley: University of California Press, pp. 147–62.

Pécoud, A. (2004), 'Do Immigrants Have a Business Culture? The Political Epistemology of Fieldwork in Berlin's Turkish Economy', *The Journal of the Society for the Anthropology of Europe* 4(2): 19–25.

Pellat, C. (1992), 'Liwāt', in A. Schmitt and J. Sofer (eds), *Sexuality and Eroticism among Males in Moslem Societies*, Binghamton, NY: Haworth Press, pp.152–67.

Pels, T. (2000), 'Muslim Families from Morocco in the Netherlands: Gender Dynamics and Father's Roles in a Context of Change', *Current Sociology* 48(4): 75–93.

Peneff, J. (1985), 'Fieldwork in Algeria', *Qualitative Sociology*, 8(1): 65–78.

Peristiany, J. G. (1965), *Honour and Shame: The Values of Mediterranean Societies*, London: Weidenfeld and Nicolson.

Philips, M. (2006), *Londonistan*, London: Gibson Square Books.

Pipes, D. (1981), 'The Politics of Muslim Anti-Semitism', www.danielpipes.org/article/161 (accessed 8 June 2004).

Pipes, D. (1983), *In The Path of God: Islam and Political Power*, New York: Basic Books.

Pipes, D. (1997), 'The New Anti-Semitism', www.danielpipes.org/article/288 (accessed 25 November 2005).

Poole, E. (2002), *Reporting Islam*, London and New York: I.B. Tauris.

Price, D. (2002), 'Past Wars, Present Dangers, Future Anthropologies', *Anthropology Today* 18(1): 3–5.

Qureshi, K. and Moores, S. (1999), 'Identity Remix. Tradition and Translation in the Lives of Young Pakistani Scots', *European Journal of Cultural Studies* 2(3): 311–30.

Qureshi, R. B. (ed.) (1983), *The Muslim Community in North America*, Edmonton: University of Alberta Press.

Rabinow, P. (1977), *Reflections on Fieldwork in Morocco*, Berkeley: University of California Press.

Radcliffe-Brown, A. R. (1922), *The Andaman Islanders: a Study in Social Anthropology*, Cambridge: University of Cambridge Press.

Rahman, F. (1984), 'The principles of Shura and the role of the Umma in Islam', *American Journal of Islamic Studies* 1(1): 1–9.

Rapport, N. (1993), *Diverse World-views in an English Village*, Edinburgh: Edinburgh University Press.

Rapport, N. (1997), *Transcendent Individual: Essays Toward a Literary and Liberal Anthropology*, London: Routledge.

Redfield, R. (1956), *Peasant Society and Culture*, Chicago: Chicago University Press.

Riddell, P. G. and Cotterell, P. (2003), *Islam in Context: Past, Present, and Future*, Grand Rapids MI: Baker Academic.

Roald, S. A. (2001), *Women in Islam: The Western Experience*, London and New York: Routledge.

Roberts, H (2002), 'Perspective on Berber Politics: On Gellner and Masqueray, or Durkheim's Mistake', *The Journal of the Royal Anthropological Institute* 8: 107–126.

Robinson, N. (2002), 'The Fascination of Islam', *Islam and Christian-Muslim Relations* 13(1): 97–110.

Roded, R. (2006), 'Alternate Images of the Prophet Muhammad's Virility', in O. Lahoucine (ed.), *Islamic Masculinities*, London: Zed Books, pp. 57–71.

Rogers, S. C. (1978), 'Women's Place: A Critical Review of Anthropological Theory', *Comparative Studies* 20(1): 123–62.

Rosaldo, R. (1989), *Culture and Truth: The Remaking of Social Analysis*, Boston: Beacon Press.

Rosaldo R. (1993), 'Grief and a Headhunter's Rage: on the Cultural Forces of Emotions', in R. Rosaldo, *Culture and Truth*, London: Routledge, pp. 1–24.

Rosen, L. (2002), *The Culture of Islam: Changing Aspects of Contemporary Muslim life*, Chicago: University of Chicago Press.

Rosenthal, F. (1991), *Science and Medicine in Islam: a Collection of Essay*, Aldershot, Hants: Variorum.

Roy, O. (1996), 'Le neofondamentalisme islamique ou l'imaginaire de l'oummah', *Esprit*, April: 43–55.

Roy, O. (2002), *Globalised Islam: The Search for a New Ummah*, London: Hurst & Company.

Sabbah, F. A. (1984), *Woman in the Muslim Unconscious*, New York: Pergamon Press.

Said, E. (1978), *Orientalism*, New York: Pantheon Books.

Said, E. (1985), 'Orientalism Reconsidered', *Cultural Critique* 1(1): 89–107.

Saifullah-Khan, V. S. (1975), 'Asian Women in Britain: Strategies of Adjustment of Indian and Pakistani Migrants', in A. Desouza (ed.), *Women in Contemporary India*, New Delhi: Manohar, pp. 16–88.

Saifullah-Khan, V. S. (1976a), 'Pakistani Women in Britain', *New Community* 5(1–2): 99–108.

Saifullah-Khan, V. S. (1976b), 'Pakistanis in Britain: Perceptions of a Population', *New Community* 5 (3): 222–9.

Saifullah-Khan, V. S. (1979), 'Pakistanis and Social Stress: Mirpuris in Bradford', in V. S Saifullah-Khan (ed.), *Minority Families in Britain: Support and Stress,* London: Macmillan, pp. 37–58.

Salih, R. (2000), 'Shifting Boundaries of Self and Other: Moroccan Migrant Women in Italy', *The European Journal of Women's Studies* 7(3): 321–35.

Salih, R. (2001), 'Moroccan Migrant Women: Transnationalism, Nation-States and Gender', *Journal of Ethnic and Migration Studies* 27(4): 655–71.

Salvatore, A (1997), *Islam and the Political Discourse of Modernity,* London: Ithaca Press.

Sampson, E. E. (1985), 'The Decentralization of Identity: Toward a Revised Concept of Personal and Social Order', *American Psychologist* 40: 1203–11.

Sampson, E. E. (1988), 'The Debate on Individualism: Indigenous Psychologies of the Individual and Their Role in Personal and Societal Functioning', *American Psychologist* 43: 15–22.

Sampson, E. E. (1989), 'The Challenge of Social Change for Psychology: Globalization and Psychology's Theory of the Person', *American Psychologist* 44: 914–21.

Sanadjian, M. (2001), 'Witnessing an Islamic Rite of Passage and a Local/Non-Local', *Social Identities* 7(2): 203–19.

Sanjek, R. (1990), *Fieldnotes: The Makings of Anthropology*, Ithaca and London: Cornell University Press.

Scarce, R. (1994), '(No) Trial (but) Tribulation: When Courts and Ethnography Conflict', *Journal of Contemporary Ethnography* 23: 123–49.

Schmalenbach, H. (1922), 'Die Soziologische Kategorie de Bundes', *Die Dioskuren,* Vol 1, München, pp. 35–105.

Schmidt, G. (2005), 'The Transnational Umma – Myth or Reality? Examples from the Western Diasporas', *The Muslim World* 95: 575–86.

Schmiduke, S. (1999), 'Homoeroticism and Homosexuality in Islam: A Review Article', *Bulletin of the School of Oriental and African Studies, University of London* 62(2): 260–6.

Schwartz, M. S. and Schwartz, C. G. (1955), 'Problems in Participant Observation', *American Journal of Sociology* 60: 343–54.

Segal. R. (ed.) (2006), *The Blackwell Companion to the Study of Religion*, Oxford: Blackwell.

Sen, A. (2004), 'Mumbai Slums and the Search for "a Heart": Ethics, Ethnography and Dilemmas of Studying Urban Violence', *Anthropology Matters* 6(1): 2 – 6.

Shankland, D. (2003), *The Alevis in Turkey*, London and New York: Routledge Curzon.

Sharpe, M. (2005), 'Maghrebi Migrants and Writers: Liminality, Transgression and the Transferal of Identity', *Dialectical Anthropology* 29: 397–421.

Shaw, A. (1998), *A Pakistani community in Britain*, Oxford: Blackwell.

Shaw, A. (2002), 'Why might young British Muslims support the Taliban?', *Anthropology Today* 18(1): 5–8.

Shweder, R. A. (1984), 'Preview: a colloquy of culture theorists', in R. A. Shweder and R. A. LeVine (eds), *Culture Theory: Essays on Mind, Self, and Emotion*, Cambridge, Cambridge University Press, pp. 1–24.

Silverman, D. and Gubrium, J. F. (1989), 'Introduction', in J. F. Gubrium and D. Silverman. (eds), *The Politics of Field Research: Sociology Beyond Enlightenment*, London: Sage, pp. 1–12.

Siraj, A. (2006), 'On Being Homosexual and Muslim: Conflicts and Challenges', in O. Lahoucine (ed.), *Islamic Masculinities*, London: Zed Books, pp. 202–16.

Sluka, J., Chomsky, N. and Price, D. (2002), '"Terrorism" and the Responsibility of the Anthropologist', *Anthropology Today* 18(2): 22–3.

Smith, R. J. (1985), 'A Pattern of Japanese Society: *Ie* Society or Acknowledgment of Interdependence?' *Journal of Japanese Studies* 11: 29–45.

Smith, R. (1999), 'Reflection on Migration, The State and Construction, Durability and Newness of Transnational Life', in L. Pries, (ed.), *Migration and Transnational Social Spaces*, Aldershot: Ashgate, pp. 187–219.

Sofer, J. (1992), 'Sodomy in the Law of Muslim States', in A. Schmitt and J. Sofer (eds), *Sexuality and eroticism among Males in Moslem Societies,* Binghamton, NY: Haworth Press, pp. 131–49.

Sökefeld, M. (1999), 'Debating Self, Identity, Cultural Anthropology', *Current Anthropology* 40(4): 417–47.

Sonn, T. (2004), *A Brief History of Islam,* London: Polity Press.

Souilamas, N. G. (2000), *Des 'beurettes' aux descendantes d'immigrants nord-africains*, Paris: Editions Grasset.

Spiro, M. E. (1966), 'Religion: Problems of Definition and Explanation', in M. Banton (ed.), *Anthropological Approaches to the Study of Religion*, New York: Praeger, pp. 85–126.

Stewart, F. H. (1994), *Honor*, Chicago: University of Chicago Press.

Strathern, M (1982), 'The Village as an Idea: Constructs of Village-ness in Elmond, Essex', in A. P. Cohen (ed.), *Belonging: Identity and social organization in British rural cultures*, Manchester: University Press. pp. 247–77.

Street, B. (1990), 'Orientalist Discourses in the Anthropology of Iran, Afghanistan, and Pakistan', in R. Fardon (ed.), *Localizing Strategies: Regional Traditions of Ethnographic Writing,* Edinburgh and Washington: Scottish Academic Press, Smithsonian Institution Press, pp. 240–59.

Sundar, N. (2004), 'Toward an Anthropology of Culpability,' *American Ethnologist* 31(2): 145–63.

Syed, J. (1981), *The Origins and Early Development of Shi'a Islam*, London: Longman.

Tahir, M.A. (1987), 'Review of Ahmed 1986', *Muslim World Book Review* 8(1): 8–10.

Tajfel, H. (1979), 'Individuals and Groups in Social Psychology', *British Journal of Social and Clinical Psychology* 18: 183–90.

Tapper, N. and Tapper, R. (1987), 'The Birth of the Prophet: Ritual and Gender in Turkish Islam', *Man* (n.s.) 22: 69–92.

Tapper, R. (1988), 'Review of Ahmed 1986', *Man*, 23(3): 567–8.

Tarr, C. (1993), 'Questions of Identity in Beur Cinema: from Tea in the Harem to Cheb', *Screen* 34(4): 321–42.

Tarr, C. (1995), 'Beurz n the Hood: the Articulation of Beur and French Identities in the *Le thé au harem d'Archimède* and *Hexagone*', *Modern and Contemporary France* 3(4): 415–25.

Tarr, C. (1999), 'Ethnicity and Identity in the cinéma de banlieue', in P. Powrie (ed.), *French Cinema in the Nineteen Nineties: Continuity and Difference*, Oxford: Oxford University Press, pp. 172–84.

Thomas, N. M. (2005), 'On Headscarves and Heterogeneity: Reflections on the French Foulard Affair', *Dialectical Anthropology* 29(3–4): 373–86.

Triandis, H. (1989), 'The Self and Social Behavior in Differing Cultural Contexts', *Psychological Review* 96(3): 506–20.

Triandis, H. C., Bontempo, R., Villareal, M. J., Asai, M. and Lucca, N. (1988), 'Individualism and Collectivism: Cross-Cultural Perspectives on Self-Ingroup Relationships', *Journal of Personality and Social Psychology* 54: 323–38.

Tribalat, M. (1995), *Faire France*, Paris: La Découvert.

Tucker, J. (ed.) (1993), *Arab Women, Old Boundaries, New Frontiers*, Bloomington: Indiana University Press.

Turner, V. W. (1967), *The Forest of Symbols: Aspects of Ndembu Ritual*, Ithaca: Cornell University Press.

Turner, V. W. (1969), *The Ritual Process: Structure and Anti-Structure*, Chicago: Aldine.

Tylor, E. (1871), *Religion in Primitive Culture*, New York: Harper & Row.

Tylor, E. (1881), *Anthropology: An Introduction to the Study of Man and Civilization*, London: Macmillan.

Varisco, M. D. (2002), 'September 11: Participant Webservation of the "War on Terrorism"', *American Anthropologist* 104(3): 934–7.

Varisco, M. D. (2005), *Islam Obscured: The Rhetoric of Anthropological Representation*, Basingstoke and New York: Palgrave Macmillan.

Vetrovec, S. (2001), 'Trasnationalism and Identity', *Journal of Ethnic and Migration studies* 27(4): 537–82.

Voltaire, F. A. M. (1736/1905), 'Mahomet', in F.A.M. Voltaire, *The Works of Voltaire*, Vol. XXVII, Akron, OH: Werner Co.

Waines, D. (1995), *An Introduction to Islam*, Cambridge: Cambridge University Press.

Warren, C. A. B. (1998), *Gender Issues in Field Research*, London: Sage.

Warren, C. A. B. (2001), 'Gender and Fieldwork Relations', in R. M. Emerson (ed.), *Contemporary Field Research*, Long Grover: Waveland Press, pp. 203–23.

Watson, J. L. (ed.) (1997), *Between Two Cultures: Migrants and Minorities in Britain*, Oxford: Blackwell.

Watt. W. M. (1956), *Muhammad at Medina*, Oxford: Clarendon Press.

Weber, M. (1920/1958), *The Protestant Ethic and the Spirit of Capitalism*, New York: Scribner's.

Weber, M. (1968), *Economy and Society: an Outline of Interpretative Sociology*, New York: Bedminster Press.

Welsch, W. (1990), 'Identität im Übergang', in W. Welsch (ed.), *Ästhetisches Denken*, Stuttgart: Reclam, pp. 168–200.

Werbner, P. (1979), 'Avoiding the Ghetto: Pakistani Migrants and Settlement Shifts in Manchester', *New Community* 7: 376–89.

Werbner, P. (1980), 'Rich Man, Poor Man, or a Community of Suffering: Heroic Motifs in Manchester Pakistanis' Life Histories', *Oral History* 8: 43–8.

Werbner, P. (1981), 'From Rags to Riches: Manchester Pakistanis in the Textile Trade', *New Community* 9: 216–29.

Werbner, P. (2002), *Imagined Diaspora among Manchester Muslims*, Oxford: James Curry.

Whitehouse, H. (2004), *Modes of Religiosity: A Cognitive Theory of Religious Transmission*, Walnut Creek, CA.

Whittaker, E. (1992), 'The Birth of the Anthropological Self and Its Career', *Ethos* 20(2): 191–219

Wikan, U. (1984), 'Shame and Honour: A Contestable Pair', *Man* 19: 635–52.

Wikan, U. (1999), 'Culture: A New Concept of Race', *Social Anthropology* 7(1): 57–64.

Wikan, U. (2002), *Generous Betrayal: Politics of Culture in the New Europe*, Chicago: University of Chicago Press.

Wiktorowicz, Q. (2005), *Radical Islam Rising: Muslim Extremism in the West*, Oxford: Rowman and Littlefield Publishers.

Wilson, A. (1981), *Finding a Voice: Asian Women in Britain*, London: Virago.

Woodward, M. (1989), *Islam in Java: Normative Piety and Mysticism in the Sultanate of Yogyakarta,* Tucson: University of Arizona Press.

Wright, J. W. Jr and Rowson, E. K. (1997), *Homoeroticism in Classical Arabic Literature,* New York; New York University Press.

Wyn, M. D. (1988), *Knowing One Another: Shaping Islamic Anthropology*, London and New York: Mansell.

Yaqoob, S. (2003), 'Global and Local Echoes of the Anti-War Movement: A British Muslim Perspective', *International Socialism* 100 Autumn, http://pubs.socialistreviewindex.org.uk/isj100/yaqoob.htm (accessed 10 September 2006).

Ye'or, B. (1978), *Dhimmi People: Oppressed Nations*, Genève: World Organization of Jews from Arab Countries.

Ye'or, B. (1984), *The Dhimmi: Jews and Christians Under Islam*, London: Associated University Press.

Ye'or, B. (1991), *The Decline of Eastern Christianity Under Islam: From Jihad to Dhimmitude*, Paris: Cerf.

Ye'or, B. (2002), *Islam and Dhimmitude: Where Civilizations Collide*, Madison, NJ: Fairleigh Dickinson University Press.

Yip, A. K. T. (2004a), 'Embracing Allah and Sexuality?: South Asian Non-heterosexual Muslims in Britain', in P. Kumar and K. Jacobsen(eds), *South Asians in the Diaspora*, Leiden, The Netherlands: E. J. Brill, pp. 294–312.

Yip, A. K. T. (2004b), 'Minderheit in der Minderheit: nicht Heterosexuelle Britische Muslime', in *Muslime unter dem Regenbogen: Homosexualitat, Migration und Islam*, Berlin-Brandenburg e.v. (Hg.), Berlin: Queverlag GmbH, pp. 128–42.

Yip, A. K. T. (2004c), 'Negotiating Space with Family and Kin in Identity Construction: The Narratives of British Non-heterosexual Muslims', *Sociological Review* 52(3): 336–349.

Young, W. (1988), 'Review of Ahmed 1986', *American Journal of Islamic Social Science* 5: 2.

Zavella, P. (1996), 'Feminist insider dilemmas: constructing ethnic identity with "Chicana" informants' in D. L. Wolfe (ed.), *Feminist Dilemmas in Fieldwork*, Boulder, CO: Westview, pp. 138–69.

Zola, I. K. (1982), *Missing Pieces: A Chronicle of Living with a Disability*, Philadelphia: Temple University Press.

Zubaida, S. (2003), 'Is there a Muslim society? Ernest Gellner's sociology of Islam', in B. Turner (ed.), *Islam: Critical Concepts in Sociology*, London: Routledge, pp. 31–70.

# Index

## MUSLIM CONTRIBUTORS/ INFORMANTS